INTERNET SECURITY YOU CAN AFFORD: USING UNTANGLE™ AS YOUR INTERNET GATEWAY

CHRISTOPHER DAWSON

Cengage Learning PTR

D1408632

CENGAGE
Learning®

Professional • Technical • Reference

Australia • Brazil • Japan • Korea • Mexico • Singapore • Spain • United Kingdom • United States

CENGAGE
Learning®

Professional • Technical • Reference

Internet Security You Can Afford: Using Untangle™ as Your Internet Gateway
Christopher Dawson

Publisher and General Manager, Cengage Learning PTR: Stacy L. Hiquet

Associate Director of Marketing: Sarah Panella

Manager of Editorial Services: Heather Talbot

Product Manager: Heather Hurley

Project Editor: Kate Shoup

Technical Reviewer: Serge Palladino

Copy Editor: Kate Shoup

Interior Layout Tech: MPS Limited

Cover Designer: Luke Fletcher

Indexer: Kelly Talbot Editing Services

Proofreader: Kelly Talbot Editing Services

> For product information and technology assistance, contact us at
> **Cengage Learning Customer & Sales Support, 1-800-354-9706.**
>
> For permission to use material from this text or product, submit all requests online at **cengage.com/permissions.**
>
> Further permissions questions can be emailed to **permissionrequest@cengage.com.**

Untangle is a trademark of Untangle, Inc. All other trademarks are the property of their respective owners.

All images © Cengage Learning unless otherwise noted.

Library of Congress Control Number: 2012930797

ISBN-13: 978-1-4354-6136-9

ISBN-10: 1-4354-6136-3

Cengage Learning PTR

20 Channel Center Street

Boston, MA 02210

USA

Cengage Learning is a leading provider of customized learning solutions with office locations around the globe, including Singapore, the United Kingdom, Australia, Mexico, Brazil, and Japan. Locate your local office at: **international.cengage.com/region**.

Cengage Learning products are represented in Canada by Nelson Education, Ltd.

For your lifelong learning solutions, visit **cengageptr.com**.

Visit our corporate website at **cengage.com**.

Printed in the United States of America
1 2 3 4 5 6 7 16 15 14

This book is dedicated to all of the educators, makers, developers, and open source supporters who know that if you want something done, you need to do it yourself. Whether or not it's done right is always up for debate.

ACKNOWLEDGMENTS

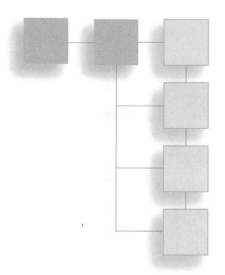

I would like to acknowledge the sharp, dedicated folks at Untangle, both for supplying a test appliance and for continuing to innovate on a very powerful product. My editors at Cengage Learning PTR deserve much more than an acknowledgment for their patience and perseverance. Most of all, I want to acknowledge my kids for their understanding of my experimentation with our connection to the information superhighway (and the various game servers that reside there) and my wife for her understanding of, well, me.

About the Author

Christopher Dawson grew up in Seattle, back in the days of pre-antitrust Microsoft, coffee shops owned by someone other than Starbucks, and really loud, inarticulate music. He escaped to the right coast in the early 1990s and received a degree in information systems from Johns Hopkins University. While there, he began a career in health and educational information systems. Positions at Johns Hopkins and at a large biotech company in Cambridge, several years teaching and managing technology in his local school district, and an executive leader position in a virtual classroom company have culminated in his current work consulting, writing, and bootstrapping educational startups. He has written and broadcasted extensively for ZDNet, Ziff Davis, CRN, and Edukwest. He now lives in New England with his wife, kids, and an assortment of farm animals who care far less about technology than he does.

Contents

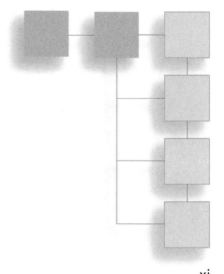

INTRODUCTION

For several years, in addition to writing for various technology publications, I managed networks and computing environments for my local school district. Because it was a public school district, it meant that I needed to find ways to save money while still putting as much technology into students' hands as possible. When, after much searching, I stumbled across Untangle, I was thrilled! Even as far back as 2007, Untangle worked pretty well to keep students out of places they shouldn't be during the day and from getting back in at night.

Ultimately, our district opted for a complete, integrated package for all our schools that bundled Internet connections and another brand of combination Internet gateway/ firewall/content filters for one tolerable price. Untangle went by the wayside. Occasionally, however, I revisited Untangle, torturing my kids by experimenting with it at home and otherwise staying abreast of developments in the software.

After a while, I left the school district and started consulting for educational organizations. Eventually, I landed a job as VP of business development for WizIQ, which provides a virtual classroom and learning network to independent educators and major universities alike.

As I became more immersed in the world of independent education, I met a lot of people who called themselves *edupunks*. Like cyberpunks, edupunks lived and worked outside the confines of traditional paradigms. They were willing to use whatever tools available (usually technological, progressive, and utterly engaging) to make sure learners (who might be third graders or 65-year olds) got what they needed from an educational standpoint. I was so excited to have found like-minded people who really wanted to disrupt the way we educated our kids (and others), and who were passionately independent!

As I began to spend more time consulting with schools, startups, and various media outlets, I couldn't help but turn my attention back to open source projects, innovative Internet tools, and a variety of technologies that could help change the way schools did business. Untangle was on my radar for a serious, in-depth review. Edupunks weren't so worried about keeping kids off of Facebook or Wikipedia, but porn had to be left at the door (even if that door was virtual) and sensitive data still needed protecting. So I combed through the software, and was even more impressed.

Around the same time, a fellow member of the Internet Press Guild, which is a group of independent writer types, most of whom worked on a freelance basis, mentioned that he'd heard of a publisher who was looking for an Untangle expert to write a book. (Thanks, Bryan!) I thought, "That's me!" You can probably guess what happened next, because here I am, and here is this book.

Long story short, I want this book to be *the* resource and reference that would have been oh-so helpful when I was first exploring Untangle. I'd also like it to be a good read. It might not be *Cryptonomicon* (my favorite book of all time), but hopefully you'll find it enriching and entertaining! Just because you're reading about an open source Internet gateway written by a big geek doesn't mean you have to be frowning and playing with your pocket protector the whole time.

WHAT'S IN THIS BOOK?

As we've established, this is a book about Untangle, an Internet gateway for your network that keeps the bad guys out, the good guys in, and generally protects everyone and everything that connects to the Net through it. The beauty of Untangle is that, in its basic form, it's free. The free version, however, comes only with community support and not much in the way of instructions, best practices, troubleshooting, or walkthroughs. Most of these can be found in various obscure corners of the Internet or picked up over a few years working in networking and information technology. They can also be found in this book.

Note

As I was writing this book, Untangle rebranded its Internet Gateway as the Untangle Next Generation Firewall, or just Untangle NG. It's more than a firewall, though, and, frankly, it's more than a gateway. In fact, Untangle, Inc., generally refers to the gateway as a separate device (like a DSL or cable modem). But modems and the like are more akin to on-ramps on a highway. Gateways control access to the driveway on a lot of levels. Hence, the subtitle of this book, 'Using Untangle as Your Internet Gateway.' While this book is primarily concerned with Untangle NG, it also covers Untangle's other products at least in passing, so you'll find references to general Internet gateways as well as Untangle's specific gateway and firewall offerings—both free and otherwise. Regardless of the specific nomenclature, this book is about how to get Untangle software between your network and the rest of the world.

To successfully use Untangle, you need to be able to do the following:

- Build, salvage, select, or otherwise find a suitable computer to run the software.
- Install a Linux-based operating system on said computer.
- Get said computer routing traffic on your network.
- Decide on and implement policies for the way your network is accessed and used.
- Automatically inform users about said security policies.
- Deal with violations of said policies.
- Implement new software configurations to prevent further violations.
- Identify problems and issues on your network.
- Troubleshoot your server.
- Decide when a DIY server just isn't going to do the trick anymore.

While you could just buy an Untangle appliance from the company, along with lots of extra software and top-notch support, people and organizations on a budget can often meet their Internet security needs quite nicely with the free version of the Untangle Next Generation Firewall and the so-called "Free Package" of software modules. Everything you need to get up and running with Untangle—and then actually use it effectively in your organization—is right here. By the time you finish reading this book, you should not only be able to handle the basic hardware and software tasks around using Untangle, but should also have the ability to make good decisions for your organization and then make those decisions come to life with the gateway you've built.

WHO SHOULD READ THIS BOOK?

It might actually be easier to start with who shouldn't read this book. Here's my take on it:

- My wife. She hates technology, doesn't know a browser from a search engine (yes, she types URLs into Google and then follows the link), and would become Amish if she could take a hot shower every morning and keep her Roomba vacuuming robot
- CTOs of Fortune 500 corporations looking at solutions for deep packet-level content filtering and highly customizable bandwidth shaping
- Small children who have just completed the "My Baby Can Read" program

OK, that might be an oversimplification, but the audience for this book is actually pretty large. This is, in fact, what makes Untangle so interesting. It will work just as well for the computer-savvy mom who wants to make sure her kids can use the Internet safely at home (without learning things they definitely don't teach in sex ed) as it can for a small to medium-sized business looking to cut costs but still protect sensitive data and equipment.

Could you install or upgrade Windows on your own computer if you needed to? If your answer is yes, then this book isn't going to be too full of geeky mumbo jumbo to be of use to you.

Could you re-image 60 machines at the same time as you set up LDAP replication to a branch office? Good for you! Way to multitask! And you can still probably find something very useful in this book.

The only real prerequisites here are:

- You have computer users that you support, employ, gave birth to, or want to help.
- The places those users can go on the Internet needs to be restricted in some way.
- You need/want to protect those users and/or the computers on your network from any number of bad things on the Internet (viruses, spam, ads, phishing attacks, etc.).
- You want to do this cheaply and/or you want to do it yourself.

While not prerequisites, this book is also up your alley if:

- You need a free router or firewall.
- You need to manage traffic in some reasonable way on your network.
- You're at least as big a geek as I am and you love to find new uses for aging computers.

- You believe in the power of open source software.

- You need a VPN solution to give outside users safe access to your network.

- You need or want to see what's happening on your network.

- You're a student learning about computer networking. (I didn't want to leave you out if you're reading this book because you had to buy it for a class.)

In the article "Is Do-It-Yourself Deployment Right for You?" available at www.untangle .com, the folks at Untangle have outlined a few thoughts of their own on who should tackle building an Internet gateway with their software:

- You already have hardware available or identified for your software appliance.

- You are comfortable with technical deployments like installing an OS on a new machine.

- You have a good understanding of your network and a plan for running Untangle as a transparent bridge or router. (Don't worry if you don't know what a transparent bridge is. We'll get to that.)

So there you go. That covers a lot of people. Chances are, you wouldn't have picked this book up if you weren't one of them, so read on!

How to Use This Book

This book lends itself to being read in order, chapter by chapter. It also works well for teaching both Untangle and the basics of firewalls and gateway devices when read in order. That being said, I encourage you to skip ahead and read the chapters that matter to you if you're that guy (or gal) above who's reading in his (or her) spare time while configuring directory services for a branch office network. It's OK. I won't mind.

And don't worry if you have to read every chapter and look up terms on Wikipedia. Wikipedia is awesome, no matter what anyone says. Read this book from front to back, mark chapters you find especially useful, and then use it as a reference in the months and years to come.

While my experience with Untangle was in education (and now in my house and various small businesses and schools), there's no reason that this tool can't be used across lots of jobs and industries, by parents and instructors, by edupunks and straight-laced school district CTOs, or by lawyers and accountants.

Oh, one more thing. As noted above, this book focuses on the open source, downloadable version of Untangle. It's free and is the basis for more advanced toolsets and actual hardware that the company, Untangle, Inc., sells to fund further development of Untangle. Learn the free version and you'll be able to quickly pick up on how to use the paid software and appliances that provide additional features. The underlying principles and interface are the same, so this book should be kept handy when and if you decide to upgrade.

Speaking of principles, most chapters include some tidbits on networking, the Internet, Internet service providers, computer hardware, DIY computing, and all sorts of other information technology stuff (for lack of a better word). Working with Untangle is an outstanding introduction to a whole host of computing concepts, assuming you have at least a rudimentary understanding of basic IT. I'll try to stick with general principles as much as possible so that anything you learn here is more broadly applicable, whether you are learning about Cisco routers, Linux, the World Wide Web, or anything in between.

BUT CAN'T NORTON JUST DO THE JOB?

No.

I thought about just leaving it at that and going on to the next topic but decided against it. It's probably a good idea to say a few words about what Untangle does, what Norton (and other desktop anti-malware software) does, and why tools like Untangle become increasingly important as the size of your network (or the importance of computing to your business) grows.

Threats to Your Network and Users

Whether you are a concerned parent or a growing business, the users on your network and the equipment with which they work are your primary responsibility. Some analysts report that unprotected computers can be compromised in as little as 15 minutes after they are connected to the Internet. "Compromised" in this case refers to infection by some sort of malware, most likely an automated bot that can harvest information from the computer or turn the computer to nefarious purposes—spamming, attacks on other networks, etc.—all without any action by the user.

The potential financial gain for the organizations that create this sort of malicious software is so great that they invest countless dollars and man-hours developing new ways to attack both consumers and businesses. Millions of compromised consumer PCs can, for example, be used to generate so-called denial of service (DoS) attacks on Internet sites, flooding them with messages from around the world, sent by infected PCs.

The MyDoom worm was perhaps the best-known such software. However, it is believed that such malware is quite widespread, sending, for example, the vast majority of spam emails worldwide. Sending large quantities of spam (even unwittingly) often results in a particular network or server being blacklisted Internet-wide, causing long-term problems when those networks need to be used for legitimate email and communications purposes.

While the threats presented by malware in all its incarnations can be devastating in terms of productivity, data loss, and communications capabilities, direct human attacks are not uncommon. This is true even for comparatively low-profile targets like schools, which deal with sensitive data, or startups, which tend to be heavy on intellectual property (even if they are light on significant financial assets). For lack of a better term, "hackers" target organizations large and small for potential financial gain, mischief, disruption, and even simply to show that they can.

Finally, the Internet is full of more passive threats. Schools and libraries, for example, must make a good-faith effort to prevent minors from accessing objectionable material via their networks if they want to continue to receive federal funding. Parents, private schools, and even many businesses may make far more sweeping decisions about access to sites deemed objectionable or dangerous, or even those that might be a threat to productivity. It can, in fact, be a full-time job to ensure that corporate policies, federal law, or parental wishes are enforced. The Internet, after all, is a vast playground (for both adults and children), just as it's the most important educational and business resource of our time.

What Untangle Does

Untangle is primarily concerned with three things:

- Keeping bad guys (both automated and living/breathing) out of your network (firewall)
- Keeping your users out of bad places outside your network (content filter)
- Keeping the computers on your network free of viruses, Trojans, scareware, and all other manner of electronic nastiness collectively known as 'malware.'

It does plenty of other things, too, like blocking phishing attacks if your users are fans of Outlook and other mail clients or providing a simple VPN portal for users to access your network remotely. However, most of the functions of Untangle fall into the realm of keeping your network and the computers that live on it safe and functional. The other functions can basically be categorized as content filtering and are the sorts of services that kids spend countless hours trying to thwart so they can get on Facebook.

What Norton *et al* Do

Norton, McAfee, Malwarebytes, Kaspersky, and many other software companies make products designed to protect individual computers from the various software threats that abound on the Internet. They can clean those PCs after they've been infected and even prevent a fair amount of inbound infections. However, protecting servers and other resources on your network can require much more expensive software. By the time you're thinking about protecting servers, you also most likely have intellectual or financial assets that require a degree of electronic protection.

Even the maintenance of anti-malware software on every PC on your network is time-consuming and expensive. I'm not saying that all your computers shouldn't be running some sort of antivirus software, by the way. I am saying, however, that there are ways to make such software less critical and to be able to leverage lower-cost solutions without worry that their protection will be inadequate. The same goes for tools to protect those less-tangible assets from unauthorized access.

Most modern operating systems have built-in firewalls that prevent unauthorized software from accessing important bits of the OS. However, they generally lack the ability to effectively monitor all inbound and outbound traffic, actively looking for potential problems—from employees accessing unauthorized sites to hackers trying to infiltrate important systems. You'd be hard-pressed to find any business other than the least computerized mom and pop that doesn't employ some sort of firewall between the network and the outside world. The problem is that these can be either prohibitively expensive or cheap and utterly ineffective.

Whether you're a parent who just refuses to clean the malware from her kid's PC one more time (even though you paid for that stupid 15-month subscription to Bob's Virus Protection, the trial version of which came with said kid's new computer) or a small business owner who just can't afford an enterprise-level firewall, it's worth reading on.

Note

Friends don't let friends buy Norton for every computer in the house, office, or school. Given that unprotected computers can be compromised within minutes by simply sitting on the Internet, though, you can't just say, "Well, that Dawson guy said not to buy Norton." I'd rather you said, "Well, gee, Dawson, tell me what I should do instead to save some cash and keep my computers running along happily."

Norton vs. Untangle and the Battle for Your Network

I keep singling out Norton anti-malware products because they dominate the PC market, along with McAfee, which tends to come pre-installed on a whole lot of computers. They aren't bad products and they are a far better choice than an unprotected PC. However, even home networks generally contain many more devices (or nodes in networking parlance) than just a Windows PC or two. Smartphones, Macs, iPads, Internet-connected gaming consoles and DVD players, Chromebooks, and even refrigerators can access the Internet. As such, they can harbor and transmit malware, even if they aren't susceptible to malicious code primarily written for Windows.

Increasingly, developers of this sort of software are, in fact, targeting non-Windows operating systems, including mobile devices. While there are commercial solutions available for just about every mobile and desktop operating system, Norton Internet Security on a Windows PC remains something of the standard bearer for anti-malware. So I talk about Norton, despite all of the other anti-malware software to be had.

Regardless of the actual protection you choose for the devices that land on your network (if you even have a choice, as various laptops, tablets, phones, and other potential vectors access your network, whether with remote workers or kids' friends), some sort of overarching nod to security is probably in order. If I can draw a crude analogy, so-called client-side anti-malware software (like Norton) is like the condoms that some school districts make available to students. When used properly, they are fairly effective at preventing all sorts of problems. But making sure that they are used properly and universally is incredibly difficult. Untangle, then, is the comprehensive sex ed program the district has in place. It casts a wider net and, when delivered correctly, can be very effective in helping students make good choices.

A bit of a stretch, to be sure, but the presence of Untangle (or similar firewall/content filter devices) takes a bit of the pressure off client-side tools. Instead of Norton or McAfee, suddenly the open source Clamwin just might do the trick. Windows Defender (built in to Windows 7) is probably comprehensive enough. And the stray unprotected device has a decent layer of protection every time it's on your network. (See Figure I.1.)

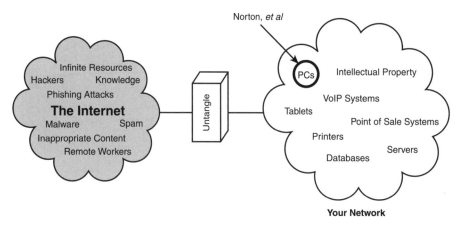

Figure I.1
Commercial anti-malware software only protects a fraction of the devices on your network from a portion of the threats on the Internet.

There are highly sophisticated appliances that actually scan every device that enters your network. Anything that's infected doesn't get access. These devices are very powerful, very expensive, and very worthwhile when you have an entire enterprise to protect. When you have a home, small business, or school network to protect, the substantial investment becomes much harder to justify, as does the cost of diligently protecting and maintaining every device on the network. Enter Untangle.

I CAN'T JUST BUILD AN INTERNET GATEWAY! WAIT, WHAT'S AN INTERNET GATEWAY?

Wait a minute and I'll tell you. But first…

An Incredibly Brief History of the Internet

The Internet is a giant network of connected networks. Welcome to the Department of Redundancy Department, right? Actually, it's neither as bad as it sounds, nor as redundant (even though the Internet was designed to be redundant). The Internet was born in the 1960s from the need to connect research universities and ultimately military installations and facilities over a more robust connection than phone lines could provide. Long story short, some very smart folks designed a system called "packet switching" that allowed large amounts of data to be broken into packets, sent over a communications infrastructure, and then reassembled at the end of their journey into a copy of the original data.

As the military became increasingly involved with development of this communications infrastructure, then called ARPANET, it became clear that in the event of a nuclear strike, key parts of this infrastructure could be destroyed, meaning that these packets needed a means to be routed and rerouted if the network was badly degraded. Notice that word *route* I keep using? That's why we call devices that connect various computer networks to each other "routers."

The rest is history. Lots of us now have broadband connections to the Internet, which has grown into a worldwide network of networks, connecting everything from Web servers to home PCs to telemedicine devices for remote surgical operations.

ROUTERS, TRANSCEIVERS, AND GATEWAYS...OH MY!

In their simplest form, routers are generally referred to as "gateways." Full-featured routers can manage traffic at many levels and connect many networks (one of which may be the Internet itself). Gateways generally just connect a single network to the Internet. Some of this is merely semantics, but for our purposes, we'll refer to Untangle as an Internet gateway since it does not perform more robust routing functions.

The cable or DSL modem that most likely provides your Internet connection might also function as a router, depending on its configuration. In fact, however, this equipment is technically a transceiver that provides a relatively dumb connection to the Internet. A gateway or router device (like an Untangle appliance) adds significant levels of functionality—most importantly the ability to route traffic from many devices on a network to the modem and off to the Internet.

So why add a gateway or router when a simple transceiver gets you online just fine? Because as your needs become more sophisticated, that plain old DSL modem just isn't going to cut it. For the average home user, there is little need to do more than just "get online." But when home use turns to business use or when little Junior is getting just a little too curious about the nether regions of the Internet, having layers of functionality separating networked computers from the Internet starts to make a lot more sense. Those layers of virus protection, intrusion prevention, and content filtering all just happen to be freely available in the Untangle Internet Gateway.

CAN'T I JUST PAY SOMEONE TO TAKE CARE OF ALL THAT INTERNET SECURITY STUFF? OR, 'FREE? WHAT'S THE CATCH?'

We all know that "free" doesn't really mean free. There is no such thing as a free lunch, and there is no such thing as a truly free Internet gateway. There will be costs associated with DIY network protection. You'll need a computer, time, and electricity, and it will even cost you a bit in terms of network performance. After all, this little gateway you're about to build can only look at all of those packets flying into your network so fast.

The thing is, though, there really isn't a particularly good alternative. You can't just go buy some software or pay the Best Buy Geek Squad to take care of Internet security for your home, business, or school. You can, in fact, pay certain companies sizable chunks of money to worry about the security of your network for you, but you know what they're going to do? Install a gateway, router, and/or firewall between your network and the Internet. And when they do, I guarantee it's going to cost more than a cheap computer, some time, and some power.

So there's no catch to the "free" in the free version of Untangle. People who spend their days thinking about software licensing (a fun bunch, I might add) talk in terms of "free as in beer" and "free as in freedom." Untangle's Lite version is both. The company gives it away for free just like a friend might give you a beer without expectation of payment. The software is also open source and its users are free to do with it as they please as long as whatever they do doesn't change its fundamental "freeness." So, no catch, except for the DIY nature of setting up and maintaining the gateway. Kind of like when your friend didn't offer you the free beer until you'd helped him move.

PART I

OKAY, I'M CONVINCED. NOW WHAT?

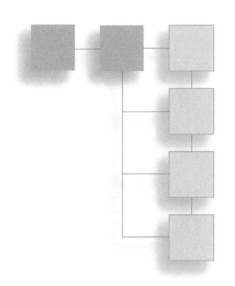

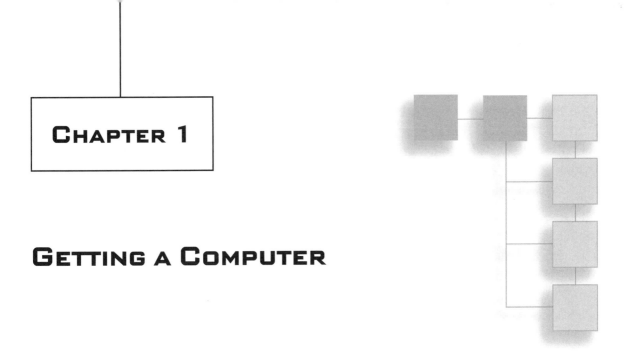

CHAPTER 1

GETTING A COMPUTER

WHY DO I NEED TO DO ANYTHING SPECIAL?

Routers and gateways sold to consumers, schools, and businesses tend to be small, specialized devices. These devices are, at their core, little computers, with many of the input/output capabilities, graphical interfaces, and software found on traditional desktop and laptop computers stripped away, leaving only the basic functionality needed to connect one network to another. Such little computers can consume very little power and need little in the way of fast processors, memory, storage, graphics subsystems, or interfaces that come standard on the average computer.

They don't need to accept a mouse or keyboard, they don't need to drive a monitor, they don't need a card reader to upload photos to Facebook, and they definitely don't need a Blu-ray player. All they really have to do is move packets of data as fast as they can to the right places. Interestingly, though, they don't tend to be cheap. In fact, they can be quite expensive considering how little they actually do.

Of course, the very limited set of tasks they do tends to be utterly critical and the speed with which they do that set of tasks can have more impact on the performance of a network than the bandwidth of the Internet connection they negotiate. Not only do they need to be fast, but they need to be utterly reliable. They generally need to support at least one outbound connection and potentially several inbound connections. Manufacturers are increasingly bundling Web servers (for administration of their functions), firewalls, basic content filters, and other software to differentiate them from their competitors.

Therefore, if you want to create your own Internet gateway, there are very different hardware considerations than if you simply want to build your own computer. It isn't impossible to just go to your local big box store, buy a cheap computer, make some minor hardware additions, and have a perfectly acceptable machine for running Untangle. However, it's quite possible to create a better-suited, cheaper, specialized machine that will run Untangle more efficiently and will better emulate the appliances sold by other vendors (and by Untangle, for that matter).

This approach isn't for everyone. Many individuals will be best served by simply using the modem provided by their Internet service provider (ISP) and going about their business. The same is true for many businesses and organizations without the time or wherewithal to create their own robust devices for content filtering and intrusion prevention. These same businesses should investigate commercial solutions as their networked assets become increasingly critical to their operations. However, for those with a bit of time, a bit of computing savvy, and a copy of this book, there is money to be saved and networks to be protected for less money, for a more interesting experience, and with greater control than most low- to mid-range commercial solutions on the market. If you fall into this category, read on.

What Exactly Do I Need? (Or How Cheap Can I Be?)

Truth be told, you can be pretty cheap. Hardware costs continue to drop quickly and Moore's Law is alive and well. Your Untangle appliance doesn't need to be the fastest, biggest, most tricked-out computer on the market. Far from it, in fact, since it's only going to have a limited number of functions. Instead, the machine needs to be fast in a few key areas; the rest of the components can safely be the bargain-basement variety.

Moore's Law

In 1965, Dr. Gordon Moore, co-founder of Intel, first described a trend in integrated circuitry (essentially the basis for all computing hardware, including the computers you'll be building and working with in this book). As it turns out, this trend has carried on to today and is expected to continue until somewhere around 2020. He noted that more and more transistors could be inexpensively placed on integrated circuits every year. The end result of his observation, which became known as Moore's Law, was that the power of computer hardware roughly doubles every two years but the cost of the hardware remains about the same. Thus, a computer you can buy for $500 today is four times more powerful than a computer you could purchase for $500 four years ago.

Fortunately, the expensive parts of a computer tend to relate to graphics processing, high-end central processing units (CPUs), and the latest trends in solid-state storage, none of which are necessary for Untangle to run well. Of course, as the amount of traffic the appliance needs to process increases (e.g., as the size of your network increases or your users' Internet utilization grows), the faster the machine will need to be.

First, let's take a look at the basic components of any computer and then discuss each of these considerations in detail. You'll get to exactly what happens inside an Untangle box in Chapter 4, "What's Happening Inside My Untangle Gateway?" For now, it's important to understand the basics at a hardware level so you can choose appropriate components. Figure 1.1 shows a basic PC component schematic.

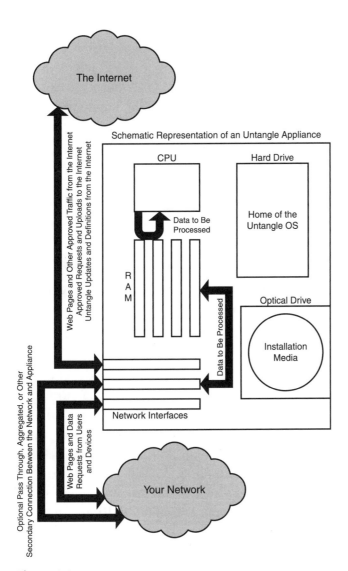

Figure 1.1
Basic PC component schematic.

Essentially, the appliance needs to review each packet of data that users request from the Internet. Keeping in mind the idea that packet switching is the basis for all communications on the Internet, Untangle must quickly assemble incoming packets into usable, identifiable chunks; do something about them if they have a problem (such as a malware payload or keywords that administrators have identified as prohibited); and pass them back on to users if they are "okay" (whatever okay means for individual types of traffic). The Untangle server must also evaluate each request from every user. For example, if a user enters http://www.naughtysite.com into his Web browser, Untangle compares that URL to a list of unacceptable domains before even initiating a transfer from the requested site. (See the section "Router Versus Bridge and Other Router-Setup Considerations" in Chapter 4 for more information.)

None of this has the appliance writing much information to a disk. Untangle just needs to receive, process, and then transmit data. Over and over. *Ad infinitum.* Untangle runs on a version of Debian Linux, one of many flavors of the open source operating system. Debian is inherently multithreaded, meaning it can use multiple processors simultaneously. All of this processing, then, can be done faster the more processors you throw at Untangle. The latest trend in CPUs is the use of multiple cores in a single chip, essentially turning one processor into as many as six or eight, all handling data at the same time. Intel also offers proprietary technology in many of their chips called *Hyper-Threading*, which effectively doubles the number of cores in Intel's processors. Thus, a four-core processor with Hyper-Threading would be able to process eight sets of instructions simultaneously.

Similarly, this data needs to live somewhere as it is processed, so memory (RAM) becomes very important to the process, as do architectural features of the processor called *cache* that hold small amounts of data for short periods of time without wasting precious microseconds being passed in and out of RAM.

Again, just how many cores or processors and how much RAM you need depends on how much data you expect to be processing—i.e., how much Internet traffic your organization will be filtering. However, keep in mind that the highest-end appliance sold by Untangle, designed for corporate deployments with thousands of users, has two Intel quad-core chips with Hyper-Threading on each, enabling the appliance to operate as though it has 16 processors. For average home, educational, and small-business customers, between two and four cores should be more than sufficient. In fact, as you begin to explore throughput in more detail, you'll see that several other factors limit the practical effectiveness of more expensive processors, reaching the point of diminishing returns fairly quickly in most applications.

Table 1.1 Hardware Recommendations

Resource	Processor	Memory	Hard Drive	NICs	Notes
Minimum	Intel/AMD-compatible processor (800+ MHz)	512 MB	20 GB	Two	
1–50 users	Pentium 4 equivalent or greater	1 GB	80 GB	Two or more	
51–150 users	Dual core	2 GB	80 GB	Two or more	
151–500 users	Two or more cores	2+ GB	80 GB	Two or more	
501–1,500 users	Four cores	4 GB	80 GB	Two or more	64-bit
1,501–5,000 users	Four or more cores	4+ GB	80 GB	Two or more	64-bit

Untangle makes some general recommendations for DIY applications, the specific reasons for which are discussed in subsequent sections. Table 1.1 outlines these hardware recommendations.

As you can see, relatively archaic hardware will get the job done for very small deployments. However, because hardware is fairly cheap, it is possible to build or buy a robust Untangle server that can be repurposed later or serve multiple purposes in addition to Internet security if necessary.

There are a few key considerations when choosing hardware for Untangle:

- Throughput
- Reliability
- Efficiency

Throughput

Throughput is the server's ability to move data through the machine in either direction (from users to the Internet and/or vice versa). While the processor and memory considerations outlined previously have a significant impact on overall throughput, there is no greater determination of this parameter than internal and external bandwidth. The bottleneck on a single 3 Mbps DSL connection will most likely not be the processor you choose. It will be the Internet connection itself. Similarly, internal networking running on older cable, utilizing hubs or early switches, or traversing long distances, will introduce an additional bottleneck that faster hardware inside the Untangle server won't be able to address. Finally, the network hardware on the server itself is critical to delivering data to the processor quickly for routing and filtering.

Networking hardware will be discussed in detail in Chapter 2, "Networking 101," but at this point, there are two take-home messages as you determine appropriate hardware for your appliance:

■ Make sure that your network is in order before you even start down this road. If you aren't sure that your home/office/school network is up to snuff or you don't know what constitutes "up to snuff," read Chapter 2.

■ Make sure that the network interface cards (NICs) on your machine support 1,000 Mbps or so-called *gigabit Ethernet*.

This second bullet is particularly important. The fastest networking equipment widely available runs at 1,000 Mbps. There is faster equipment to be had, but it's incredibly expensive and tends to be reserved for large data centers. Google's server farms don't use gigabit Ethernet. But guess what? They don't use Untangle, either. Gigabit Ethernet cards are fairly inexpensive, will largely future-proof your server for any upgrades to your network (at least for the life of the machine), and will provide that processor with a steady stream of data to crunch and filter. Even if individual computers on your network don't support gigabit Ethernet, it only takes a few slower machines streaming video and downloading large files to start pushing the limits of a single gigabit connection.

Fortunately, Untangle supports more than just a single connection to your internal network. In fact, with some add-on software, it supports multiple connections to the Internet as well and does a nice job of balancing the work that each connection handles. While Untangle only needs one connection to the Internet and one connection to the internal network to work, a second or third internal connection can do wonders for throughput. Do yourself a favor and spend the extra $40 on a third network card. You'll see shortly (in Chapter 3, "Downloading and Installing Untangle," and Chapter 6, "Implementing Networking Best Practices [or Not] with Untangle," to be exact) how that will work exactly, but Figure 1.2 shows the movement of data at a high level that is enabled by additional cards.

Aside from the network interface cards, other internal components of the Untangle server can also negatively affect throughput. All the data moving from the NICs, across the motherboard, through the processor, and into and out of memory can hit bottlenecks at many points that are much harder to identify. Cheap motherboards often only support lower-speed RAM, for example, limiting the rate at which the processor can read and write data to memory. While a high-end motherboard is hardly necessary, look for RAM running at least at 1,033 MHz. This won't be hard to find, but the cheapest of computers

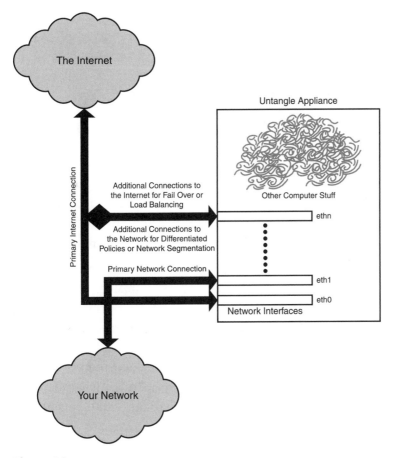

Figure 1.2
Data-flow schematic for Untangle gateways.

(or older computers if you are repurposing an aging machine) will tend to be a bit more sluggish in this area. Although this is no problem for a very small network, it will become an issue as your network grows.

Reliability

Your Untangle server is most likely going to be on all the time. Full-blown servers from major original equipment manufacturers (OEMs) are designed to run 24×7 for several years; the average PC is not. Of course, the average server also costs several thousand dollars. Somewhere, there is a good balance between price, performance, and reliability. As you've seen, performance doesn't need to be extraordinary, especially outside network interface hardware. This gives a little more room to work in improved reliability.

All computers, regardless of their purpose, have the same basic set of components, each of which has a particular likelihood of failure as the number of usage hours increases. While hardly an exact science, these components are listed here, roughly in order of their age-related failure rates. This ranking is specific to an Untangle use case, given that certain components will be used far less than they might be in a mainstream computer.

- **Power supply.** The average PC is not used 24 × 7, allowing the power supply to cool down, potentially pull in less dust, etc. Such is not the case for an Untangle gateway—hence the need for beefed up and/or redundant power supplies (as most servers have). Power supplies are usually sold by the peak wattage they can provide to various PC components. Higher-wattage power supplies, even if not necessary due to the generally low-power requirements of a gateway, will tend to hold up better to years of constant use, as they can operate cooler at a given wattage than a small power supply.

- **Motherboard.** Motherboards basically run everything. If your computer won't boot, it's hardly a rarity for the motherboard to be the issue. Even under normal use, motherboards bear the brunt of a whole lot of electrical current zapping about between components. When data moves, it does so via the motherboard. When a CPU starts pulling extra power under heavy load, that power is delivered via the motherboard. You get the idea. This component has a tendency to fail when consumers are using a PC frequently. Again, a 24 × 7 application like an Untangle gateway will take its toll on a cheap motherboard.

- **Hard drive.** While solid-state drives are becoming more common on consumer PCs, they're still quite pricey. For your purposes, standard hard drives (i.e., those with spinning magnetic disks and mechanical parts for reading and writing data) are perfectly suitable because the drive doesn't see especially heavy use with Untangle. Preferences and logs are stored there, as is the Untangle OS, but reading and writing large files is rare. That being said, the presence of moving parts makes them susceptible to failure. The drive itself need not be the largest or the fastest, but it shouldn't be the cheapest, either. Fortunately, decent hard drives are quite inexpensive, especially as solid-state drives continue to put pressure on the market.

- **Network cards.** Network cards aren't generally prone to failure. Configured properly and paired with the right drivers, network interface cards usually just work. These fairly low-maintenance parts, though, are the most critical components in an Untangle appliance in terms of throughput and avoiding bottlenecks. There are a few considerations worth noting in your search for reliable, fast, cost-effective network cards.

First, most motherboards come with an integrated network interface. Cheap motherboards carry cheap NICs, often running at only 100 Mbps. Spending a bit extra on the motherboard will usually get you a gigabit network chip, speeding throughput by 10 times and ensuring that half of the required two network interfaces is already running at the recommended speed. This usually has the side effect of getting you a higher quality motherboard with greater performance optimization.

The second consideration, coincidentally, involves the second required network interface. Unless you are purchasing a server-class motherboard (not recommended, since it simply isn't a necessary expense for your purposes), most will only have a single network interface built in. Thus, any additional NICs will need to be add-on cards. These cards will need to fit the motherboard (PCI slot types are discussed later in this chapter, in the section titled "A Basic DIY Setup"), but can otherwise be fairly inexpensive units. They are, unlike the integrated network interface on the motherboard, easily replaceable.

■ **RAM.** High-end motherboards can support very fast RAM in large quantities. Neither is necessary for this application. However, buying a single stick of RAM in the size required for your application (most likely 4 GB) or two matched sticks (sold as matched pairs of, for example, 2 GB each) will tend to result in better performance and greater reliability. Minor mismatches in voltage or speed caused by using unmatched pairs can have long-term detrimental effects on reliability and short-term effects on data throughput.

Efficiency

As noted, these gateways are going to be on all the time, whether you are using them or not. This is hardly the greenest approach to computing and, as larger businesses and schools know, power consumption can be one of the more expensive long-term components to server total cost of ownership. While a single Untangle gateway running 24 × 7 will hardly break the bank, there is no reason to choose inefficient components or to overbuild the computer with components that are more powerful than necessary.

One significant area of energy savings is the lack of a dedicated monitor. Untangle includes its own Web server that facilitates all administration so, after initial setup, the server can run "headless." In fact, it doesn't even need a keyboard or mouse; everything can be managed from the Web interface. Without a monitor, the Untangle box only needs basic graphics capabilities integrated into the motherboard for setup and trouble-shooting. A dedicated graphics card is unnecessary from a cost and function standpoint and wasteful in terms of energy consumption.

The cost of multi-core, high-speed processors continues to drop rapidly. Those of you who have built your own computers in the past know that the usual game is finding the fastest processor possible in a given budget with as many processing cores as possible. Being able to maximize performance on a tight budget is one of the key reasons to build a computer instead of simply purchasing one. However, when building a server yourself, the game is choosing the best components for the job. In this case, selecting a processor with a lower clock speed or fewer cores because the size of your network only requires two cores, for example, means being able to effectively filter Internet traffic while using far less energy than a more exciting eight-core beast from AMD or Intel.

Similarly, spending a nominal extra sum on a motherboard that supports granular power management settings can pay significant dividends in power consumption later on. Finally, choosing a motherboard that supports reporting of component temperatures allows for the careful adjustment of case fans to provide enough cooling to protect components but avoid wasting energy on excessive cooling; this can also help optimize power utilization.

Noise

Corporations and large businesses frequently have a server room or data center where servers and appliances like an Untangle box can live happily without disturbing anyone. For most individuals and organizations thinking of building an Untangle gateway, though, such a specialized area is a luxury that simply won't exist. More often than not, the device will sit under a desk, on a desk, or in whatever room happens to have an incoming connection to the Internet.

Modern computers purchased off the shelf tend to be fairly quiet, with only the light hum of a power-supply fan and possibly a small case or CPU fan. Because Untangle can run very well on a homegrown PC assembled from a kit, from components, or on a repurposed older machine, the sound insulation and passive cooling (i.e., no fans to move air across the computer parts) of new PCs may not be available on the machine you choose to use. This isn't a problem, exactly, but is a consideration. For example, if your incoming Internet connection is in a conference room, beside a home-theater setup, or even under your desk, the constant hum may be an issue. The solution, of course, is to use a new, low–power consumption computer or to build a computer with components that enable low-noise applications. This tends to cost a bit more, but the joy of building the device yourself is being able to make choices around function, cost, and scalability.

New, Used, or DIY?

New computers are easy. You buy them, bring them home (or have them delivered), open the box, plug them in, run through a wizard or two, and you have a perfectly functioning computer (usually). However, when buying a computer off the shelf, no matter how inexpensive, there are usually operating-system costs included in the price. Untangle replaces the operating system with its own Debian Linux–based OS, meaning that those licensing fees built into the cost of off-the-shelf computers is wasted.

New computers, especially inexpensive ones, also tend to be limited on expandability. They have no need for the extra expansion slots required by higher-end machines for added graphics cards or disk controllers. Those same slots are needed to accommodate the extra network interface cards discussed earlier. This isn't to say that a new computer can't work well as an Untangle appliance, but *caveat emptor* is in full effect. At the very least, those choosing to go this route must ensure that one or two additional NICs can be accommodated by the motherboard.

While efficiency and throughput are essential in larger setups (schools, offices with more than 15–20 users, etc.), creation of an Untangle server for home, instructional, experimental, or other non-production uses can tolerate a less optimized setup. This is where a repurposed machine comes in. Most desktop PCs manufactured within the last four or five years meet the criteria outlined earlier for a minimal setup. In fact, reliability will be a larger issue than their performance in small-scale settings, given that a realistic lifespan for a desktop computer is about four years before components start wearing out.

While Untangle maintains that up to 50 users can be supported by the minimal configuration (single-core Pentium or AMD and 1 GB of RAM), this would only be suited to very light Internet usage. More typical usage (such as what a good-sized family would create or what might be expected in a church or very small library) would be well served by this low-end setup, but most others would probably find that the system became a bottleneck online.

That being said, many people don't wait four or five years to upgrade their computers. It isn't hard to find a hand-me-down or unused machine that is only a couple years old for free or a nominal price that would work well for a small office or a library with 15–20 computers. The only expense then would be an extra network card. Similarly, most computers built before 2010 will easily accommodate inexpensive PCI network cards, making upgrades and additions easier than in many brand-new computers that tend to be focused on small form factors and cosmetics rather than upgradeability.

While this book was written around a reasonable DIY machine that would work well for 75–100 users, my first forays into Untangle were with salvaged machines from an old high-school lab; I was easily able to demonstrate the use, function, and setup of the gateway. With the rapidly evolving technology of personal computing, there may, in fact, be no better use for aging machines than ensuring some protection for a network and experimenting with products like Untangle (or a file server, a Web server, authentication protocols, or any such important enterprise tools that don't require advanced graphics or the latest, fastest processors).

A Basic DIY Setup

While you will find precise setup instructions for three different do-it-yourself Untangle appliances (one ultra-cheap, one repurposed, and one high end for large deployments) in Appendix B, "Building Your Own Computer," the following is the setup upon which this book is based and that I used for testing purposes throughout (and to which I subjected my kids, thwarting their attempts to reach the nether regions of the Internet for months of writing).

There is nothing particularly sacred about any of the components listed here. They were meant as exemplars that would satisfy a few key requirements:

- Be able to provide nearly transparent content filtering for 50 users at high load or 100 users at moderate load.

- Be able to handle both filtered and unfiltered network segments.

- Provide DNS and DHCP for at least 100 users.

- Be relatively efficient (i.e., generally operate under peak capacities).

- Be compact and suitable for location just about anywhere.

- Avoid the need for anything other than standard air cooling.

- Include widely available commodity components.

- Do not exceed $350.

- Be sufficiently robust to have a three- to four-year lifespan under daily, continuous use.

- Be suitable for repurposing later as a solid desktop system for Web surfing and productivity tasks.

The components listed in Table 1.2 shouldn't be seen as an endorsement of any particular platform. AMD and Intel processors both have merits and detriments and, for our purposes, the choice between these two components should largely be driven by available prices for a given performance level. (The same can be said of the other manufacturers represented here, but the AMD versus Intel debate is as old as the Mac versus Windows debate, so was worth calling out.) All of these parts (or similar) are also widely available from any number of online or brick-and-mortar retailers and, even a year or two after this book is published, will still be easy to find (although most will be significantly cheaper; prices below are rounded, as they will obviously fluctuate).

Table 1.2 Bill of Materials for the DIY Machine Used for This Book

Component	Quantity	Description	Price
AMD Athlon II X3 455 with fan	1	Triple core processor; compromise between dual and quad core	$80
Thermal gel	1	Provides thermal conductivity between processor and fan	$5
Screw and accessory kit	1	A good just-in-case item; many motherboards and cases include appropriate parts to assemble components, but if they don't, having a complete kit is a big help	$15
Linksys LKG-6100 gigabit network adapter	2	Inexpensive and designed to fit the compact case	$30
Western Digital Caviar Green 1TB SATA hard drive	1	1 TB is more than will ever be needed for Untangle but this will allow the computer to function as a file server later	$55
Sony Optiarc DVD-RW SATA drive	1	The DVD-RW function is not necessary, but prices on these devices are very low and an eye to later repurposing influenced this decision	$20
Case fan	1	Not strictly necessary with the heat output of this setup, but the case was not designed specifically for passive heating, so increased airflow will help ensure longevity	$5
Biostar GeForce 7025 motherboard	1	An inexpensive motherboard that still included onboard graphics, supported later processor upgrades, and gigabit networking	$50
Crucial 4 GB DDR3-1333 MHz memory	1	4GB is more than sufficient for these needs; slower memory would have been adequate, but the cost differential made faster memory a better choice	$25
Cables to go dual SATA power splitter	1	The power supply above only had a single SATA power connector; two were needed for the hard drive and DVD-RW	$7

(Continued)

Table 1.2   Bill of Materials for the DIY Machine Used for This Book (*Continued*)

Component	Quantity	Description	Price
Ultra SATA II/III 12-inch cables	2	Cables to connect the hard drive and DVD burner to the motherboard; these are generally not included with inexpensive motherboards or kits	$14
Apex Micro ATX computer case	1	The Micro ATX form factor allows relatively easy expansion but keeps the overall footprint small for installations in a variety of locations	$50
		Total:	**$356**

SETTING UP THE COMPUTER

Assembly of these components is relatively intuitive and takes about 20 minutes. Many DIY setups can be purchased as complete kits and even people who have never spent much time inside a PC will have little trouble following basic directions to assemble the kit. Similarly, for those repurposing a machine or upgrading a new machine with the appropriate networking equipment, it should be relatively intuitive to add the network cards required for the server.

Two rules of thumb:

■ If there isn't a slot on the motherboard that matches the size of the card or component you are trying to attach, stop, check the directions, and proceed with caution. There are several standards for internal connections, not all of which are universally supported. For example, many networking cards follow the PCI standard, but many newer computers only have one regular PCI slot (or none at all), favoring instead enhanced PCI standards of varying speeds and sizes.

■ Discharge static electricity before touching internal components. It seems a trivial thing—most computer parts are relatively resistant to small amounts of static—but working in socks on a shag rug in the middle of winter is probably not an optimal environment for playing with the inside of a $500 PC. While there is special equipment to discharge static, all that is really necessary is to touch an external metal object before heading inside the computer.

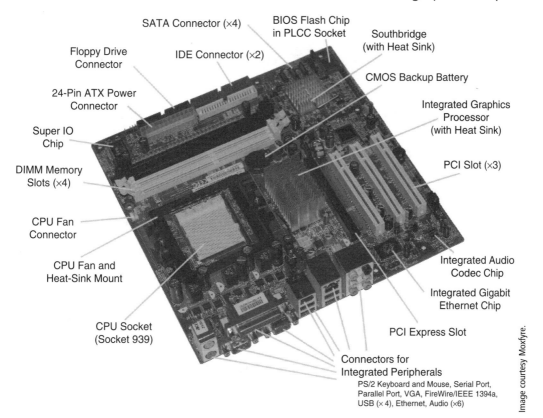

Figure 1.3
A typical motherboard.

Figure 1.3 shows a typical motherboard. While it looks fairly dense, there are only so many places where various components can be attached. Even better, most motherboards are labeled (if somewhat cryptically), taking away most of the guesswork.

Figure 1.4, however, shows a standard PCI network card. There are three slots on the motherboard in Figure 1.3 in which this card could be inserted. However, most compact motherboards (ideal for an Untangle application) and many newer computers and motherboards lack the large slots required for standard PCI cards, opting instead for much smaller (but faster) PCIe slots. Ensuring compatibility between hardware components (particularly between the motherboard and network controllers, in this case) will be the only aspect of assembling or upgrading a PC for your purposes that might be a bit challenging. When ordering network interface cards, be sure you know which size slots your motherboard contains. This is easy when ordering a kit, because the specifications of the motherboard will be readily available, but will tend to be more obscure when repurposing an older computer. Figure 1.5 shows the three most common types of PCI slots on a motherboard.

Figure 1.4
A standard PCI network card.

Figure 1.5
Common PCI slots.

Location and Environmental Issues

As noted previously, servers really belong in a climate-controlled, dust-free environment so that they can run mission-critical applications 24 × 7 for an organization. However, the reality of server location for most of the people reading this book—whether a school IT manager, a student, a parent, a librarian, a small business owner, or just about anyone else who isn't in enterprise information systems—is that the Untangle server is probably going to go wherever there happens to be space.

Mine is currently sitting in my basement, next to the cable modem and Airport, tucked as far behind the television as possible so it doesn't offend my wife's aesthetic sensibilities any more than it has to. (She considers it a necessary evil for throttling the kids' access to Facebook when there are chores to be done.) Having worked in the public schools for some time, I've seen far more mission-critical servers scattered about, crammed in book closets, holding up tabletops, and propping open doors. Seriously.

The point of all of this is that the Untangle gateway you are building—even if used for educational, experimental, or hobby purposes—has the potential to stand between you, your computers and other connected devices, and the big bad Internet. It can handle a variety of networking functions more transparently and robustly than your broadband modem or existing routing equipment (assuming you already have consumer-level wireless hotspots, cable/DSL Internet access, etc.) and has the potential to be a critical piece of compliance with various regulations and the safety of your network.

Given that, it's worthwhile to find a spot for the Untangle appliance (no matter how little one spends on it) where it will be all of the following:

- Cool
- Dry
- Relatively free of dust
- Inaccessible to prying hands, tripping feet, spilled coffee, etc.

Even a cheap box represents an investment of time, and more importantly, will most likely end up becoming a critical part of the network upon which you and your users rely, whether for readily available external access to the network (through its integrated VPN), for its DNS and DHCP capabilities, or for its content filtering.

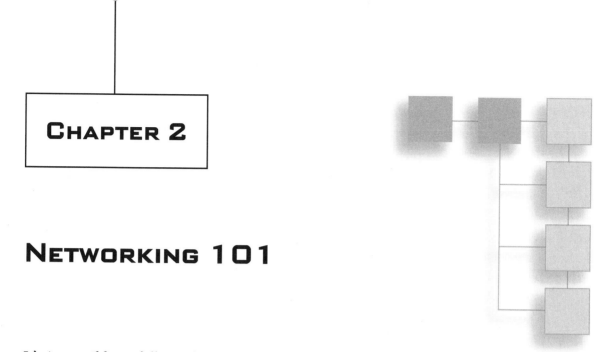

CHAPTER 2

NETWORKING 101

It's impossible to fully understand the use, setup, and function of Untangle without first having a basic understanding of networking technologies. Although a deep understanding of network protocols and topologies is not a prerequisite for setting up an Untangle gateway or, for that matter, using this book, Untangle is a useful entry point to networking applications.

This chapter provides high-level overviews of the technologies and best practices associated with the creation and maintenance of computer networks suitable to small and home offices, schools, libraries, and other scenarios that match the scope of this book and DIY Untangle gateways.

Note

> This is one of those chapters that can be easily glossed over by experienced network and system administrators who really just want to understand Untangle. On the other hand, it's a chapter that could form the basis of a computer networking or information technology course with a fully functioning Internet gateway and well-documented network as the final outcome. You be the judge, but if words like DNS, DHCP, TCP/IP, node, and topology don't roll of your tongue, you should probably make sure you read and understand this chapter. It's near the beginning for a reason; the rest of this book will assume comprehension of the topics in this chapter.

EVALUATING YOUR NETWORK

Before I launch into the technical nitty-gritty of network topologies and protocols, it's important to recognize that most of you already have at least a rudimentary network in place. A network is simply an interconnected system of computing devices. Do you have a computer and a printer connected to your Internet router or modem? Then you have a network. Have a wireless hotspot connected to your router, a desktop PC hardwired to the router, a printer shared from the desktop PC, and a Nintendo Wii using the wireless connection? Then you have a network. Do you have five computer labs, a rolling cart of laptops, wireless routers in every corridor, and three servers handling operations in your school? Then you also have a network, albeit a much larger one than the home networks I just described.

In any case, there is some infrastructure in place supporting communication between various devices connected to each other and, most likely, to the Internet. Routers, switches, hubs, wireless access points, and the like—along with cabling that connects these components to each other and to the devices they serve—make up the underpinnings of a network.

The devices themselves are referred to as *nodes*. Anything that has its own identity on a network—whether a laptop, a desktop, a printer, a mobile phone with WiFi, an Internet-connected TV, or any other device that sends and receives traffic of some sort via the infrastructure—counts as a node. In fact, if you stop to think about all the devices that connect to your network, you may realize that the network is far larger and more critical to your professional, educational, and entertainment needs than you previously thought. Even for those who already administer larger networks and understand their significance and complexity, a complete inventory of connected devices can be surprising, revealing the need to control and monitor access (if that isn't happening already) and adjust bandwidth to accommodate a larger-than-expected number of nodes.

Introducing the Systems Development Life Cycle

The systems development life cycle (SDLC), shown in Figure 2.1, is a familiar topic to information-technology students and professionals, as well as those managing technical projects in an enterprise setting.

The SDLC has been visualized and explained in many ways over the years and can be implemented informally or formally. Regardless of the details, it is essentially a system of ongoing evaluation and development designed to solve a problem or create and maintain a system that meets a particular need. In this case, you're evaluating existing network infrastructure and nodes to do several things:

- Determine the size, scope, and relative functionality and health of your existing network.
- Define requirements for upgrades, changes, and maintenance in the existing network to accommodate the successful use of Untangle.

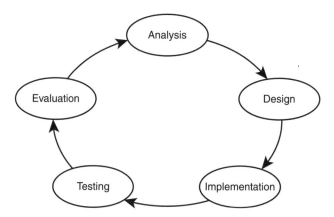

Figure 2.1
The systems development life cycle.

■ Define requirements for an Untangle appliance.

■ Document the network topology, a critical baseline for any networking project.

Most likely, a network already exists to which you will be adding Untangle to improve the network's function, safety, and reliability. While *evaluation* is technically the last step in the SDLC, the circular, cyclical structure of the SDLC implies that any system is always subject to evaluation and improvement. Thus, evaluation of your existing, Untangle-free network is really the first step of the SDLC for your purposes.

Evaluation: What You Already Have

This step is going to either be painful (for larger networks) or trivial (for small networks). Do it anyway. In this phase, you fully diagram and document your existing infrastructure and nodes. This will be incredibly useful (and, in fact, quite necessary) as you get deeper into managing networks with Untangle and will provide an opportunity to decide if the existing topology is appropriate or if another should be implemented as you begin using Untangle. (Larger networks may already have a network diagram in place, but it's remarkable how many don't!)

So what should a network diagram look like? There isn't a set formula; different texts and references will point you to different conventions. For your purposes, it really doesn't matter. The network diagram must merely document infrastructure and nodes, with basic information about each.

Network diagrams can be one of three types:

■ **Physical.** Physical diagrams are schematics showing detailed connection information (e.g., PC-XYZ has a dynamically assigned IP address and is connected to wall jack

A1, which is connected to port 22 on switch 3 in wiring closet 2; switch 3 is connected to port 4 on switch 1 in the server room; etc.). Don't worry if all the terms in that parenthetical note don't make sense; these are covered in detail later in this chapter, in the sections "Network Equipment" and "IP Addresses, TCP/IP, DNS, and DHCP." What is important to note is that a physical network diagram is concerned with actual, specific connections and is quite useful for network troubleshooting.

- **Logical.** Logical diagrams are concerned with the high-level function and segmenting of a network. They are more useful from the perspective of designing a network around an Internet gateway like Untangle that can divide infrastructure and nodes into separate functional units (e.g., a group of PCs for library patrons, a group of PCs for librarians attached to a library information system server, and a wireless access point serving several WiFi-connected e-readers). Such a diagram will usually describe particular network attributes for each group, such as address blocks, DNS, and DHCP properties. Again, without concerning yourself with the details of computer networking just yet, note that logical diagrams address function rather than form, as is the case for physical diagrams.

- **Hybrid.** While highly complex networks should have separate physical and logical documentation, most networks managed by an Untangle gateway can be well documented with a hybrid diagram that categorizes detailed physical network data by its logical/functional units.

To make these distinctions clearer, Figure 2.2, Figure 2.3, and Figure 2.4 show physical, logical, and hybrid maps, respectively, for a small, fictional community library using an Untangle gateway to manage all network services and handle gateway antivirus and content filtering. The library has 10 PCs for patron Internet access (these must be filtered for offensive materials to meet federal regulations), three kiosks that access only the library information system server (also located onsite), two PCs for librarian use only (these do not need to have Internet access filtered), and a cart of Android tablets that can be checked out by patrons.

Note that very effective network diagrams can be developed with basic graphics software, various specialized software, or even with spreadsheets. Figure 2.5 shows the hybrid map from Figure 2.4 represented by a spreadsheet. Using a spreadsheet allows for a high degree of implementation detail, but can be difficult to comprehend at a glance. Best practice, in fact, dictates that both a diagram and a detailed spreadsheet (or other similar tabular data)

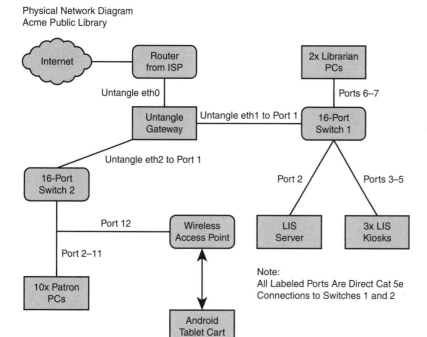

Physical Network Diagram
Acme Public Library

Figure 2.2
A physical network diagram.

be maintained for complete network documentation, but this is rarely necessary or practical in settings outside the enterprise.

For graphical representations of a network, the following applications are freely available:

- Google Drawings, which is part of Google Apps; user-submitted templates include network diagrams (http://www.google.com/google-d-s/drawings/)

- LibreOffice Draw (http://www.libreoffice.org/download/)

- Inkscape (http://inkscape.org)

More sophisticated drawings can be achieved with specialty software like eDraw or Omni-Graffle (the latter is only available for Mac OS but is noteworthy for its ease of use and available specialized templates), but for the purposes of this text, freely available drawing programs are more than adequate. In general, logical network diagrams will be used throughout this book, with hybrid drawings used as appropriate for specific examples.

Logical Network Diagram
Acme Public Library

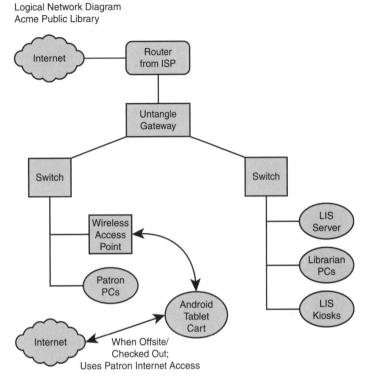

Figure 2.3
A logical network diagram.

Evaluation: Requirements

The second component of the evaluation phase involves determining requirements in four major areas:

- Untangle hardware configuration (necessary performance and number of network interfaces)

- Untangle software configurations (required modules, functions, degree of filtering, etc.)

- Necessary network infrastructure upgrades to support robust content filtering and to ensure high performance

- Desired network upgrades, segmentation, and topology changes to be completed using the new capabilities of Untangle

Putting an Untangle gateway in front of your network provides a great opportunity to look at the overall form and function of your network and decide whether the technology

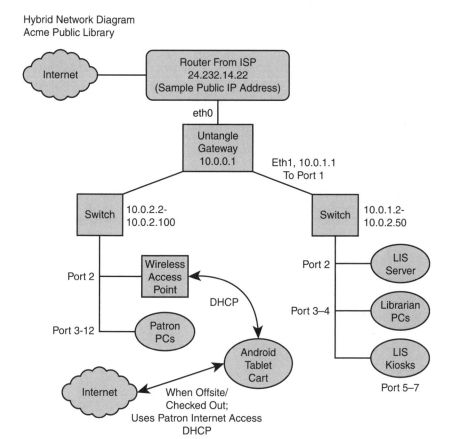

Figure 2.4
A hybrid network diagram.

	A	B	C	D	E	F	G	H	I
1	Hybrid Network Map								
2	Acme Public Library								
3									
4	**Node/Device**	**IP Address**	**IP Block**	**Connected to**	**Origin port**	**Destination port**	**Notes**		
5	Router	24.232.14.22	N/A	Untangle gateway	N/A	eth0	Example public IP address		
6	Untangle gateway	10.0.0.1	N/A	Router	eth0	N/A	The spreadsheet introduces some redundancy		
7		10.0.1.1	10.0.1.2-10.0.1.50	Switch 1	eth1	1			
8		10.0.2.1	10.0.2.2-10.0.1.100	Switch 2	eth2	1	Unfiltered zone		
9	Switch 1	Unmanaged	10.0.1.2-10.0.1.50 via gateway/DHCP	LIS Server	2	N/A			
10				Librarian PCs	3-4	N/A			
11				LIS Kiosks	5-7	N/A			
12	Switch 2	Unmanaged	10.0.2.2-10.0.2.100 via gateway/DHCP	Wireless access point	2	N/A	Configured in bridge mode		
13				Patron PCs	3-12	N/A			
14	Wireless access point	Bridge mode	Draws from Switch 2/eth2 pool	Android tablets and patron personal computers	N/A	N/A			
15									

Figure 2.5
A spreadsheet with a hybrid map.

within Untangle should be used to engineer a more efficient, more secure, and/or more usable network.

This is tied to the choice in hardware, as well. If, as will be discussed in the coming sections, it makes sense to segment your network, additional network cards will be necessary. Applying differential content-filtering policies to different devices or physical locations on the network, allowing remote access to specific network assets, and the creation of guest networks are the most common reasons for segmentation.

Similarly, as discussed in Chapter 1, "Getting a Computer," larger or more complex networks require faster components, more RAM, etc. Upfront definition of requirements will ensure that the Untangle server is built appropriately to meet the needs of your network.

A note about developing requirements: It's okay for requirements to exist in your head. For large systems, for systems requiring major purchasing decisions, or for systems bumping up against procurement rules, requirements deserve some solid documentation and justification. However, for the purposes of most of the readers of this book, the important thing is the thought process and the realization that just any old computer won't do here. The choice in computer (or computer components) shouldn't be just be a guess; instead, it should be driven by the needs of the system it supports.

Network Configurations

This book uses the terms *network configuration* and *topology* interchangeably and in a less formal sense than many texts on computer networking might. Formally, network topologies are often described by their underlying technologies as well as the manner in which they connect to each other physically. They can include token ring, bus, and star configurations, among others. However, because most modern networks (and certainly the vast majority of networks that readers of this book will support) are Ethernet networks, I will use the configuration and topology terms to refer to the arrangement of nodes in both logical and physical groups. Other formal topologies are well outside the scope of this book.

A few words about Ethernet, however, *are* within this book's scope. Ethernet has a variety of specific implementations, standards, and related equipment, all of which operate on the principle of CSMACD (carrier sense, multiple access, collision detection). Essentially, Ethernet is a communications protocol in which electronic bits of data travel via cable or wireless signal, and that automatically retransmits bits as needed if they do not reach their destination because of a so-called "collision."

Now that the strictly technical bits are out of the way, what, precisely, do I mean by network configurations? In the previous section, I talked about segmenting a network such that groups of computers could fall under different sets of rules for exposure to the Internet, content filtering, etc. The idea of segmentation is also reflected in the logical network maps discussed earlier. While Untangle supports differentiation among computers via their addresses, login information from their users, and various rules set up in the Untangle interface, it is often more efficient, easier to manage, and, most importantly, easier to conceptualize if different network policies are applied to different physical portions of a network.

For example, I have several computers, tablets, smart phones, servers, and printers on my home/office network. A wireless router that my kids access with their laptops and game consoles is attached to one network card on our Untangle server. This interface is heavily filtered for inappropriate content and a number of ports related to peer-to-peer networking are blocked. (Remember Napster? Neither do my kids.) My Web server is attached to another interface with policies set up to forward all incoming HTTP and FTP requests to the Web server, while blocking all other traffic. Finally, a third interface is attached to a wireless access point for the "big people" in the house. This interface has no content filtering and supports remote access to my desktop PC.

Not only does this approach just make sense from a parenting and getting-work-done-at-home perspective, but it also helps manage traffic bottlenecks by exploiting three fast interfaces. While we have only a single connection to the Internet, the kids will tend not to experience any lag on their online console games, even if I'm moving large files onto the Web server, for example. Similarly, I can prioritize my own traffic to ensure that three kids watching YouTube videos doesn't interfere with my video conferencing.

Similar segmentation can be applied at scale in settings like those in the figures earlier in this chapter. While not necessary to take advantage of Untangle's content filtering, firewall, virus protection, and other gateway services, the use of multiple interfaces is an especially useful feature of the gateway.

Thus, for your purposes, *network configuration* and *topology* refer to the physical segmentation of an Ethernet network, the arrangement of hardware on those segments, and the software rules that manage traffic on them.

NETWORK EQUIPMENT

Throughout the introduction and first two chapters of this book, I have mentioned several types of infrastructure hardware. Switches, cabling, routers, wireless access points, and network interface cards all play a role in connecting network nodes to each other and to the Internet.

Adding Untangle to a network rarely requires hardware changes, but there are certainly considerations when adding a layer of services that can introduce latency. *Latency* is the delay between transmission and receipt of data. The services built into Untangle, no matter how quickly executed, can slow network performance, especially at peak loads. Ensuring that the remaining infrastructure is optimized wherever possible reduces other sources of latency and can make the introduction of Untangle relatively transparent to users.

The most likely bottleneck for Internet traffic is the incoming connection. Standard DSL and cable modems provided by ISPs are meant for consumer use and will rarely be connected to a device like an Untangle server. The modem remains the single point of connection to the Internet. I discuss bandwidth and connection issues in the next section, but bear in mind that most stock devices provided by the ISP will only support 100 Mbps internal connections to the rest of the network and are often locked down such that users cannot optimize or modify their settings.

A variety of broadband modems that address these deficiencies can be purchased at any electronics or computing retailer. As discussed earlier, it is possible to optimize internal traffic to some extent with multiple network interfaces, but it becomes quite expensive to have multiple Internet connections. (See the section on load balancing and bandwidth aggregation in Chapter 9, "Advanced Topics," if you would like to know how to support that with Untangle.) Thus, a higher quality modem than that provided by most ISPs is generally a worthwhile investment for homes and small businesses that rarely purchase enterprise-grade Internet connections.

Inside your network, there are likely a number of components that can be inexpensively upgraded to improve overall performance and ensure the best experience for your users, even as content filtering, bandwidth shaping (prioritizing access to Internet connectivity for particular traffic), and anti-malware inspection put pressure on Internet performance. As the size of the network increases, infrastructural upgrades obviously become less trivial, but schools and libraries can generally leverage eRate, a federal program that provides reimbursements for these types of upgrades. Small and medium-sized businesses have the moral equivalent: tax deductions. Interestingly, to be eligible for eRate reimbursements, schools and libraries must have a content filter like Untangle in place.

As you talk about larger and larger networks, the concept of the *backbone* becomes important. The backbone is generally one or more high-speed switches that may be daisy chained together to provide connectivity to the most critical nodes or subnetworks. Segmented networks may actually have multiple backbones. Direct connections between the backbone and a network node are called *home runs* and provide the simplest high-speed connection from a user to the gateway and on to the Internet. (See Figure 2.6.)

Note that Figure 2.6 shows a logical diagram. The thick line represents a single, multiport switch, while the thin lines represent cabled connections back to the switch. You neither know nor care how long these cables are (as long as they meet Ethernet cabling

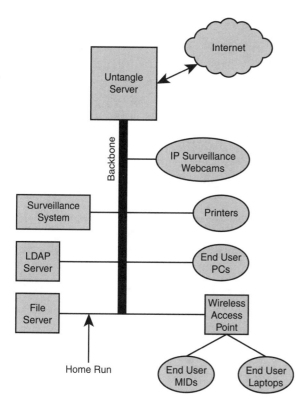

Figure 2.6
A simple network backbone topology.

standards; an excellent description of cabling standards, terms, and equipment is available at http://www.zytrax.com/tech/layer_1/cables/tech_lan.htm). The switches that make up the network backbone should be as large as is feasible and necessary. For example, a single 48-port switch is preferable to two 24-port switches daisy chained together. Similarly, these switches should at least support gigabit speeds where they connect to each other and to the Untangle server; increasingly, switches with gigabit speeds at all ports (instead of 100 Mbps speeds) are both common and relatively inexpensive.

As noted previously, Ethernet has a number of standards utilizing the same underlying technology. These standards extend to the types of cable used to connect Ethernet devices. Cable now is usually Category 5 Enhanced (Cat5e) and, unlike older Category 5 (Cat5) cables, supports gigabit data transmission. Category 6 cable is also becoming more common. In any case, Cat5 cable should be replaced whenever possible, as should any cabling that is kinked, abraded, cut, or otherwise damaged. Wherever practical, it should not run near fluorescent lights or other sources of electromagnetic interference like microwave ovens or PA speakers.

Finally, most networks include at least one wireless access point (and potentially several). As with other Ethernet hardware (wireless access points still use CSMACD, even if they don't use Ethernet cabling), several legacy standards exist that can drastically increase latency for wireless devices, particularly as the number of users increases. All wireless Ethernet follows the so-called 802.11 standard, but varying speeds and wireless frequencies are associated with 802.11a, 802.11b, 802.11g, and 802.11n. While 802.11g devices provide acceptable performance and are usually quite inexpensive, 802.11n devices are drastically faster and generally have far better range. Thus, whenever financially feasible, wireless access points should be replaced with 802.11n access points.

Bandwidth and Internet Connections

In many locations, no matter how completely one optimizes an internal network, the actual connection to the Internet will be a far more significant bottleneck than anything else. With or without the filtering and security services offered by Untangle, bandwidth is all too often a scarce and precious commodity.

While a growing number of communities can access very fast Internet connections at home, at businesses, and at schools, others limp along with painfully slow DSL or even dial-up. For those with access to high-speed Internet connections, the cost may simply be too high to take advantage of it. The bottom line is that dial-up Internet users shouldn't bother implementing content filtering or the other services offered by Untangle. The additional overhead will cripple an already archaic means of connecting.

Those with connections in the 1–3 Mbps range should carefully consider whether an Untangle appliance makes sense in their context. A relatively fast server will provide fairly transparent filtering, but the Internet connection itself will not support more than a couple moderate users at a time, making the investment in a sufficiently fast server of questionable value. Those readers looking to use Untangle as an educational or enthusiast project or who are looking to, for example, carefully monitor their children's Internet usage in ways that other commercial products can't support will find the investment worthwhile. A small office limited to a fairly slow connection may be better served using the rudimentary tools that ISPs usually build into their modems.

One exception is what is called a *leased line*. These are dedicated connections to the Internet that schools and other organizations may purchase when less expensive options are unavailable. While leased lines can be incredibly fast, these very expensive connections are usually limited to universities or large corporations. Slower leased lines (called *T1 connections*) usually don't exceed 3 Mbps in throughput (the actual speed with which data moves back and forth from the Internet) but have considerable bandwidth (the number of streams of data potentially available through the connection), making them suitable for use with Untangle and likely to be used in settings where inexpensive content filtering is a must.

Higher speed connections (e.g., cable or fiber optic) make the actual Internet service a less likely bottleneck. As noted before, Untangle also supports load balancing across multiple incoming connections, effectively improving bandwidth for a network. However, this comes at an additional cost for Untangle (this component is neither free nor open source) as well as the extra cost of multiple Internet connections.

IP Addresses, TCP/IP, DNS, and DHCP

If the title of this section looks like alphabet soup to you, read on. If you can calculate subnet masks in your sleep, feel free to turn the page now.

The Internet essentially works via two important protocols: Transmission Control Protocol (TCP) and Internet Protocol (IP). These form the basis of what is known as a *packet-switching network* and can be compared to the function of the postal service. Say for example, that you have a large document that you need to send to someone. If you only have letter-sized envelopes, the document won't fit into a single envelope. Therefore, you must break the document into sections of sufficiently small size to be placed in multiple envelopes. Each of these envelopes needs to be addressed, stamped, and mailed to the intended recipient of the large document.

The postal services in most countries aren't known for their efficiency. It's entirely possible that the individual letters will arrive over multiple days. When all the envelopes finally reach their destination, the recipient needs a system by which he or she can reassemble the document in its original order, regardless of how it arrived. Data transmitted on the Internet are handled in much the same way. TCP breaks up data into manageable parts called *packets*. IP basically handles addressing so that the packets can reach their intended recipient, even as millions of other packets are flying around a network. Then TCP provides a mechanism for reassembly of the individual packets into meaningful data; it also handles verification and can request retransmission of lost data. These two protocols are generally referred to together as TCP/IP because neither is particularly useful without the other.

Domain Name Service, or DNS, associates text addresses with the numeric addresses that Internet Protocol uses, called *IP addresses*. In other words, DNS makes IP addresses useful to and readable by humans. (This is actually a gross oversimplification of DNS, but it works for your purposes.) DNS requires the continuous worldwide replication of such associations—knowing that cnn.com, for example, is associated with the IP address 157.166.226.25—as well as management of these types of associations internally on a network, where chrisdawsonpc.local might be associated with 192.168.128.2.

Finally, DHCP, which stands for Dynamic Host Control Protocol, is closely related to IP. It handles the assignment of IP addresses automatically. IP addresses can be assigned manually to a particular device, but most often, this is reserved for servers and other critical hardware. DHCP starts with a predefined range of IP addresses and then hands them out to devices as they connect to the network. It then takes away their addresses and reassigns them on predetermined intervals, making the management of addressing fairly transparent to system administrators and end users.

What does this have to do with Untangle? Untangle not only inspects the packets that move across its interfaces for signs of malware and for origins in forbidden regions of the Internet, but it also handles DNS and DHCP on the network if you choose to configure those services. Chapter 3, "Downloading and Installing Untangle," and Chapter 4, "What's Happening Inside My Untangle Gateway?" deal with the setup and use of these features in greater detail, but for now, know that Untangle can handle virtually all of your network-management features as part of its NG Firewall Free package.

PROXY SERVERS

As a final note about network configurations and hardware, proxy servers deserve a few moments of your time. *Proxy servers* essentially add layers of control and anonymity to requests for pages and content on the Internet. Computing devices can be set to make requests for Web content from a proxy server instead of directly from the Web server itself. The proxy server then requests the content and sends it back to the original device.

While this might seem overly complicated, it enables a variety of important functions. For example, the circuitous route for requesting Web pages lets Untangle check to see if a particular file has been downloaded before. If it has, a locally cached version of the file can be used, avoiding a time-consuming and potentially expensive download in the case of metered Web services.

There is also a more unpleasant side to proxy servers. Many such servers exist on the Internet that can be accessed simply from a Web browser and allow students to bypass content filtering. Untangle supports blocking such sites and allows system administrators to blacklist such sites as well, since students (and staff at small and medium businesses, but it's the students who tend to be both savvy and motivated in this respect) are increasingly setting up their own proxy servers that wouldn't otherwise be known to Untangle. In fact, end users could set up their own Untangle servers at home with all content filtering turned off, set their Web browsers to use these servers as proxies, and then, ironically, bypass Untangle if the content filter didn't have a mechanism for blacklisting these external servers.

Chapter 3

Downloading and Installing Untangle

Can it really be that easy? Just download some software and all of a sudden you have a firewall and content filter that keeps the kids from going where they shouldn't online or keeps the computers on a small business network free of malware?

To answer that question: No. It isn't quite that easy. Most things that are free come at some sort of price, even if that price is just a bit more work than you might otherwise expect. However, making the leap from computer parts or repurposed PC to functional content filter and firewall isn't as hard as you might expect.

Start Downloading and Start Burning

If you've ever installed a Linux operating system on a computer—whether as an experiment, to save money on a DIY system, to eke an extra bit of life out of an old system, or because you prefer the open source operating system—then you've probably burned an ISO image to a CD-ROM or DVD-ROM. The same goes for those of you who have managed and deployed volume-licensed software from Microsoft. You may have even made one if you created an archive of a home movie DVD or backed up software or music DVDs.

An International Organization for Standardization (ISO) image is an exact copy of an optical disk (a CD-ROM or DVD-ROM) that can then be written to a blank disk. These can also be written to USB drives, although the easiest method, using software that is generally already installed on most PCs, is to simply burn a CD or DVD from the image. The Mac OS Disk Utility, various Roxio software often installed on new PCs, and Free ISO Burner (http://www.freeisoburner.com/) for Windows will all create optical disks from disk images. Once you have an optical disk with the Untangle installation media on it, you're ready for the next step.

An ISO, BIOS, and Boot Sequence Primer

For those of you who have never installed an operating system on a computer before, the idea of an ISO is important because it allows users to create CDs or DVDs from which computers can boot. I'm going to get extra basic here for a minute to make sure you're on the same technical page, so (as with some sizeable chunks of this chapter) feel free to skim or skip the next couple of paragraphs if you frequently reimage computers, build or maintain computers for a living, or otherwise fully understand the boot process of a PC. Otherwise, read on for a quick primer.

When a computer boots, it looks for an operating system to load into memory and launch all of the interfaces and functions with which you're familiar. The *operating system*, or *OS*, provides the interface between users and the computer, between applications and the computer, and, to some extent, between users and applications. (See Figure 3.1.) Generally, the operating system resides on a hard disk, but most computers can also be set to look for CD-ROMs or DVD-ROMs that contain a bootable operating system or associated installer. The aforementioned ISO images contain just such a bootable operating system.

To set a computer to look at its optical drive for a bootable OS before it looks at its own hard drives, you may need to modify the BIOS. BIOS, which stands for basic input output system, essentially enables the OS and various peripheral devices to communicate at a basic level with the computer's underlying hardware. Among other things, the BIOS establishes the order in which the computer checks for bootable devices. By default, most newer computers look first to their internal hard drives, then to optical drives, USB drives, 3.5-inch floppy drives (if present), and even to a computer network.

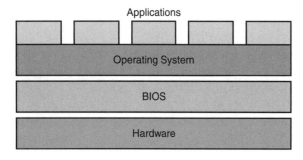

Figure 3.1
Schematic of a PC operating system.

If the PC in question was built from scratch and contains an empty hard drive, then the computer will skip the hard disk and pick up the optical drive—which, in your case, will contain an Untangle ISO. It will then jump automatically to the Untangle installer (more on that later). However, if the PC has been repurposed, recycled, or bought new with an operating system already installed, or if it becomes necessary to reinstall Untangle for whatever reason, then it will ignore the bootable CD or DVD in the optical drive and boot to Windows (or whatever OS was previously installed) unless the computer's BIOS instructs it to look at the optical drive first.

You access the BIOS settings immediately at system startup by pressing a particular key, which invariably is different for every computer you encounter (or build). Most PCs quickly display the required key to "Enter Setup" as they start; press this key (often Delete, F10, F12, or F2), and you will be presented with a BIOS setup interface. Again, this is rarely standardized and is not a graphical interface, meaning that it must be navigated with keystrokes. However, the necessary keystrokes are generally detailed somewhere on the screen; a bit of experimentation will yield a section of the setup application that allows users to change the boot sequence. Setting the optical drive to the first position will allow the computer to boot from a CD or DVD and run the Untangle install (or any OS install for that matter).

Figure 3.2 shows a common BIOS setup sequence for changing the boot order on a PC; the actual sequence and appearance will depend on the age of the computer and the manufacturer of its motherboard, but this figure gives a sense of the interface you can expect.

Yes, Untangle Is an OS

Untangle is not software that runs within an operating system like a typical antivirus utility. Rather, it's a complete operating system that runs a number of applications designed to protect an entire network and handle a variety of networking functions. Untangle is based on Debian Linux (as are Ubuntu and Mint, the two most popular versions of desktop Linux) but bears little resemblance to what you typically think of as an operating system.

Untangle provides a very basic console to launch its services, shut down the machine, and assign simple options. Untangle has a built-in Web server and all administration happens via a Web browser. In fact, when the Untangle server is launched, a browser simply opens full screen and users never have to touch the underlying Untangle OS. More likely, users will be able to run the server "headless"—i.e., without a monitor, accessing the administrative tools from another PC. (Any Web browser on a PC connected to the network will

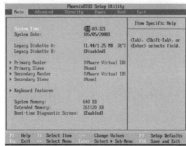

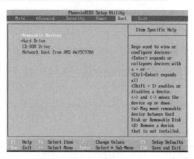

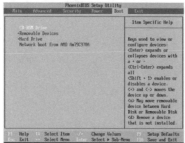

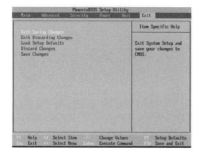

Figure 3.2
Common BIOS interface for changing the boot order of a PC.

work, as will remotely connected machines. I'll cover remote administration and the setup required for access to the server from outside the network in Chapter 9, "Advanced Topics," in the section on remote administration.)

The key message here? Installing Untangle will wipe out anything that already existed on the computer you are using. It requires no additional software to run and, in general, is meant to run by itself on a dedicated computer, just as one would generally run Microsoft Windows by itself on a dedicated PC.

Choosing and Burning the Disk Image

Okay, disk-image experts, start reading again here.

All that background aside, it's time to actually get the Untangle ISO and burn it to a CD or DVD. It doesn't matter which medium you use; the ISO looks the same to a computer regardless. Obviously, if you are using DVDs, the computer doing the burning needs to have a drive capable of writing DVDs and the computer that will become the Untangle server needs to be able to read them.

You can download the Untangle ISO from www.untangle.com/get-untangle. It is available in both 32-bit and 64-bit versions. The 32-bit version will run on any PC hardware and is suitable for most applications. The 64-bit version is a better choice if you intend to process larger amounts of data or expect that your appliance will be used in more demanding settings (with a higher numbers of users, with greater volumes of traffic, etc.).

32-Bit Versus 64-Bit

As a rule of thumb, a 64-bit operating system is required to access 4GB of RAM or more. Untangle recommends 2GB of RAM or more for more than 150 users and 4GB of RAM for 500–1,500 users. Thus, as the number of users on your network approaches 150 users, you should plan to use 64-bit Untangle to ensure scalability. Smaller networks will not be negatively impacted by the use of 64-bit Untangle if you have an appropriate 64-bit processor.

If you aren't sure which to pick, go with the 32-bit version. Performance will be indistinguishable for small office or home applications. The 64-bit download requires compatible hardware (all AMD Athlon, Phenom, Opteron, and FX processors and most Intel Core and Xeon processors; check manufacturer Web sites for details), but will scale better as loads increase and will be able to address larger amounts of system memory. (Anything greater than 3.5 GB of RAM requires a 64-bit OS to be available to the system; 32-bit versions will work if the PC has more RAM, but will not be able to recognize it.)

Once you download the ISO, instructions for burning the image to a DVD or CD vary by operating system, as well as by any software previously installed on the burning computer.

■ In Windows 7 and 8, the Windows Disk Image Burner is included by default and can usually be accessed by right-clicking the ISO file. Many users have reported that the burner software is easily displaced by other software that can also burn image files, so an easy solution is to simply download the free ISO Recorder software at http:// alexfeinman.com/isorecorder.htm. It isn't fancy, but works well.

■ In Mac OS X, the Disk Utility will handle burning tasks. It can be found in the Utilities folder in Applications.

■ Linux users can download any number of disk-burning applications using Apt, Synaptic, or whatever software management utility is installed in their particular choice of distributions; K3b is a particularly powerful and popular choice for disk burning on Linux.

Tip

A wide variety of available software can be found on CNET (http://download.cnet.com/1770-20_4-0.html? tag=mncol%3Bsort%3Bda&query=disk+burning+software&searchtype=downloads&filter=&sort=date Added +asc&rpp=10).

Follow the instructions specific to your software and create the CD or DVD and then read on.

INSTALLATION

Once the BIOS setup is complete and the disk is burned, insert the disk into the Untangle server's drive and restart it. When it boots, you will be greeted with the screen shown in Figure 3.3 (although on some hardware, this screen may take some time to appear).

The normal graphical install option is fine for most applications. Occasionally, if using very limited hardware with minimal graphics support or 500 MB or less of RAM, the text installer will be necessary. Expert mode provides access to advanced configuration options up front. You'll set up the advanced options after the installation. (Advanced options are discussed later in this book.)

Pressing Enter launches a wizard with entirely self-explanatory options that will be very familiar to anyone who has installed a graphical Linux operating system before. Language, dialect, keyboard layout, and time zone selection screens all bring you to a system test screen. Untangle will scan your system hardware and alert you if there are hardware

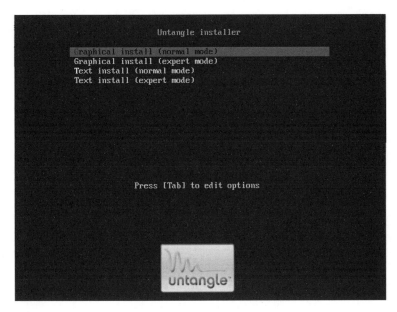

Figure 3.3
Startup screen.

problems that will prevent Untangle from running (for example, insufficient memory or an inadequate processor).

Assuming your hardware passes muster, click Continue. As shown in Figure 3.4, you will be asked if you want to proceed and format your disk. You don't actually have a choice if you want the installer to continue, but it's worth mentioning that this is the last chance to *not* erase the entire hard drive on the computer. While this is irrelevant for newly built PCs, any machines being repurposed should be completely backed up if there is any possibility that something of value may exist on the computer. Telling a lawyer—even in your cheeriest tone—that although three years of briefs were wiped out, the law firm is now protected from malware will not make you the IT hero that Untangle claims its solutions will on their Web site.

The Untangle installer will chug for a bit, formatting the hard drive and installing the OS. The time it takes to install will depend upon the hardware. When it has completed the installation, the installer will prompt you to remove the CD/DVD and will reboot automatically. If everything went as planned, you will be greeted with the GRUB boot loader screen when the computer reboots. (See Figure 3.5.) GRUB is a standard open source application for choosing from multiple operating systems or different interfaces to a single OS. In this case, you will be able to choose from high- and low-resolution versions of Untangle and two recovery options. The default low-resolution choice will be chosen automatically if you do nothing; this is generally the best choice anyway.

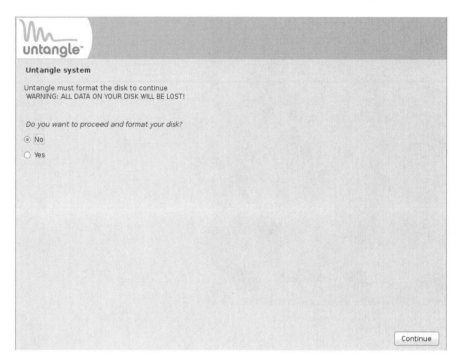

Figure 3.4
Last chance to save items that might be saved on a computer destined to be an Untangle appliance.

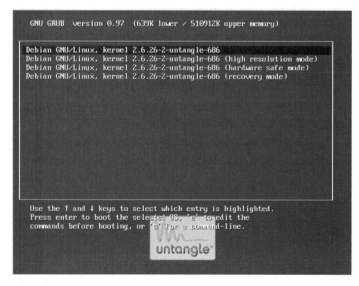

Figure 3.5
GRUB boot loader.

It may take as long as two to three minutes during the first boot after installation for the initial splash screen to be displayed. When the Untangle server boots, users gain access to a basic set of functions. Much of the underlying Debian Linux operating system is hidden and is of no real concern (unless users have an interest in advanced uses of the Untangle appliance or extending the functionality of the software).

As shown in Figure 3.6, users are presented with eight choices after boot:

- Launch Client
- Change Resolution
- Turn On Screensaver
- Turn Off Screensaver
- Reboot
- Shutdown
- Recovery Utilities
- Terminal

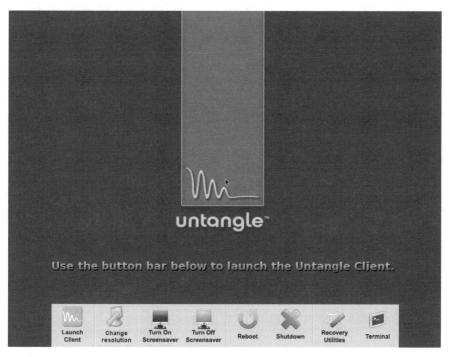

Figure 3.6
Opening splash screen.

The "client" to be launched is nothing more than a Web browser configured to display a Web front end to Untangle. It runs in the open source browser Iceweasel, which, as its name suggests, will be very familiar to Firefox users. This browser can be minimized, enabling users to access a stripped-down version of the Debian desktop, but at this point, let's focus on the browser.

The Change Resolution, Turn On Screensaver, Turn Off Screensaver, Reboot, and Shutdown buttons are self-explanatory, and the latter two may be the only buttons you ever need to click on this screen. The recovery utilities are available to advanced users who need to repair broken or corrupted installations. The Terminal button launches a command prompt and is the most direct means of accessing the OS.

This leads to a brief digression from the flow of installing Untangle to provide a warning and a glimpse into the underlying operating system. The use of the terminal requires a reasonable understanding of Linux to be useful—or, in fact, to be something that anyone should attempt to access. The terminal is the most robust way to manipulate the file system, providing so-called "root" access to the server. In Linux nomenclature, the *root user* is a super-administrator with the ability to change, manage, override, or otherwise manipulate functions of the operating system, security settings, and file management. The root user, not surprisingly, can do a lot of damage. An experienced Linux administrator, however, would be crippled without root access at a terminal shell and could easily extend the functionality of an Untangle server or perform advanced troubleshooting from the command line. Even you will use it to diagnose potential networking issues, but you must take care when accessing the OS in this way.

The first time the terminal is launched, users are prompted to create a root password (see Figure 3.7). Note that this is different from the Untangle administrator password that you will create in the next section. It should be a strong password and kept someplace where you will be able to find it later. If it's already been set and you need to access the terminal again but can't remember it, you will need to reinstall Untangle.

Returning to the installation flow, on the first boot of the operating system, Iceweasel will launch automatically after a few seconds and prompt users to complete the system setup, all of which happens in the browser from here on. (See Figure 3.8.) On subsequent boots, the user will need to click the Launch Client button in the splash screen to access Untangle (or any of the other buttons described earlier to access additional functions). However, even when the browser window is active, it can be dragged to the bottom of the screen so that users can access the splash screen and shut down the computer, launch a terminal session, etc.

Figure 3.7
Dire warnings about accessing the command prompt.

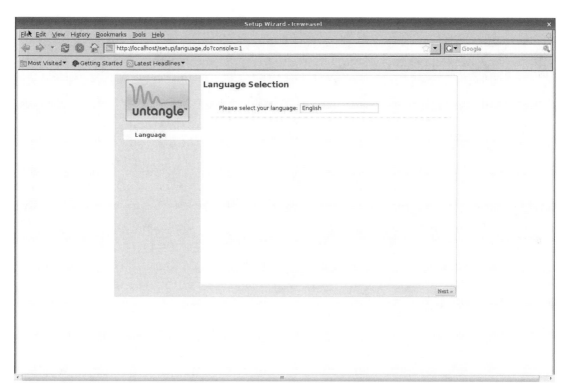

Figure 3.8
Browser-based setup begins.

The initial part of the setup requires little explanation. Selecting a time zone, language, etc., is a standard part of any operating-system setup. You will also be prompted to create a password for the Admin user (not the super-administrator mentioned in the earlier discussion of the terminal prompt, but the main administrative user of Untangle). This should be a very strong password given that Untangle is ultimately responsible for the security of your network. A weak password would expose the network to intrusion and could also allow determined users to bypass content filtering and other restrictions on the use of the network. Best practice dictates that this password be at least eight characters long and include both upper- and lower-case letters, numbers, and special characters.

The next step, however, is where the Untangle-ness appears in the setup. At this point, you must map the multiple network interfaces to their various possible functions. Before you do, let's take a step back to talk about identifying them and examine the function of each (depending upon how many were installed).

Eth 1? Eth0? What Do I Plug In Where?

Linux designations for network connections will look a bit unfamiliar to those accustomed to Windows and Mac operating systems. Particularly in Untangle, though, given the number of connections you will be supporting and the varied roles they may take on, the nomenclature and assignments are important. They are, however, not terribly intuitive.

Figure 3.9 shows the network interface detection screen. Untangle presents all active interfaces that it can detect and shows whether they are connected to a cable. Notice that Figure 3.9 shows three interfaces, as suggested in Chapter 1, "Getting a Computer." Your setup will show only two if that is all you installed. Regardless of how many interfaces are installed (Untangle can support up to seven physical network connections, but must have a minimum of two), Linux numbers them sequentially, with the prefix *eth* and beginning with the number 0. Thus, the three interfaces on the test machine pictured in Figure 3.9 are eth0, eth1, and eth2. If any of the interfaces are wireless (neither preferred nor recommended, but workable in specific situations), they will also be numbered sequentially from 0, but with the prefix *wlan*.

As the setup screen suggests, it isn't always possible to know which designation (i.e., eth0, eth1, etc.) corresponds to which actual jack in the Untangle server. However, because each is capable of serving a distinct function, it is important to know which is which—particularly at this step, where those distinct functions are assigned at a very basic level. The only way to actually know which physical interfaces map to particular logical interfaces (where *physical* refers to the network jack itself and *logical* refers to the eth/wlan interfaces used by the OS) is trial and error.

As noted, computers and motherboards frequently come with an integrated Ethernet jack. Often, these end up being eth0, while add-on cards are assigned subsequent numbers.

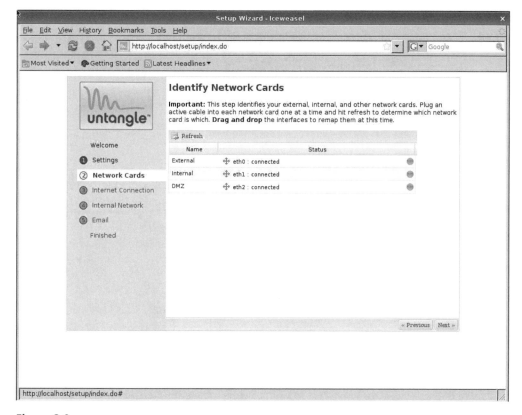

Figure 3.9
Identifying network interfaces.

However, the steps outlined on the setup screen are a better means of accurately determining mappings:

1. Unplug any network cables.

2. Plug a single cable into your modem/router.

3. Click the Refresh link on the setup page. Only one interface should show a "connected" status.

4. Repeat this process until all connections have been identified.

These jacks should be labeled physically on the box with their logical identifiers so they can be connected to appropriate network segments when setup is complete. Notice that you have the option to remap the logical interfaces to particular functions in this screen by dragging and dropping them. Thus, eth0 could be remapped to the DMZ, for example.

(More on what that means shortly.) While it rarely matters which physical interface has which function on the server as long as the mappings are known, there may be some cases related to the location of the jack or a particular arrangement in which it simply makes sense to assign a specific physical/logical mapping to a certain function. In general, though, all that is necessary is to document which jack is assigned to the internal and external interfaces (and any other interfaces that might be present).

Isn't the DMZ in Korea?

So what exactly are those functions? The internal and external interfaces are intuitive, but DMZ may not be. The DMZ is not just the demilitarized zone between North and South Korea established at the end of the Korean War, but also a quarantine network location where best practices dictate that publicly facing computers be located. These computers most often include Web and FTP servers.

If you only have two network interfaces, the DMZ won't appear. If, however, you have more than three interfaces, then—in addition to the default internal, external, and DMZ interfaces—you can choose whether the extra interfaces are used to connect to the Internet (external), connect to a network segment (internal), or provide more DMZs. Note that using more than one external interface requires additional paid modules from Untangle (see the section on load balancing and bandwidth aggregation in Chapter 9).

Figure 3.10 illustrates the extreme case of seven interfaces with theoretical use cases for each. Figure 3.10 shows types of interfaces and their potential functions. Notice that once you get beyond internal, external, and the first DMZ interface, all other interfaces are referred to as "DMZ" by Untangle, even if they are not serving a DMZ function. The external interface, though, should always be used to connect Untangle to the Internet, and the internal interface should always connect to at least one of the internal "networks." (This can be a single computer or device if appropriate.)

Web servers and other computers can be located on a single DMZ, but as you will discover soon, there may be situations in which one would want to apply different rules to different servers. This is most easily accomplished with separate interfaces. Similarly, connecting separate networks to different interfaces provides the most expedient (and the most efficient, in terms of managing traffic) means of applying different rules to different groups of computers.

As a simple example, a parent could have an interface connected to a wireless router to which only he or she has the password. Another interface could be connected to a wireless access point that only the kids use. Traffic on the parent's router could be prioritized and

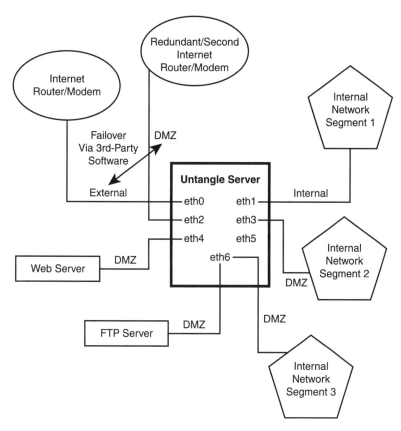

Figure 3.10
What to do with all of those interfaces.

otherwise unfiltered, while traffic from the kids' interface could be deprioritized and fil-tered for explicit content and illegal file sharing. There are more sophisticated ways of accomplishing this in Untangle with a single interface, but often, pairing the physical interface with logical rules and policies or functions can create the simplest, most robust experience—particularly for less technical users (to which Untangle and this book should appeal).

FINISHING THE INSTALL AND INITIAL CONFIGURATION

At this point, the Web-based installation is nearly finished. A few key steps remain, however. The next screen prompts users to determine how the IP address of the external interface is set. The options are static, dynamic, or PPPoE. (See Figure 3.11.)

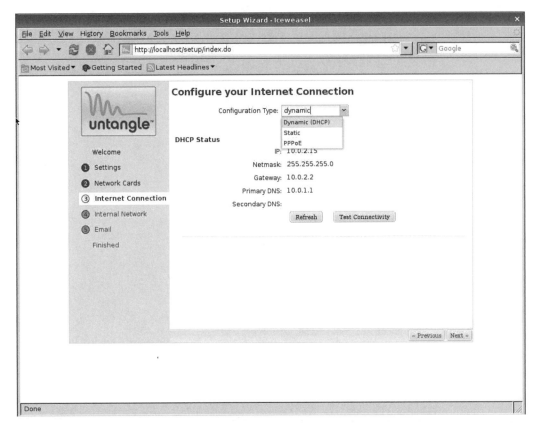

Figure 3.11
Choosing the external interface connection type.

For a static IP address, the user sets an address and other related DNS and gateway information manually. This information will be provided by your ISP if you've paid for a static IP address as part of your Internet service (this is uncommon for consumer-grade service but very common for business-class service). This is quite useful in larger networks and makes remote administration of the Untangle server much easier, as well as facilitating remote access to other network resources. Keep in mind that Untangle can be set up as gateway to an internal network segment, as well—e.g., only a portion of the network is filtered or managed by the Untangle appliance. The external IP address used for this portion of the setup will then be obtained from the organization's network administrator if he or she chooses to assign it a static IP.

More often for home users and small businesses, the external IP address is assigned by the ISP dynamically, just as individual nodes on most networks often receive their addresses via DHCP. In this case, simply choose Dynamic when setting up the external connection and Untangle will negotiate a connection and obtain an IP address from the ISP.

Untangle gets an external IP address on the fly that DNS (handled somewhere on the network, potentially by Untangle, but more likely by the router) resolves as needed for other computers to communicate with the server. This is a reasonable choice if Untangle is intended to act only as a content filter rather than implementing all of its gateway functions, particularly if the filtering will only happen inside a network (i.e., not for mobile devices that will access Untangle as a proxy server).

The final option is not recommended by Untangle and would rarely be necessary, but Untangle does support Point-to-Point Protocol over Ethernet (PPPoE). This is required when there is no modem or router present to handle negotiation of communications with certain types of Internet service. Its configuration and use are outside the scope of this book; it is assumed that a transceiver will be enabled on all networks so that PPPoE isn't necessary.

After users select either a static or dynamic IP configuration for the external interface, they must choose whether the server will act as a transparent bridge or a router. (See Figure 3.12.)

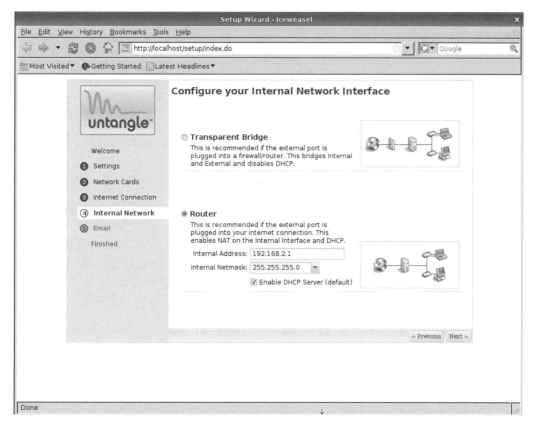

Figure 3.12
Bridge versus router.

Because this fundamentally affects the function of the Untangle server, it's worth a few moments of consideration. In Transparent Bridge mode, traffic is simply routed through the server and anything behind the server on a configured interface is filtered or managed by Untangle. Overall addressing and routing of traffic across the network is handled by another device (typically a dedicated router or firewall or a modem with routing capabilities). This is appropriate if the server will largely be used for content filtering or if there are network segments where filtering, protection, or other types of intervention are either unimportant or take a back seat to ultimate performance—for example, if the network already has a router and a Web server (that would otherwise not require filtering anyway) with heavy traffic that must be exposed to the Internet. The Web server would not even be attached to a DMZ interface, while segments of the network with user devices would have content and malware filtering enabled. This is also an easy default setup in home or test setups where most users are likely to already have a router in place and another router could cause conflicts and unwanted traffic slowdowns.

Untangle, however, is capable of functioning as a full-blown router and firewall. The Router option assumes that whatever transceiver is connecting the network to the Internet does not have any routing functions enabled. Untangle is then the first device connected to the transceiver (a CSU/DSU, a modem with routing disabled, or another device that simply makes a connection to the Internet without further handling of IP traffic). This is one area where Untangle can save larger organizations a fair amount of money by combining the functions of separate expensive devices. If you are looking for "one device to rule them all" (to paraphrase Tolkien), then you should choose the Router setup.

Most of the internal workings and administration of Untangle remain unchanged regardless of the setup chosen. Routing simply adds a new layer of functionality and is the most robust, cost-effective setup. Therefore, the remainder of this book assumes that the router function was chosen at setup unless otherwise noted.

Once this function is determined in the setup, Untangle runs through final, self-explanatory housekeeping steps and then reboots. The initial splash screen again appears after reboot and choosing to launch the client brings users to the main Web-based administrative interface where you will spend the remainder of this book.

Running the Software: Basics of the UI

As noted before, all administration of an Untangle server takes place in a browser. (Look ahead to Figure 3.15.) Before users reach this interface, they will be prompted to create an Untangle account. This account is used on the Untangle Web site and allows the server to

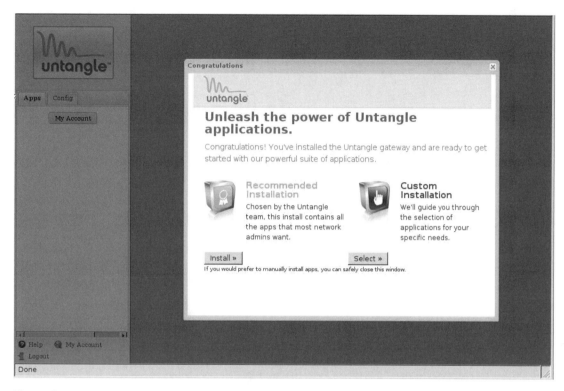

Figure 3.13
Choosing a pre-configured package of apps.

download updates, patches, and additional packages directly from Untangle servers. A brief wizard leads users through the account creation and prompts them to install either a "recommended" or "custom" configuration. (See Figure 3.13.) The recommended configuration installs a variety of modules automatically in Untangle, most of which are free. Paid modules are not open source and can be activated if users choose to pay for them. These are covered in detail in Chapter 9, in the section about paid features. For now, choose the recommended configuration and, once through the creation of an Untangle account, click the Install Now button (see Figure 3.14).

Again, a number of things happen automatically and in the background. The end result is the user interface shown in Figure 3.15. Untangle presents to users an imaginary rack of virtual devices representing installed software. These devices are accessed in the left pane of the interface. The pane has two tabs: Apps and Config. The Apps tab shows the

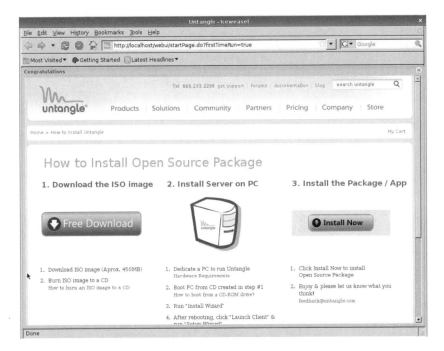

Figure 3.14
The Install Now button.

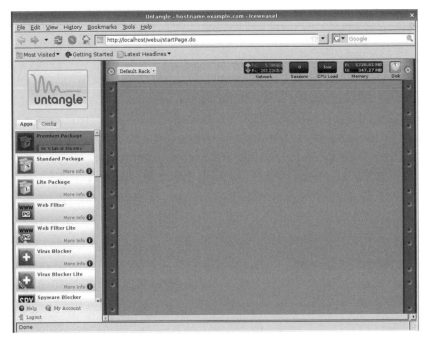

Figure 3.15
The Untangle user interface.

installed software and the Config tab gives users granular control of the various networking tools that were set up either during installation or automatically by Untangle. The right pane is empty at this point, but clicking the individual apps or sections of the Config tab will populate the pane with setup screens and options for all server functions. The actual setup of these individual components is covered in Chapter 4, "What's Happening Inside My Untangle Gateway?"

PART II

So What About This So-Called "Server"? How Do I Protect My Network?

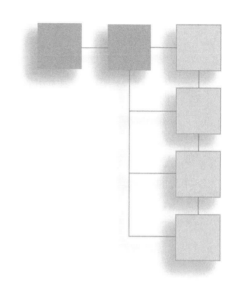

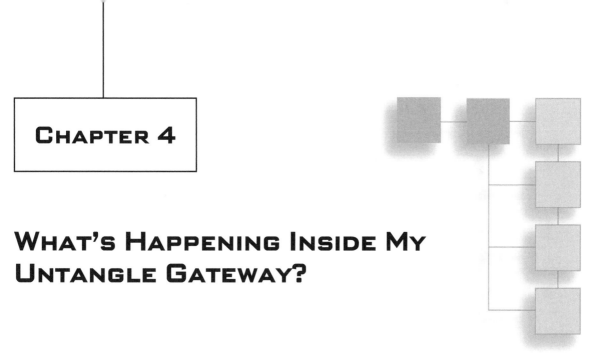

CHAPTER 4

WHAT'S HAPPENING INSIDE MY UNTANGLE GATEWAY?

By now, you should have a machine in front of you that is capable of doing everything from preventing your users from accessing pornography to keeping hackers off your network. Getting it set up hasn't been the easiest journey, but clearly it isn't rocket science either. In fact, now that you've done it once, it isn't hard to imagine doing it again for a variety of settings, with hardware ranging from the ultra-cheap for a couple of home users looking for anti-malware protection to a fairly robust computer for a school or medium-sized business.

A basic install of Untangle, however, is only as good as the settings implemented by the administrator. A much deeper understanding of the function, interface, and underlying software is necessary to fully exploit Untangle's power. Even for home users and hobbyists, this greater insight is necessary to avoid pitfalls and problems on an existing network (i.e., to not screw up something that is already working). These same users—as well as those with more significant needs in larger settings—have already invested both time and money in hardware and setup of the server. As you move forward in Part II, "So About This So-Called 'Server'…How Do I Protect My Network?," you will look at all the ways your box can enhance the security, functionality, and safety of your networks.

ROUTER VERSUS BRIDGE AND OTHER ROUTER-SETUP CONSIDERATIONS

In Chapter 3, "Downloading and Installing Untangle," you briefly considered the issue of setting up Untangle as a bridge or a router. As a router, Untangle takes on a far more fundamental function on a network than it does as a bridge. However, while this book

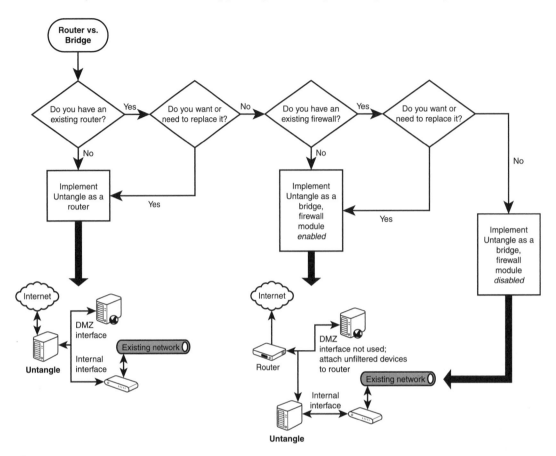

Figure 4.1
Guidelines for choosing a router or bridge configuration.

generally assumes a router setup (and most of the apps function in precisely the same way regardless of which need the server fills), in reality, many Untangle users will already have a router in place. This begs the question, should you replace your existing router with Untangle or just leave it alone?

The answer, of course, is it depends. The decision tree outlined in Figure 4.1 provides some reasonable guidelines, though. Most importantly, new Untangle administrators need to consider the following:

- How well their network is currently functioning and how important their existing investments in routers and network infrastructure are
- The level of detail required in reports on content filtering
- The size of the network
- The aspects of their network that they want to actively manage

Not to worry, by the way, if you change your mind about the decision you made in Chapter 3. That chapter was meant to get you started using Untangle as quickly as possible. If, after reading this chapter, you decide that your gateway should actually have been a router instead of a bridge or vice versa, you've invested very little in terms of setup time. Just rerun the setup, wiping out the old install, and choose the appropriate function.

For many home users or hobbyists, for example, their ISP has already kindly provided them with a router in the form of a cable or DSL modem. Often, the inner workings of these devices can't be modified by the end user. As a result, a router setup for Untangle with a whole host of networking functions enabled can introduce conflicts and cause a variety of problems on the network. Similarly, many schools already have firewalls and/or routers provided as part of the bundled services implemented by their ISP or services integrator to take advantage of a loophole in a federal funding mechanism called eRate. (eRate reimburses for Internet connectivity, but will only pay for hardware on the network if it is bundled with the Internet connection costs.) In this case as well, using Untangle as a router will introduce conflicts and create traffic bottlenecks.

On the other hand, full-blown dedicated routers and firewalls are expensive; when they fail, Untangle can serve as a very robust replacement. Many of the less expensive firewalls and routers provide only basic features and performance can be subpar as a network grows. An Untangle server can be as powerful as a user makes it, frequently at a lower cost (and without potential subscription fees that many firewalls and content filters bring with them) than a comparably performing dedicated appliance.

Using Untangle as a router, then, makes a great deal of sense for organizations implementing a new firewall/router (the functions of which are frequently combined), looking to upgrade an existing device (or devices), or replacing broken or degraded equipment. The router configuration also maximizes reporting capabilities and the granularity of these reports, although the reports in both modes are more than enough to satisfy monitoring and regulatory requirements.

At the most basic level, the router mode should be chosen when one needs to connect two separate, unrelated networks. These connections could include the Internet to an office or a branch office to a main office (while still keeping the two networks distinct). The router function can also quickly create a separate network within a single building or organization. Imagine, for example, a high school opening one of its computer labs to a community organization for adult continuing education. Placing an Untangle server in router mode between the computer lab and the rest of the network completely separates the new users from the rest of the school while maintaining existing infrastructure.

Again, at the most basic level, bridging connects computers on the same network transparently. In the case of Untangle, the server simply handles its assigned filtering tasks but is not concerned with actually assigning the destinations of data packets. From a configuration perspective, the internal connection is not assigned a specific IP address, but is left as a bridge, sharing the IP address of the external interface. (In router mode, the internal connection gets its own IP address—one within the network that it is connecting to the external network.)

So why tell you this now when, in theory, you've already selected a mode? For several reasons:

- The next couple of sections present points at which you can change the mode of the server from router to bridge and vice-versa.

- A deeper understanding of the role of a bridge versus a router is necessary to make further configuration decisions that will also be discussed in the coming sections.

- This is the best point in setup and configuration of the server to reconsider your decision.

THE APPS TAB

As you saw in Chapter 3, the Untangle UI is divided into two major panes. The left pane contains an Apps tab and a Config tab. The right pane shows a virtual server rack when the Apps tab is active and configuration details when the Config tab is active. This section focuses on the Apps tab and the server rack.

When Untangle is set up and connected to a registered account with Untangle.com, several packages can be downloaded. This book is concerned with the NG Firewall Free package, which contains only free and/or open source modules (or apps). Downloading (and paying for) the so-called Complete packages amounts to upgrading the server to a professional level. The Free package, however, is not only free, but is completely appropriate for home, small office, hobbyist, and educational uses. Untangle recommends the use of their discounted Education Complete package for schools, but the Free version meets all federal content-filtering requirements and most network-protection needs. Obviously, the larger the school, the greater the need; the section about adding paid features to your box in Chapter 10, "Paid Features," discusses points at which an upgrade would be needed.

By default, the Complete package is downloaded and recent updates to the installer make it difficult to only download the Free package. Fortunately, the Free package is a subset of the Complete package and the download is relatively quick. In any case, the Complete package contains all possible paid apps as well as all free and open-source apps. Once downloaded, you can remove any unwanted apps from the rack by clicking the Settings button on the virtual server in the rack and choosing Remove. The advantage of allowing the default Complete download is that all paid apps have a 14-day free trial so you can explore the differences between the free and paid apps and evaluate whether individual Complete apps may be worth their price for your purposes.

If you prefer to bypass this entirely, though, and just stick with the free apps, close the download screen that appears automatically and click More Info next to the Free package button on the Apps bar. You'll have the option to download only this package in the screen that appears. (Additional information on application management can be found later in the section.)

The Free package consists of the following apps:

- Web Filter Lite
- Virus Blocker Lite
- Spam Blocker Lite
- Attack Blocker
- Phish Blocker
- Spyware Blocker
- Application Control Lite
- Captive Portal
- Firewall
- Intrusion Prevention
- OpenVPN
- Reports

Each of these apps has a more advanced, robust, proprietary equivalent in the Complete package. As noted, most of these paid options come with a 14-day free trial so there is no harm in downloading the non-free packages and testing whether the more advanced apps better suit your needs. A comparison of the packages appears in Table 4.1.

As noted, the free apps are more than adequate for most needs outside the enterprise. With few exceptions, readers of this book should never need to upgrade. Similarly, these apps can be purchased *à la carte*, so it isn't necessary to pay for an entire package when

Table 4.1 Comparison of Free and Paid Untangle Packages (Included and Optional Software)

App	Description	Free/Open Source	Package		
			Lite	Standard	Premium
Attack Blocker	Prevents denial of service (DOS) attacks by identifying and blocking machines with suspicious traffic patterns and levels; legitimate, high-traffic machines can be excepted from blocking	×	×	×	×
Bandwidth Control	Provides extensive quality of service and bandwidth shaping to prioritize mission-critical traffic				×
Branding Manager	Allows organizations to add their own logos and customize Untangle pages that end users see (content blocked, logins, etc.)			×	×
Captive Portal	Forces all users to log in and consent to filtering, monitoring, logging, etc.; required in many regulated environments	×	×	×	×
Configuration Backup	Performs automatic daily backups of server settings and configurations offsite to Untangle's data center			×	×
Directory Connector	Interfaces with LDAP servers to provide differentiated access, filtering, etc., to predefined users and groups and to allow users to authenticate with their LDAP credentials			×	×
Firewall	Provides bridging, port forwarding, and port definitions to prevent unwanted or potentially harmful traffic	×	×	×	×
Intrusion Prevention	Detects and blocks attempts to access and exploit network resources	×	×	×	×
IPsec VPN	Connects to existing firewalls on a network or at branch offices to ensure secure connections			×	×

Table 4.1 Comparison of Free and Paid Untangle Packages (Included and Optional Software) (Continued)

App	Description	Package			
		Free/Open Source	Lite	Standard	Premium
OpenVPN	Provides secure remote access to network resources	x	x	x	x
Phish Blocker	Blocks phishing attacks sent via email accessed by email clients like Outlook or Apple Mail and blocks Web sites designed to solicit, steal, or exploit personal information	x	x	x	x
Policy Manager	Expands on Untangle's Local Directory configuration to provide granular control of user roles, policies, and privileges without an external LDAP server			x	x
Application Control Lite	Monitors, logs, and blocks peer-to-peer, instant messaging, and other identified types of traffic that administrators deem unacceptable	x	x	x	x
Application Control	Monitors, logs, and blocks peer-to-peer, instant messaging, and other identified types of traffic that administrators deem unacceptable; more granular control than the Lite version			x	x
Reports	Tools for reporting on usage, errors, blocked traffic, etc.	x	x	x	x
Spam Blocker	Expands on Spam Blocker Lite to reduce false positives and implement a wider range of detection technologies for email-based spam			x	x
Spam Blocker Lite	Scans email traffic (excluding Web mail) and identifies and quarantines spam	x	x	x	x
Spyware Blocker	Blocks sites identified as potentially harmful because of spyware and malware distribution	x	x	x	x

(Continued)

Table 4.1 Comparison of Free and Paid Untangle Packages (Included and Optional Software) (*Continued*)

App	Description	Package			
		Free/Open Source	Lite	Standard	Premium
Virus Blocker	Expands on Virus Blocker Lite to reduce false positives and implement a wider range of detection technologies for viruses				x
Virus Blocker Lite	Scans email and Web traffic (including software downloads) for malware and blocks and quarantines potentially infected files	x	x	x	x
WAN Balancer	Allows manual and automatic assignment of traffic to multiple Internet connections for improved performance and redundancy				x
WAN Failover	Included with WAN Balancer; automatically redirects traffic to redundant connections				x
Web Cache	Saves Web application data to improve performance for users				x
Web Filter	Expands on Web Filter Lite to improve detection and blocking of inappropriate sites with access to larger, more robust lists of sites within each category and to identify new sites that should be blocked			x	x
Web Filter Lite	Simple content filtering with categories that can be manually chosen to meet basic needs for preventing access to inappropriate or unwanted sites	x	x	x	x

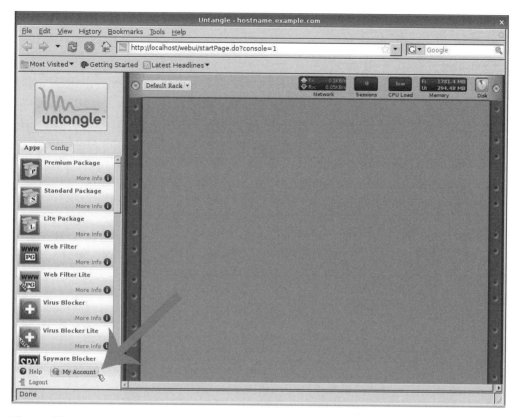

Figure 4.2
Accessing your Untangle account to obtain new apps and packages.

you need only one or two add-ons. You purchase individual apps in much the same way you buy packages.

To manage paid applications (delivered as subscription services), as well as the Untangle account that lets you populate the rack with free apps, you can access your Untangle account directly from within the Untangle interface. At the bottom of the Apps tab, there is a button labeled "My Account" (see Figure 4.2); clicking this button launches a Web browser in the content pane. Users will need to log in with the Untangle account information created in Chapter 3.

A successful login opens an account dashboard in the content pane. Within this dashboard, users can complete relatively mundane activities like changing their Untangle.com account passwords and managing billing information. (Billing information isn't necessary if you have no intention of using non-free modules or services.) Administrators can also manage installed applications. (Note that free applications included with the Free package are not displayed in this pane; application management applies only to paid, licensed software downloaded from Untangle.)

One particularly useful app—a paid app that I would recommend for a production setting—is WAN Balancer. This enables Untangle to use extra network interfaces for redundant connections to the Internet in case of failure or to improve performance. The app automatically assigns traffic to an underutilized Internet connection; alternatively, administrators can customize traffic by interface. For example, mission-critical, bandwidth-intensive traffic can be assigned to a fast cable modem, while email traffic can be handled by a slower DSL connection. I'll go through the process of installing this app in detail next; the installation procedure is the same for other apps and packages.

To install new apps and packages, follow these steps:

1. Find the app or package you want in the Apps tab (in this case, WAN Balancer; WAN Failover is another paid app than can be purchased alone but is included in WAN Balancer).

2. Free available apps will have an Install Now link; WAN Balancer has a link to more info. Click the link. (See Figure 4.3.)

3. A page describing the function of WAN Balancer appears, and you will have the option to either buy it or enter a free trial. Click the Free Trial button; the Untangle.com browser window reappears in the virtual server rack.

Note

As with all the paid apps on Untangle.com, a widget enables administrators to calculate the cost of the add-on software by entering a range of the number of devices accessing Untangle. In the case of WAN Balancer, the cost as of the writing of this book is $108/year for 1–10 PCs. (This software is licensed by the number of computers accessing the Untangle server; occasionally, apps will be licensed by the number of users.)

4. Look at the Apps tab. You can now see the WAN Balancer app being downloaded via a progress bar embedded within the app button. You can also see that WAN Failover, included with the purchase of WAN Balancer, was downloaded and installed. Once the download and installation is complete, both will disappear from the Apps tab and be active servers on the virtual rack.

5. While you can disable installed apps by simply pressing the power button on the virtual server, you can also remove them from the installation entirely. Click settings on the virtual server/application you wish to remove and click the Remove link; the app will appear in the Apps pane again, ready to be reinstalled as needed.

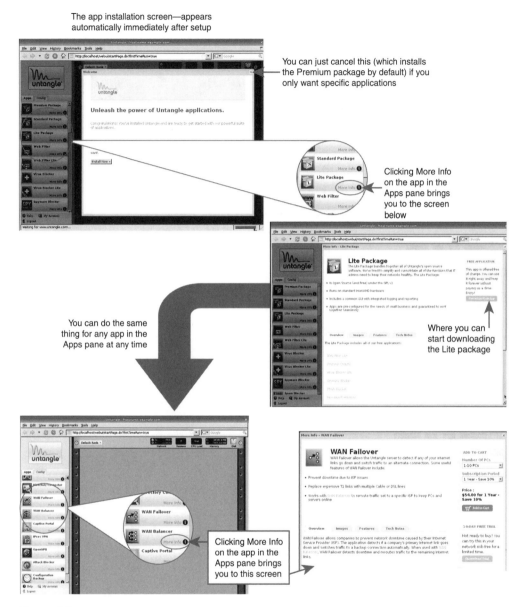

Figure 4.3
Adding apps and packages.

It is worth noting that all apps available for use with Untangle are included in the Complete package. The entire Complete package can be installed as previously described for a 14-day trial, giving you an easy meta-package to survey the functions of every Untangle app. When the 14-day trial expires, administrators can subscribe to packages individually.

Others can simply be left alone; when the trial period expires, the paid modules/apps are no longer active or usable.

To summarize, apps in the Apps tab represent installed or available modules. You can install new modules from within the Untangle interface by accessing the My Account screen using a point-and-click approach. Unused modules can be stopped and hidden from view. (More on that later.)

THE CONFIG TAB: FURTHER SETUP AND ADMINISTRATION

In addition to the Apps tab, Untangle features a Config tab. The Config tab provides direct access to most of the features that were set up during the installation of Untangle. There are also several additional configuration options that allow very granular tweaking of the gateway. These configurations are wholly separate from the setup of the individual apps and relate to the core functioning of Untangle.

There are several major configuration categories in this tab:

- Networking
- Administration
- Email
- Local Directory
- Upgrade
- System
- System Info

Clicking any of these categories in the Config tab brings up a detailed configuration screen in the right frame, replacing the virtual server rack. The settings in these screens are critical to the proper setup and maintenance of Untangle, so I'll go through each briefly.

Networking

Each configuration screen has multiple tabs for different aspects of the configuration. Shown in Figure 4.4 is the DHCP tab, in which Untangle can be set up to act as a Dynamic Host Control Protocol server, providing IP addresses to the various nodes on the network. Note, by the way, that DHCP functionality is turned on by default, providing an automatic pool of addresses based on your initial setup of the internal interface. This should be turned off or modified immediately if DHCP is already running on the network or if that service is not required.

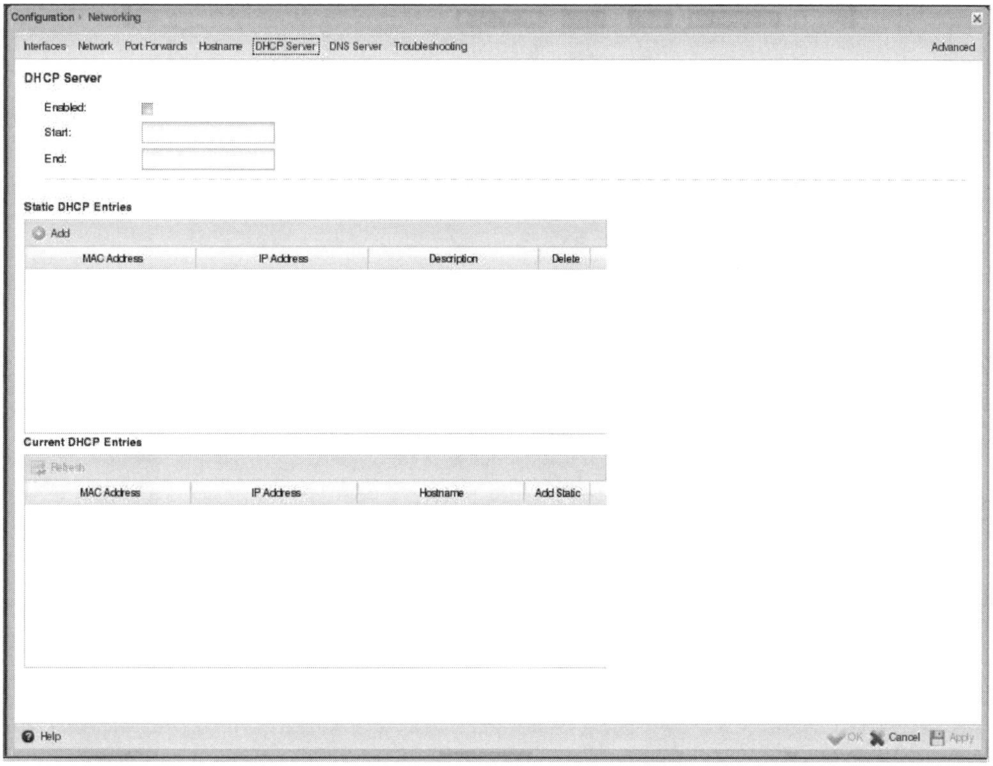

Figure 4.4
Networking configuration screen.

DHCP, along with port forwarding, host-name, and DNS configuration, are functions that can't be configured in the initial Untangle setup. The Interfaces and Network tabs are both fully configured during the Untangle installation. However, if at any time you need to reassign interfaces to individual network cards (for example, eth1 to DMZ, as described in the section "Eth1? Eth0? What Do I Plug In Where?" in Chapter 3), use the Interfaces tab. To change bridging and routing functions, assign IP addresses to interfaces, and modify other IP information, use the Network tab. Further discussion of networking configuration and related best practices is covered in this chapter and in Chapter 5, "Network and User Protection Best Practices."

Administration

The Administration configuration screen, shown in Figure 4.5, allows the assignment of superuser or admin privileges to various user accounts, enabling delegation of Untangle administration to multiple users. (See the upcoming "Local Directory" section for information about the setup of individual user accounts.) The Administration screen also

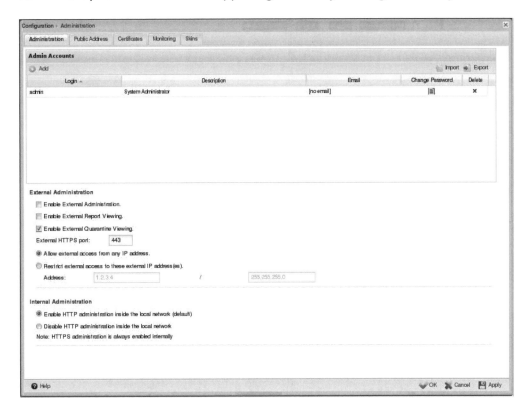

Figure 4.5
Administration configuration screen.

establishes whether the Untangle server can be administered only on the local network, outside the network, or only from the console. By default, Untangle can always be administered from a device connected directly to the same network as the Untangle box. Using a secure connection (i.e., accessing Untangle from https://<server address> instead of http://<server address>), users can always access the box from within the network served by Untangle; this screen enables administrators to turn off the secure connection requirement. A secure connection is always required to administer the server from outside the network, but even secure external access can be disabled here. External administration can also be limited to specific IP addresses (e.g., the administrator's home address).

Caution

These settings deserve an extra warning that should go without saying for experienced system administrators, but may not be second nature for many readers of this book, for whom Untangle may be their first foray into networking and security: Untangle is most likely the only thing standing between your network and the big, bad outside world. If users on your network, disgruntled ex-employees, or any number of nefarious types outside your organization (including both human and automated potential intruders) get administrative access to your Untangle box, they can compromise your entire network and bypass any of the content-related protections (many of which may be required by law) you've put in place. Carefully evaluate who should have access to the box and how and from where they should be able to access it. In general, forcing secure, internal-only access to the gateway is considered best practice. If external access is necessary, the use of the VPN can provide an additional layer of security. (See Chapter 9, "Advanced Topics," for more information.)

The Public Address tab is used to set the address at which Untangle can be accessed from outside the network. It's self-explanatory, but this would be used either for remote administration or to specify Untangle as a server through which students or employees could access a VPN and continue to have their Web content filtered even when they are off the network.

The Certificates tab is used to manage secure certificates. These are essentially digital signatures required for the https connections described earlier. Users can generate certificates on this screen or can import certificates they already have. The Monitoring tab, on the other hand, sets options for using the Simple Network Messaging Protocol (SNMP) to notify administrators of error conditions on the server, as well as notification settings of specified flags in the system log. By default, both of these functions are turned off. System log notifications can range from informational alerts to critical failures; the severity at which an administrator wishes to be notified is set on this screen as well.

The Skins tab is purely cosmetic, allowing administrators to set the look and feel of the Untangle interface.

Email

Untangle has a built-in email server that can be used to send the aforementioned alerts along with regular reports specified in the Reports settings on the virtual rack. The Email screen, shown in Figure 4.6, enables users to specify whether Untangle should send mail directly or use a Simple Mail Transfer Protocol (SMTP) server. (This is also known as an outgoing mail server, and should be familiar to people who have set up an email client such as Outlook, Eudora, or Apple Mail.) Users also need to specify the email address from which Untangle emails appear to be sent. By default, this is the email address associated with the administrator's Untangle.com account. Interestingly, the From-Safe List tab is one of the few areas of the Config tab and screens that provide information for the apps. The from-safe list is a white list of email addresses that should not be flagged as spam by the Spam Blocker app. Similarly, the Quarantine tab shows mail messages that have been flagged as infected or potentially harmful and allows administrators to manage those emails, set alerts, etc.

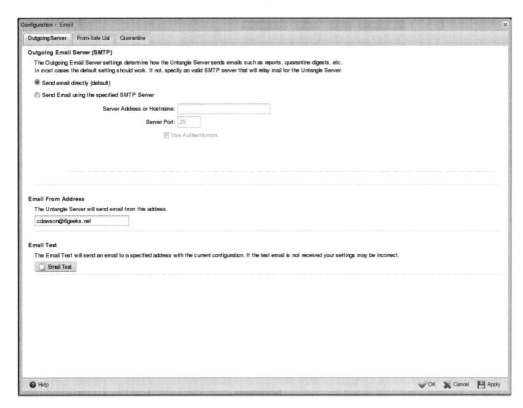

Figure 4.6
Email configuration screen.

Local Directory

Untangle can interface with a variety of LDAP systems with its paid Directory Connector app. LDAP stands for Lightweight Directory Access Protocol and refers to logical security implementations of user names, roles, and policies. Examples include Microsoft Active Directory and OpenLDAP; these are usually used on enterprise networks to handle authentication and control access to various resources or to set user privileges. Through the Directory Connector, Untangle administrators can set groups of users with differentiated security and content-filter settings without having to redefine these groups or maintain them separately in both Untangle and whatever authentication system they already use. A deep discussion of LDAP and its integration with Untangle is beyond the scope of this book; most likely, those Untangle users who aren't familiar with LDAP don't need the Connector. Those who are familiar with LDAP will be able to navigate the Connector easily.

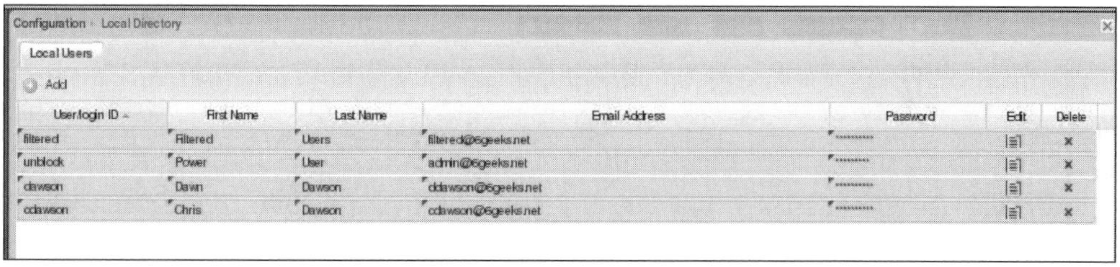

Figure 4.7
Local Directory configuration screen.

However, there are many settings where such a directory either doesn't exist or the need to differentiate among users is far less important. In many schools, for example, one only needs two sets of policies: teachers and students. Teachers have basically wide-open access to the Internet and students are filtered at a variety of levels. Home users could have parent and kid policies in a similar configuration. In these cases, simply defining a small set of users on the Untangle server is adequate.

The so-called "Captive Portal" will be covered in greater detail in Chapter 8, "User Considerations;" this facilitates user login, however, when using the local directory instead of any outside authentication system. Simply put, all teachers in the preceding example could log in with a single arbitrary username and password (e.g., username: teacher; password: teachersrock) and all students could log in with another username and password (e.g., username: student; password: studentsblock). This dual login is adequate to differentiate policies for students and teachers without any external tools or complicated authentication schemes, servers, or policies.

In Figure 4.7, there are four user accounts. Two are for specific administrators and two are general logins that define a filtered and an unfiltered group. Users who don't need sophisticated differentiation among many users and groups access the setup of local users through the Local Directory screen.

Upgrade, System, and System Info

The final three configuration screens can be addressed together, as they are relatively simple with "set it and forget it" options.

- **Upgrade.** When launched, the Upgrade screen immediately checks for available upgrades to Untangle. Administrators can choose to upgrade immediately if updates are found or defer upgrades for later. Outside of test or home settings, best practice dictates postponing upgrades until off hours to ensure that users don't experience any service disruptions.

A second tab, Upgrade Setup, gives users the option of automatic versus manual upgrades and specifies the times at which upgrades can occur (e.g., Saturday nights, when users are not likely to be accessing the Internet and leaving Sunday to test the results of the upgrade before the work/school week begins). Again, in home or test settings, automatic upgrades are generally not a problem. However, in production environments, it's generally wise to avoid automatic upgrades because even an unexpected weekend upgrade can leave users high and dry Monday morning if something goes wrong. It can also have an unexpected impact on remote users.

■ **System.** The initial tab of the System screen (Support) contains options allowing (or preventing) Untangle staff to remotely access the server for support services, manually rebooting or shutting down the server, and re-running the system setup wizard. Other tabs allow manual backup and restoration of the server configuration, options for handling particular Web protocols (e.g., HTTP, FTP, etc.), and setting the time zone and language for the interface. In the case of the Protocol Settings tab, there is considerable granularity and extensive configurability, but users are warned to leave these settings alone unless otherwise directed by Untangle support. (The Lite package does not include support, but there should generally be little or no need to change these settings.)

■ **System Info.** Administrators will rarely need to access the System Info tab. It provides basic Untangle version and license information as well as hardware information.

THE UNDERLYING OPERATING SYSTEM

Untangle is designed to be used, administered, and generally accessed via a Web browser (whether on the server itself or remotely), and it generally isolates the user from what is happening in the background. However, there are advanced levels of configuration that can take place at the operating-system level. At its heart, Untangle is just a remix of Debian Linux. Ubuntu and Mint, the most popular Linux desktop distributions, are also based on Debian, so users familiar with these should have no problem accessing the underlying OS and making more advanced modifications or finding other use cases for the Untangle server. A deep discussion of Debian Linux, even in the context of Untangle, is outside the scope of this book. However, a brief look at what can be done (and how to do it) by bypassing the Web interface and going directly to the operating system will be useful as you become more adventurous with the gateway.

As noted previously, Untangle is a Debian-based Linux operating system. It is open source and, as such, is both free and can be modified at a source-code level. You probably won't be getting that fancy, but there are a few things that can be done at the operating system level that can't be done through the Untangle Web interface.

Most interestingly, especially for the average user of this book, administrators can add extra functionality to the server through the OS via the terminal interface. As described in Chapter 3 in the "Installation" section, clicking the Terminal button in the opening splash screen gives users a command prompt with full administrative control over the operating system. This requires care and a reasonable understanding of Linux. Linux was originally designed as a command line–driven operating system without a native graphical interface, meaning that everything from software installation to Web-server management can be accomplished from the terminal.

Should you wish to get to the terminal after launching the client, simply closing the browser window will return you to the opening screen. Note that this works only when directly accessing the Untangle server. If you are just accessing the Web interface but are not physically at the server, you'll need to use SSH. (See the section on remote administration in Chapter 9.)

It is a best practice for production Untangle servers to be single-use computers, meaning that all they do is run Untangle and process network traffic. However, in many home and small network settings, it may be necessary to add functions to the server outside of Untangle to maximize the return on hardware investment or meet other computing needs. The potential options here will be discussed in detail in Chapter 9; bear in mind that the Untangle gateway is first and foremost a server. Backup, file sharing, print server, and FTP server software can all be installed, meaning that the family photos residing on a couple of computers at home can, for example, be backed up regularly to the Untangle box. As another example, libraries could install lightweight library-management systems like Koha on the existing Web server that drives the Untangle interface.

THE VIRTUAL SERVER RACK: CONFIGURING THE APPS

As noted, apps are added in the Apps tab and then displayed, configured, enabled, and disabled in a virtual server rack. Figure 4.8 shows a single app's virtual server.

Figure 4.8
A single app's virtual server.

Settings for each app/module are accessed by, not surprisingly, clicking the Settings button on the virtual server. This opens a configuration screen. In the case of the Web Filter app, there are extensive options for setting up black lists, white lists, etc., and viewing logs of bypass instances (some users can be given the privilege of temporarily bypassing blocked sites), blocked requests, and other important tools for monitoring user activity.

Taking a step back and re-examining Figure 4.8, you can see that the virtual server rack also provides, at a glance, information about the health and performance of the network and the Untangle server, including upload and download speeds, CPU load, disk usage, active sessions, and memory usage. Regardless of which apps appear in the virtual rack, these data points are always available.

It is possible to define several virtual racks. By default, the rack contains all apps, both active and inactive. However, clicking the Default Rack drop-down menu in Figure 4.8 presents the option of entering the Policy Manager. This app is discussed in greater detail in Chapter 7, "Implementing Protection Best Practices (or Not) with Untangle (a.k.a. 'The Rack')," in the section "Critical Features Missing from the Lite Package." However, it allows differentiated racks with different applied apps and settings for multiple groups of users. Thus, a teacher rack in a school might not include the Web Filter Lite (or may have much less restrictive settings) while a student rack may have highly restrictive settings on the Web Filter Lite app and may also have QoS restrictions in place on the Application Control Lite app. Also note the virtual power button on the right side of the server; this enables you to quickly and easily activate or deactivate an app without affecting the app's configuration.

Now that you know how to navigate the interface, it's time to look at best practices around the tools and configuration options available in Untangle.

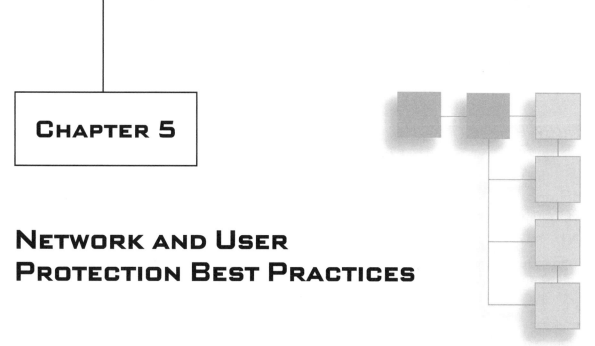

CHAPTER 5

NETWORK AND USER PROTECTION BEST PRACTICES

It's now time to take a step back and think about what you really expect from Untangle. You know how you might choose one particular configuration over another and you've completed a basic setup of all of the various components (at least for the Free package of Untangle NG Firewall), but if you've learned nothing else up until now, you should know that Untangle is extremely flexible. It can be the only network device you'll need or simply an add-on to provide content filtering on your network. It can provide a wide degree of protections and restrictions and protect your network and users from everything from malware to outside attacks.

But what's an appropriate level of content filtering for a given situation? Should you let Untangle handle DNS, or should a router or internal server do that? Should you use DHCP or static IP addresses? How aggressive should spam detection be? These are questions that need to be answered before you place an Untangle server on your network. This chapter, while not a required read for advanced users, does build a case for implementing firewall, content filtering, and other protocol control applications. Untangle just happens to provide all these tools in its free software suite and enhanced versions of the tools in its paid applications.

DHCP, DNS, AND NETWORK DEVICES

The section " IP Addresses, TCP/IP, DNS, and DHCP" in Chapter 2, "Networking 101," introduced the basic network services and protocols of TCP/IP, DNS, and DHCP. Knowing what they are and thinking about how to use them in the context of a network protected (and possibly managed) by an Untangle server, however, are two very different things.

DHCP

As discussed, Dynamic Host Control Protocol (DHCP) is the system by which nodes on an Ethernet network are provided with addresses automatically when they connect to a network. DHCP provides every node on a network with a unique IP address within the same range or subnet as all other nodes (for example, printers, file servers, etc.) that it needs to access.

While this is the easiest way to connect a device to a network, it isn't appropriate in all situations. Similarly, when configured incorrectly, it can essentially shut down multiple (or all) connections on a network. Imagine if people's homes and businesses didn't have unique addresses or if those addresses were assigned incorrectly. Duplicate addresses would mean that postal workers wouldn't know where to deliver your letters and packages. Similarly, packages without a ZIP code (the postal equivalent of a subnet) may never reach the correct post office, much less the correct address. So DHCP must assign an address on the appropriate subnet for a given device.

DHCP is not necessary, nor is it always advisable. Although network devices (be they computers, servers, printers, or something else) can usually be identified by their host-names (generally human-readable names assigned to nodes on a network—for example, Room301_printer1 or ChrisDawson_Tablet1), many nodes function optimally when they have a fixed IP address and can be located instantly via this address. Servers in particular should have fixed IP addresses, as the ability of other networked computers to locate them instantly and communicate with them reliably is critical. Fixed IP addresses are commonly referred to as "static IP addresses."

Devices that frequently move between networks, however, often must rely on DHCP to be given a different address in each location. For example, one network may have an IP address range of 10.0.0.1–10.0.0.254 (this is the typical range of Apple's Airport wireless routers), while another may have a range of 192.168.128.1–192.168.128.254. Were a laptop to retain an address of 10.0.0.122 on the second network, it would be effectively cut off and unable to access any network resources. (This is the equivalent of a postal worker trying to deliver mail in the wrong ZIP code.)

DHCP also provides other network-specific information that a device needs in order to communicate. The default gateway is the access point to the rest of the network and, in particular, the Internet. This is usually a server or router with a static IP address that any computer on the network must be able to find before it can be connected to the Internet and must be specified either manually or via DHCP. (The device can't "discover" the default gateway.)

DHCP also specifies the subnet mask for the network. Although the specifics of subnetting require a fair understanding of binary mathematics and are outside the scope of this book, the subnet mask essentially tells the computer (and the network) which parts of the IP address represent the network and which parts represent the individual devices. Going back to the mail analogy, the network part of the IP address is equivalent to the ZIP code and the device portion is equivalent to the street number. In the preceding example, 192.168.128 signifies the network and doesn't change for any computer on the network; the final set of digits (1–254) represent the 254 available individual addresses that can be assigned to devices on that network. For more detailed descriptions of subnetting, see http://www.techrepublic.com/article/ip-subnetting-made-easy/.

It is worth noting at this point that there are two types of IP addresses currently in use: IP version 4 (IPV4) and IP version 6 (IPV6). IPV4 is by far the most common, while IPV6 is emerging out of necessity. It allows for orders of magnitude more device addresses and subnets. Untangle supports both, but most network implementations of concern to readers of this book will use IPV4. The subnetting primer provided in the preceding paragraph only covers IPV4. For details on IPV6, visit http://www.techrepublic.com/blog/datacenter/breaking-down-an-ipv6-address-what-it-all-means/.

Most networks use a combination of DHCP and static addressing to give servers and other critical hardware the fixed IP addresses they require while also providing the flexibility and ease of management associated with DHCP, especially for devices that may come and go from the network. Most DHCP servers (like Untangle) include utilities for excluding a range of addresses from the range assignable by the server. Thus, the DHCP server avoids giving a server address to a client device and vice versa.

One caveat to this hybrid approach: Ensure that, whenever possible, devices are named logically and according to agreed-upon conventions. Otherwise, Untangle (or whatever DHCP server you might be using) will only be able to tell you that a device named Tablet123 with IP address 192.168.128.219 attempted to access a pornographic site, but it won't be able to meaningfully identify the actual device or device owner. Had the device been named Chris_Dawsons_Tablet1, you would have had no problem finding the user and addressing his or her online behavior in an appropriate manner. Untangle also tracks the so-called "MAC address" associated with DHCP leases. Every device capable of connecting to a network has a unique MAC address and many administrators will maintain a database of MAC addresses and the users and locations with which they are associated, allowing identification to rely less on device names.

Another option is to simply reserve a small block of IP addresses (or a separate subnet running on an extra Untangle interface) for guest devices and assign static IP addresses to any devices that rarely or never leave the network. A spreadsheet or asset-management system can then associate the fixed IP address with a particular user or physical location. This adds an extra layer of management but, for example, in a school with fixed computer labs, may be the easiest means of identifying problems with users. ("Mrs. Smith, can you tell me who was sitting in the third row, second seat from the left in the library computer lab during B period today?")

DNS

The Domain Name System (DNS), is one of the most frequent causes of difficulty in setting up and maintaining a computer network. In general, its ability to translate server and device names from a human-readable form (for example, cnn.com or dawson_macbook1. local) to IP addresses (157.166.255.18 and 10.0.0.28) is automatic and fairly transparent. Essentially, most DNS servers grab such mappings (known as records) from other DNS servers and maintain local copies of these records so that users can type cnn.com into their browsers or print to copy_room_hp2600 instead of worrying about the actual IP addresses.

However, it doesn't take many bad records to have a whole lot of people unable to print, authenticate against their network directory, or go anywhere online. If connecting to websites is taking a particularly long time on your network (or just isn't happening), try this simple test: Type http://74.125.224.72/ into a browser. If you land on Google's search page but can't get there by typing google.com, you have a DNS issue.

Again, in-depth troubleshooting of DNS issues is outside the scope of this book. However, because Untangle can act as a DNS server, it's important to understand the role of DNS in this context and with DHCP. In general, it's best to let client devices look both internally and externally for networked resources. DHCP can pass DNS server information to clients when it assigns an IP address and usually specifies a primary and secondary DNS server. The primary DNS server should be the onsite DNS (the Untangle server if that is being used for DNS or another server, router, firewall, or device that is handling this function for the network). The secondary DNS should point to a major DNS provider on the Internet such as Google, your ISP (it will provide you with DNS server information), or OpenDNS as noted in Figure 5.1.

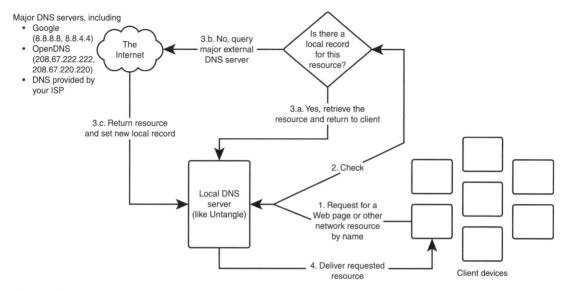

Figure 5.1
DNS (simplified schematic).

The bottom line is that the fewer devices handling DNS the better, from a management perspective. DNS is designed to be self-replicating, but in most environments in which tech support is not widely available or in which simplicity and cost containment are key requirements, the use of Untangle (or another firewall/router) to handle most DNS tasks along with DHCP is considered a best practice. While a single device represents a single point of failure, DNS replication failures and inconsistencies are common sources of network issues. When in-house expertise in DNS troubleshooting is scarce or non-existent, a single, easy-to-use, unified interface is certainly a desirable thing.

Network Devices/Nodes

Knowing which devices are connected to your network is critical to management, planning, and accountability. As noted, Untangle's advanced content filtering is of limited utility if, for example, one can't identify the user or computer accessing inappropriate content. In large organizations, the management of devices is called enterprise resource management (ERM). Even in the much smaller settings with which readers of this book will most likely be concerned, knowing who is connected via what device and where will make Untangle more useful and ensure that you, as Untangle puts it, "Own your network or someone else will."

The simplest form of management is to just create a spreadsheet. Fields for IP address (if the device in question uses static IP addressing instead of DHCP), physical location, device name, user assignment (if any), and connection information are all that are needed in most cases. Figure 5.2 gives an example of such a sheet, which should look very much like the network documentation described in Chapter 2.

	A	B	C	D	E	F	G
1	Device Name	IP Address (or DHCP)	Location	Jack location	Attached to	Assigned to user	Notes
2	Untangle server	192.168.128.1	Main office	Home run to router	Router	N/A	Bridge mode
3	file_server1	192.168.128.2	Dawson office	Home run to hall switch	Hall switch, port 2	N/A	
4	web_server1	192.168.127.2	Dawson office	Home run to Untangle DMZ port	Untangle DMZ	N/A	
5	Reserved for expansion of static IP address	192.168.128.3-192.168.128.19	N/A	N/A	N/A	N/A	
6	student_labpc1	192.168.128.20	Media center, row 1, seat 1	Media center switch	Media center switch, port 2	N/A	
7	student_labpc2	192.168.128.21	Media center, row 1, seat 2	Media center switch	Media center switch, port 3	N/A	
8	student_labpc3	192.168.128.22	Media center, row 1, seat 3	Media center switch	Media center switch, port 4	N/A	
9	student_labpc4	192.168.128.23	Media center, row 1, seat 4	Media center switch	Media center switch, port 5	N/A	
10	student_labpc5	192.168.128.24	Media center, row 2, seat 1	Media center switch	Media center switch, port 6	N/A	
11	student_labpc6	192.168.128.25	Media center, row 2, seat 2	Media center switch	Media center switch, port 7	N/A	
12	student_labpc7	192.168.128.26	Media center, row 2, seat 3	Media center switch	Media center switch, port 8	N/A	
13	student_labpc8	192.168.128.27	Media center, row 2, seat 4	Media center switch	Media center switch, port 9	N/A	
14	student_labpc9	192.168.128.28	Media center, row 3, seat 1	Media center switch	Media center switch, port 10	N/A	
15	student_labpc10	192.168.128.29	Media center, row 3, seat 2	Media center switch	Media center switch, port 11	N/A	
16							
17							
18							
19							

Figure 5.2
ERM spreadsheet.
Used with permission from Microsoft.

At the same time, all devices that belong to your organization should be physically labeled to correspond to the sheet. As configurations change, the sheet and labels should be updated. While this seems like a lot of hassle for a network of 10 computers (or even 30–40), the ability to fully leverage the various data points that Untangle gives you, as well as establish a scalable framework for tracking assets, is invaluable. Labels are often referred to as "asset tags" and can be generated automatically by ERM software or created manually for smaller networks. Asset tags should be attached to the bottoms of laptops, the backs of tablets, the sides of computers, etc., for easy identification as needed.

Depending on your configuration and network complexity, user information may be stored in a directory service (a tool for authentication and role/policy management, such as Microsoft Active Directory or OpenLDAP). Paid services available within Untangle allow the gateway to get user information from these LDAP servers, but since your focus is the free version of Untangle, you'll assume that such a system, which would generally associate particular users with devices through their logins, doesn't exist on your network. Rather, users and their devices would need to be managed through whatever ERM system (even a primitive one like the spreadsheet in Figure 5.2) you implement.

In many settings, computers are shared or at least not assigned to a single person. Thus, the spreadsheet described here is very device-centric; user information is secondary and needs to be provided only if dedicated machines are assigned to users.

The choice of a particular naming convention is irrelevant. That said, names of devices should be meaningful and readable to the average user. In virtually all manner of documentation, no matter how simple the system, one rule of thumb is the "hit-by-a-bus" rule. If you were hit by a bus, could someone else step in, look at your documentation, and understand it well enough to maintain, improve, or otherwise carry forward the system?

Firewall, Ports, Protocols, and Intrusion Prevention

Untangle divides the traditional role of a firewall (keeping a network largely separate from the other networks to which it connects, with a few carefully controlled exceptions) into multiple components, so I'll treat them separately here as well. The first is the physical and logical separation of networks. The second is focused on preventing hacking or intrusion attempts. Others block specific types of traffic that administrators choose not to allow.

Firewall

The firewall is designed to evaluate traffic both into and out of the network and to broker safe connections between networks. These networks could be subnetworks, branch offices, partner networks, or, most commonly, the Internet itself. As described on Untangle's website, "Firewalls draw the line that separates internal and external networks."

Firewalls apply sets of rules to all network traffic, allowing some to pass in a single direction, some to pass in both directions, and some not to pass at all. For example, HTTP traffic (the Internet protocol that handles requests for and delivery of websites) is generally allowed to pass both ways as web pages must be both requested and delivered. SMTP traffic (the protocol used to send email from client applications such as Outlook and Apple Mail) is generally allowed to pass only out of the network, as there should be no need for it to come into the network.

The goal of any firewall is to ensure that the bare minimum of traffic is allowed to pass, making it harder to exploit security holes and to ensure that bandwidth is used only for necessary traffic.

The firewall can also be used to implement network address translation (NAT), illustrated in Figure 5.3. Here, the concept is to send a request made to the public IP address of the firewall or router (generally the address provided by an ISP) to an appropriate internal IP address. Thus, if a web server sits behind a firewall on a network, users around the world will enter http://mygreatcompany.com into their browsers. A DNS server somewhere on the Internet will resolve that domain name to the external IP address of your network. While that address might be 32.61.228.27, the IP address of the web server is only meaningful in the context of the internal network (for example, 10.0.0.2). The purpose of NAT in this case (and a key component of the firewall) is to send all HTTP requests that hit 32.61.228.27 to the internal web server and then pass the requested web pages back to the external user. All of this needs to be transparent to the web user and needs to keep the details of your internal network safely hidden while providing safe and appropriate levels of access to the web and other networks.

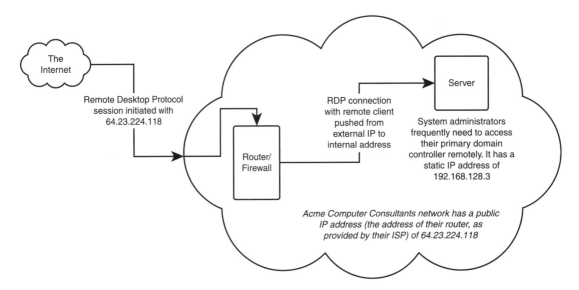

Figure 5.3
Network address translation, allowing remote access to a server.

Ports and Protocols

The preceding section mentioned the HyperText Transfer Protocol (HTTP) and the Simple Mail Transfer Protocol (SMTP). Various other protocols serve myriad functions for a network-connected computer. Each of these protocols uses what is known as a port to facilitate communications between (and within) networks. Similarly, a variety of

Internet-based applications use particular ports to form a figurative tunnel between the client computer and another server or device on the Internet.

Ports are essentially holes in the firewall and, as such, represent security risks and potential sources of wasted bandwidth. Instant messaging, peer-to-peer applications (such as those often used for illegally downloading music), and online games rely on open ports to function. Some of these ports clearly must be open. Port 80, for example, handles HTTP, while port 443 handles HTTPS (for secure online transactions). However, instant messaging not only tends to be a distraction in settings where it isn't needed, but is also a major source of infected file transfers and potential liability, depending on your use case. *World of Warcraft*? Same thing, but with fewer potential legitimate uses.

Interestingly, most of these applications don't just use a single port. Rather, they try many ports to see which might be open to establish connections. Thus, blocking specific ports is rarely an effective approach for preventing use of such applications. Many firewalls and content filters (including Untangle) can detect signatures associated with particular communication protocols or types of traffic and block the traffic regardless of the port it is attempting to use.

Ports, then, are often managed in the reverse. Whereas it is best practice to simply block all unused ports or to use a firewall capable of detecting protocol and application signatures, there are times when specific ports need to be opened up. Skype, for example, functions most efficiently when all outgoing ports above 1024 are available. If Skype is an important part of your Internet use, then at least a large group of these should be opened to ensure the highest quality connections. If applications like Skype are critical for your organization, relying on signatures and protocols instead of ports will likely yield the most reliable blocking and allowing of specific traffic. However, knowledge of ports and the applications that use them will often be necessary for fine tuning.

Intrusion Prevention

The final key function of a firewall is to prevent hackers, robots (yes, robots, but not in the Asimov sense), and others seeking unauthorized access to your network from getting in. As Untangle describes the problem:

> Most hackers are looking for computer networks that they can hijack and exploit. They cast wide nets using automated programs that sniff out exposed networks. This makes small businesses, with more limited IT budgets, particularly vulnerable.

Thus, the main problem for home networks, schools, libraries, and small businesses is not so much individuals looking to access their networks to get access to data, but rather attempts to use their network to launch attacks on bigger targets. This can lead to mail sent from your network being flagged as spam, slow performance, and legal troubles with your ISP.

While many organizations are moving their data and applications to the cloud, schools, legal offices, municipal agencies, and others often have sensitive data on site, making them targets for more traditional hacking. These same groups are also relatively common targets for denial of service (DOS) attacks. Fairly easy to implement, a DOS attack floods a network with traffic, preventing users from accessing the Internet and potentially internal resources. A motivated teenager with an ax to grind at a school can orchestrate a DOS attack, crippling a setting that is increasingly reliant on access to the Internet. Such an attack can be thwarted by the right firewall, Untangle included.

Malware Protection

Malware is a very broad term. Short for malicious software, malware can include computer viruses, Trojan horses, spyware, keyloggers, scareware, adware, worms, and many other types of software that install without the user's consent. Infections with these types of software can range from inconvenient (adware, for example, pops up ads repeatedly while users are online, can often be inappropriate in nature, and can degrade system performance) to devastating (viruses and worms can wipe out hard drives and wreak havoc on a network). So-called scareware is designed to convince users that they need to purchase a particular product (such as fake antivirus) to eliminate a threat on their computer and can lead to identity theft and unexpected charges to credit cards as people attempt to buy software to address virus alerts.

However, many commercial desktop antivirus applications are expensive, inadequate, and ineffective. Similarly, recent reviews of antivirus products for Android mobile devices showed that freely available apps were universally bad at finding malware—and that paid apps weren't much better. Macintosh products, as well, are increasingly vulnerable to infection. Although Apple users could once consider themselves safe from malware, this is no longer the case. Figure 5.4 shows the various malware threats and their potential consequences for users and the networks and organizations in which they work.

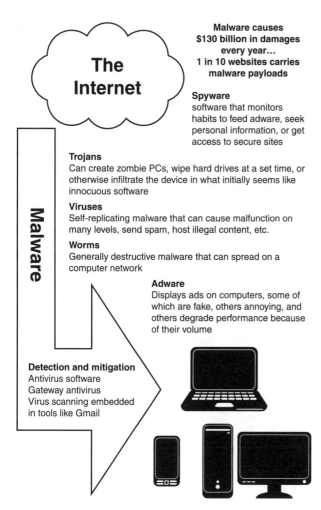

Figure 5.4
Malware threats and consequences.

Ultimately, detecting and blocking malware at the gateway level rather than on individual client devices can do the following:

- Save money in terms of anti-malware software licensing.
- Provide a single point of maintenance and updates.
- Provide superior protection for mobile devices while they are accessing the network.
- Reduce costs associated with malware removal and mitigation.
- Reduce the time spent by IT staff preventing or mitigating damage on individual PCs and devices caused by malware infection.

- Promote transparent, simple, effective malware detection.

- Enable individual users to leverage free client anti-malware applications with the assurance that most threats are managed before they ever reach the network.

- Keep end users out of the anti-malware game, allowing that expertise to be concentrated in those responsible for managing the network (and Untangle).

EMAIL PROTECTION

Increasingly, people are using webmail services such as Gmail and Yahoo! Mail to access their email. These services include virus scanning, spam protection, etc. However, many individuals still use traditional email clients such as Outlook and Apple Mail. In fact, the growing popularity of Apple products—particularly the iPhone and iPad—have brought about a resurgence of email clients, all of which use protocols that most firewalls (including Untangle) can monitor.

Email clients use Post Office Protocol (POP), Internet Message Access Protocol (IMAP), and SMTP to send and receive emails. Email remains a major carrier of malware, as well as a major source of Internet traffic and messaging overload in the form of spam. Roughly 80% of the spam sent online comes from virus-infected computers called botnets. Spam itself accounts for roughly 90% of all email messages sent (approximately 250 billion in 2011, according to maawg.org). Given that spam is estimated to cost receivers approximately 10 cents for every message, the global cost of spam is quite extraordinary.

Spam is frequently another link to malware-infected websites, may contain malware itself, and is frequently inappropriate, provocative, or otherwise unsuitable for viewing in many of the environments in which Untangle will be installed. More worrisome is the prevalence of phishing schemes in emails. Like spyware, phishing emails are designed to capture user information that can be used for credit-card fraud, identity theft, and other nefarious purposes. Unlike spyware, though, phishing involves convincing users to actively provide their personal information instead of capturing it through some sort of malicious software. As such, phishing emails are becoming quite sophisticated, professional, and personalized, unlike the Nigerian email scams of old.

USER PROTECTION AND TRAINING

In some cases, users need to be protected from themselves. I've already discussed phishing and the related possibility of identity theft and credit-card fraud. I talk about content filtering (blocking access to certain websites because of their content) in the next section.

However, it's worth taking a few minutes to think about the role the user must take to stay safe on the Internet. Although Untangle and similar products can go a long way toward automatically and transparently protecting users and the network from online threats, ultimately, the user needs to take a high degree of responsibility. This is an area that no firewall can address, but that a good administrator can handle with a few training sessions and some hand-holding.

No matter how much a content filter, firewall, or other gateway anti-malware device isolates users from the big bad world of the Internet, users will eventually encounter a phishing scam, a malware-infected website, or an email of dubious origins. In particular, as users increasingly bring their own computing devices from home, system administrators need to have some degree of confidence that those systems will be free of malware and not pose a risk to the organization's network.

Although companies can require users to install anti-malware software on personal devices, the financial and administrative reality is this simply isn't going to happen—especially for smaller businesses, non-profits, schools, etc. And although computing appliances do exist that can scan any and all devices brought onto a network for malware infections, these appliances are expensive. Even if 100% of users install and regularly maintain anti-virus software on their computing devices, new malware emerges daily, and local solutions often miss the latest threats. Again, a low-cost solution that provides the most robust network safety possible (such as Untangle) is critical to avoiding damage, loss, and the hassle associated with malware and creates a solid, multi-layered approach to security in environments where client-side anti-malware is universally maintained.

Combining appropriate devices with common-sense training for members of an organization not only empowers users and makes them responsible for their online safety, but it builds a better-educated populace more capable of dealing with cyber threats outside the relatively safe confines of a school or office.

CONTENT FILTERING

Content filtering is arguably the most important function of any gateway device, whether dedicated or combined with other features (as is possible with Untangle). Content filtering is also one of most contentious IT issues in an organization—even if that organization is a family. Filtering generally exposes a dichotomy between users who believe that access to the Internet should be unfettered and administrators, parents, and other stakeholders who see the value of restricting access to certain sites and applications.

From a user's perspective, content filtering can be lumped together with the protocol controls outlined earlier in this chapter in the section "Ports and Protocols" because both are designed to prevent unwanted activities online and both block access to properties and applications on the web. However, most gateways treat protocol control as a firewall function while content filtering is generally a separate module, application, or function. This makes sense from an administrative perspective, though, because web content is usually filtered based on blacklisted domains (for example, playboy.com and other pornographic sites) or keywords (I'll let you imagine what those keywords might be). Blocking of P2P traffic, for instance, happens via examination of requested ports or particular protocols.

Preventing access to pornography is a requirement for schools and libraries that receive certain types of federal funding (and most do, making this a mandate). Most schools also prevent access to hate speech, gaming, sites about illicit drugs, and weapons-related pages. Because most content filters allow blocking of broad categories as well as specific, manually entered sites, this is a fairly simple proposition. Untangle, like many content filters, is also relatively smart about distinguishing pornography from legitimate medical content.

Many schools and other organizations also block access to entertainment sites, social media, and video sites. The justification is that such filtering prevents distractions and limits scarce bandwidth to mission-critical web traffic. While it's beyond the scope of this book to debate the relative merits of permissive versus more Draconian filtering—that's a policy decision that must be made internally with input from all stakeholders—it's worth noting that if bandwidth is the primary reason for blocking certain websites, Untangle and other similar devices have so-called quality-of service (QoS) rules that prioritize certain types of traffic over others. For example, a web-based accounting application would never be slowed down by other users watching videos on YouTube. The use of QoS tools is generally preferred over more aggressive content filtering, but many choose to ensure that students, children, and other users aren't accessing sites with potentially objectionable content and aren't distracted by the countless shiny objects that inhabit the Internet.

Some organizations take this a step further and, instead of blacklisting categories and sites, block everything and then whitelist specific categories and sites. While this is a fairly extreme approach, it may be necessary for certain churches, orthodox religious schools, and families with young children. It's difficult for a six-year-old to find trouble on the net if they can only access Club Penguin.

Most content filters do, however, allow the ability to apply different policies to different users or for designated users to bypass content filters. While it's possible to have every user authenticate against the filter, often connecting the server to another directory server on the network, it is usually sufficient to set up two logins: one with very permissive policies and the other more restrictive. Parents, for example, may want to be totally unfiltered while their children are aggressively kept out of the nether regions of the Internet. This can also be accomplished by applying different policies to different network interfaces and assigning adults to one zone and kids to another. This approach could also, for example, allow teachers access to instant messaging for internal communications but prevent cheating and distraction by blocking students from the ports on which IM runs.

Use Case Matrix: Recommendations by Environment

I've already identified the core audience for this book. While most of the readers will share common characteristics, they will be implementing Untangle in many different environments. The most likely environments for readers appear in Table 5.1, along with particular recommendations and best practices for implementation of specific gateway features. Obviously, every situation is different, but this provides a starting point as you move into Chapter 6, "Implementing Networking Best Practices (or Not) with Untangle," and begin walking through the actual setup and detailed configuration of these features. In all cases, email and malware protection should be turned on and configured with aggressive settings. This may result in some false positives, but that is preferable to network-wide infestations or security compromises.

Table 5.1 Key Use Cases and Filtering Guidelines for Untangle

Environment	DHCP/DNS	Firewall	Content Filtering
School/library	Hybrid—DHCP for mobile or BYOD (Bring Your Own Device) devices and static IP for computers that don't leave the building	Block all P2P ports and proxy traffic that can be detected at the firewall level	Filter pornography, extremist and hate sites, gambling and drug-related sites Blacklist proxy sites that aren't picked up by the firewall (these sites allow users to bypass the content filtering) Blacklist other sites and categories consistent with internal policy and government regulation Ensure that adults can bypass filters as needed

(Continued)

Table 5.1 Key Use Cases and Filtering Guidelines for Untangle (*Continued*)

Environment	DHCP/DNS	Firewall	Content Filtering
Non-profit	DHCP except for servers, printers, and other fixed assets	None, unless sensitive data are present; then block all ports except those required for communications and web access	In general, none, although certain faith-based non-profits may require aggressive filtering
SMB—tech	DHCP except for servers, printers, and other fixed assets	Block all ports except those required for P2P, IM, remote access, and other web communications	None
SMB—non-tech	DHCP except for servers, printers, and other fixed assets	Block all ports except those required for P2P, IM, remote access, and other web communications	None
Home	Static IP addresses for all users; DHCP for guests	Block all ports except those required for communications (web, Skype, IM, etc.)	Set according to the age of the child and create differential policies for parents or older children
Student	DHCP except for servers, printers, and other fixed assets	None	None
Enthusiast	DHCP except for servers, printers, and other fixed assets	None	None

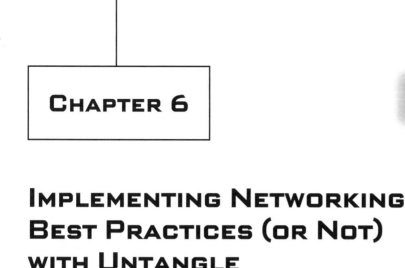

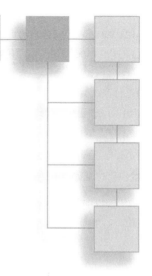

CHAPTER 6

IMPLEMENTING NETWORKING BEST PRACTICES (OR NOT) WITH UNTANGLE

Okay. So far, you now know:

- How to choose appropriate hardware for an Untangle server in a given setting
- How to build an Untangle gateway from parts or a repurposed computer
- How to navigate the Untangle web interface
- How to configure Untangle at a basic level and get it working on your network, whether as a bridge or as a router
- The key concepts of modern computer networking including DHCP, DNS, and other protocols such as TCP and IP
- The basic types of interfaces supported (internal, external, and DMZ) and how they map to physical network interfaces in the gateway
- How to manage apps and racks to customize the interface and functionality of Untangle
- Basic vocabulary and best practices around network protection

Obviously, you've covered a lot of ground. Now, however, is where the rubber meets the road, so to speak. It's time to put all these pieces in place and begin protecting your networks and your users.

This chapter is called "Implementing Networking Best Practices (or Not) with Untangle" because it's quite possible that there are areas of network protection with Untangle that aren't compatible with your existing infrastructure, organizational policies, or other factors that might lead you to implement "less than best" practices. There may also be fundamental disagreements about what represents a best practice, particularly in the areas of user consent and content filtering. I'll get to those arguments in Chapter 7, "Implementing Protection Best Practices (or Not) with Untangle (a.k.a. 'The Rack')." However, by the end of this chapter, you will have the skills and knowledge to make conscious, informed decisions about your use of Untangle and to act accordingly in your implementation, regardless of your particular situation.

NETWORK CONFIGURATION OVERVIEW

As mentioned, Untangle can manage as many as seven physical Ethernet interfaces. It can also, technically, function with only one, acting as a so-called rerouter. When rerouting, the Untangle appliance accepts traffic through its single interface, applies whatever policies have been set, and then passes traffic back out through that interface to its destination.

This configuration, which is neither recommended nor supported by Untangle, is inefficient at best and unstable or unusable at worst. Success with this approach depends on relatively unsophisticated network hardware. (More modern hardware actually detects rerouting as spoofing and tends to prevent related traffic because it can be a sign of a rogue device on a network.) Until 2010, Untangle supported a standalone software product called Untangle for Windows that could be installed on a standard Windows PC on a network and that would provide content filtering through rerouting. Untangle for Windows was never completely stable, but it was actually many users' first introduction to the product. The intention was also quite good: Provide a free product that used an existing Windows computer to manage content filtering on a small network. While this was a parent's dream (Untangle for Windows could run on Mom or Dad's PC and all Junior would ever know was that he couldn't go on those naughty websites anymore), it simply couldn't be used reliably or extensively.

So why bring up rerouting if we shouldn't do it? Because Untangle supported it in the past, and it remains a common inquiry on forums and discussion boards. It is also instructive to better understand why Untangle requires at least two network interfaces and useful to put the issue to rest up front.

Fortunately, as you've already seen, it's extremely inexpensive to configure a repurposed or very inexpensive PC to function as a standalone Internet gateway, using the recommended two network interfaces (one internal, one external). Especially in home networks, where there will most likely not be a web server or guest network that would require a third interface (the DMZ interface), this in-and-out, two-card setup is the easiest, cheapest way to establish content filtering. In the Untangle interface, a two-card setup looks like Figure 6.1.

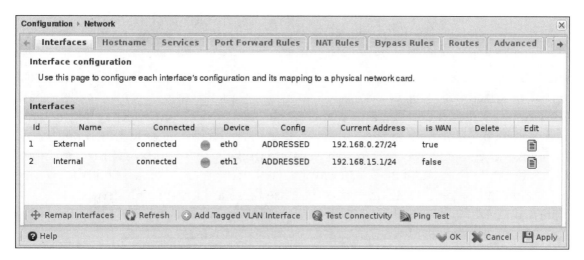

Figure 6.1
Two-card setup, as shown in the Network Configuration Interfaces tab.
Source: Untangle, Inc.

Note that the pictured device has been set up in routing mode. The external interface is set to dynamic, and the internal interface has been assigned a static IP address. Again, this is the easiest setup with the sort of modem or router that one is likely to find in a home, small business, or school. In these situations, by default, a modem or router is generally functioning as a DHCP server, so you can allow the external interface to be assigned any IP address by the router DHCP server. Because the internal interface has its own IP address and Untangle is acting as a router itself, the activities of the modem are isolated from the network and Untangle can provide DHCP services on the internal interface. (In general, multiple DHCP servers on a network cause a world of problems, but Untangle effectively creates a new network, so there is no such conflict.)

The key message here is that, with rare exceptions, all internal interfaces should have a static IP address. This prevents confusion, makes it easy to identify network segments, reduces reliance on DNS (one of many possible points of failure on a network), and eases documentation needs. It also makes it easier to manage network address translation

(NAT)—discussed in the upcoming section "NAT"—when one needs to make connections between networks.

The external interface can be set to static as well, but you will then need to choose an address for the interface that is compatible with those on the network defined by the modem and that will remain unique. For example, if another network device is connected to the modem but not to the Untangle server and its IP address is a duplicate of the Untangle server's, neither will be able to connect to the Internet.

Notice that the internal interface is on a completely different subnet from that of the external interface. All devices connected to what is in this case a cable modem have addresses of 192.168.0.x. In many instances, the only device connected to the modem/router will be the Untangle server. However, there may be instances in which one would want network segments to be completely separate from the network(s) defined by Untangle. For example, if an Untangle gateway had only two interfaces, a public-facing web server could not be on a DMZ interface (because there are not enough network cards to support a DMZ) and would therefore have to be connected directly to the network defined by the modem. This scenario is pictured in Figure 6.2.

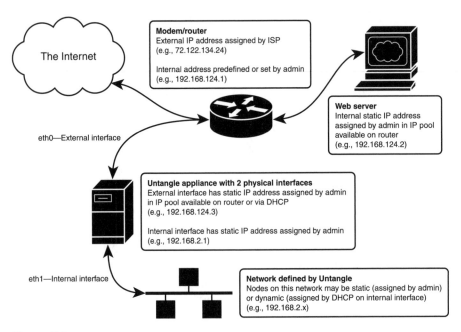

Figure 6.2
Creating a DMZ on the primary Internet connection.

While having three or more interfaces is considered a best practice when setting up an Untangle box to allow for expansion, an internal DMZ, and/or network segmentation, the use of two interfaces is a common setup, especially among casual or home users of Untangle.

For the vast majority of use cases, three network interfaces are sufficient. As noted, Untangle supports only three types of network connections: external, internal, and DMZ. Interfaces beyond the first two are named sequentially (Interface 3, Interface 4, etc.), but can be renamed to suit your needs. Figure 6.3 shows the network configuration page for a server with three interfaces. While it is quite similar to the page shown in Figure 6.1, the third interface (renamed to DMZ) is attached directly to a web server with a static IP address.

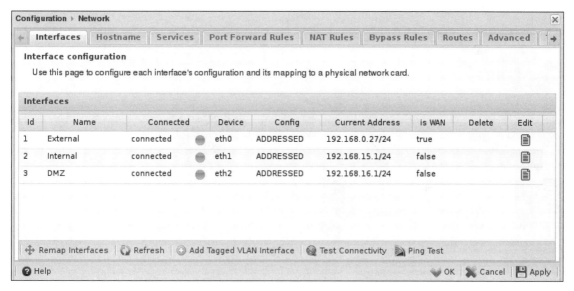

Figure 6.3
Three-card setup.
Source: Untangle, Inc.

Again, the static IP address is not required; DNS and DHCP can work together with NAT to ensure that web traffic bound for the web server makes it to its destination via the server's hostname (for example, cad_webserver1.6geeks.net) instead of an IP address. However, DNS remains one of the most common sources of network difficulty and is, perhaps, the hardest for less-experienced network administrators (that is, the core audience of this book) to navigate. A static IP address removes at least this one potential complication from the setup and, again, makes documentation even more straightforward. Even for experienced network administrators, however, servers of any sort tend to operate on static IP addresses.

NAT

Network address translation (NAT) is a technology that deserves its own, albeit brief, section in this book (or, for that matter, any book on introductory networking). It is particularly critical and germane to this discussion because it is what enables, for example, an HTTP request from a web user somewhere in the world to reach a web server that sits on an internal network behind a firewall/router (like an Untangle appliance). Figure 6.4 outlines the function and flow of NAT.

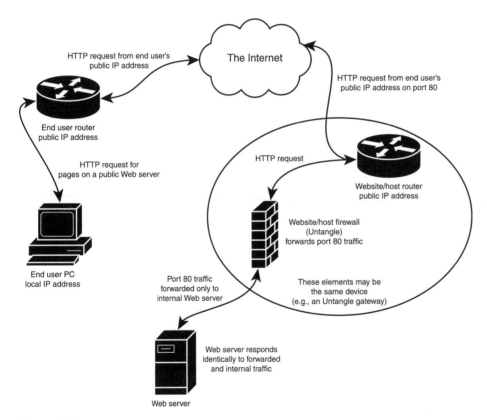

Figure 6.4
NAT on a typical network.

A more concrete definition of NAT is a set of specific changes made to TCP/IP data that allows the flow of packets between networks with different IP address pools. There are several types of NAT, all focused on allowing one network (for example, an office local area network with addresses of the form 192.168.128.*x*) to request and receive data from another network (for example, the Internet, with a very wide range of subnets and disparate IP pools).

The most relevant (and simplest) form of NAT for our purposes is called port forwarding. As noted, ports allow one to differentiate types of network traffic, and each protocol (for example, TCP, HTTP, and FTP) runs on a specific port. For example, Hypertext Transfer Protocol (HTTP), used for the majority of web traffic, runs on port 80. Thus, when a user in his home in Wichita requests http://cnn.com on his iPad (which, in this hypothetical situation, has an IP address of 192.168.0.12 on his home network), a DNS server (perhaps embedded within his cable modem if he has visited CNN before) easily translates his request to http://157.166.255.19/.

This is all well and good, but there are millions of computers running on networks that have addresses like 192.168.0.12. How can the CNN web servers send their pages back to the correct house in Wichita and then to the correct iPad inside that house? More importantly, how can the CNN servers respond to HTTP requests but not allow an FTP request from someone wanting to download the entire CNN website or upload their own content?

The answer to both of these questions is NAT. NAT modifies the so-called headers in TCP packets (equivalent to the return and mailing addresses on an envelope) so that the path to CNN and back to that iPad in Wichita can be maintained. Similarly, when the firewalls and routers at CNN's data centers (which are far more sophisticated than your little Untangle boxes but operate in much the same way) receive a request from Wichita (or wherever), they see it on port 80. All port 80 requests are translated (or forwarded) to the server farm that hosts the website through NAT rules established on the routers. FTP, however, runs on port 21. The firewall has no such NAT rule for handling traffic on port 21, so these requests aren't forwarded.

NAT, then, serves both a security and addressing function. In fact, enabling NAT on a given internal interface by selecting the NAT Traffic Exiting This Interface (and Bridged Peers) option in the Edit Interface screen will actually prevent that internal network from reaching other internal networks without creating a specific port forward rule (see the upcoming section). This is useful for isolating users, servers, and various resources from each other and strictly controlling the flow of traffic between subnets.

NAT is automatic on the external interface and enabled by default. This is necessary to ensure that the internal address requesting a particular website is translated to the public IP address of the network on which Untangle runs. It also ensures that the public IP address is translated back to the correct internal IP address so that the requested web page is delivered to the right computer.

POINTING TRAFFIC TO A WEB SERVER (PORT FORWARDS)

As noted in the preceding section, NAT can be used to forward TCP/IP traffic on port 80 (or any port) to an internal web server, ensuring the security of your network while still allowing you to expose a website to the public Internet. The same is true for an FTP server you might host to allow downloads of files by external users (instead forwarding port 21) or to ensure that mail reaches an internal mail server (forwarding port 110 for POP3 mail or port 143 for IMAP).

If you assume that a web server is connected to the DMZ (as is the intended best practice to further ensure the safety and integrity of other network resources), then this is set up through the Network configuration interface, working in the Port Forward Rules top tab. Untangle comes with a few common types of rules already specified, although they are disabled by default. Figure 6.5 shows an edited version of the built-in rule to forward web traffic to an internal web server. It detects incoming web traffic at the gateway on the external interface based on its port number and translates the external public IP address to the internal address of the web server. Also note that you can specify an internal port number. Although web traffic normally runs on port 80, multiple sites can be hosted on a web server by (among other methods) associating their content with different ports. Thus, you could specify that traffic from a particular external address could be routed to port 81, serving up a different website than that associated with port 80.

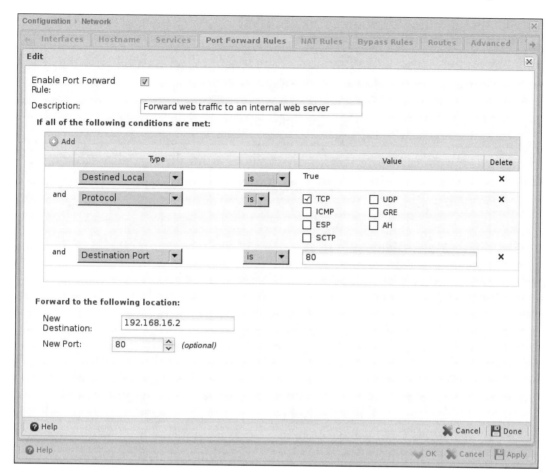

Figure 6.5
Port-forward setup for an internal web server.
Source: Untangle, Inc.

DHCP CONFIGURATION

DHCP is critical to network scalability. Although every node on your network can have a static IP address—and many, such as servers, printers, and scanners, should have static IP—dynamic IP allows the easy addition of new computers, guest computers, etc. For example, consider a school. If students bring their own devices, then wireless routers throughout the school could be configured on the DMZ with restrictive content filtering (see the section "The Application Control" in Chapter 7) and DHCP so that the individual machines need not be configured one at a time. Other school-owned devices could be configured with static IP on the internal interface for easy documentation and management and to ensure that internal traffic is managed separately and protected from student devices.

DHCP works through the definition of pools. These pools contain addresses that are available for assignment to devices on the network and are created through the Edit Interface dialog box on the Network Configuration > Interfaces tab. As a result, each interface can have its own DHCP server with its own pool of addresses. Different implementations of DHCP handle the creation of these pools in a variety of ways and many allow the creation of multiple pools. Untangle works a bit differently from most DHCP servers, though, by supporting only a single DHCP pool per interface. Static IP addresses that need to be assigned on that network, then, are specifically excluded from the pool through the creation of an entry in the Static DHCP Entries section of the Networking dialog box, which you access via the Config > Network > Advanced > DHCP Server subtab (look ahead to Figure 6.6).

According to Untangle's documentation:

> It is best practice not to assign a static IP address from the middle of a DHCP address pool. An address pooling scheme should be defined that incorporates servers, printers, dynamic workstation addresses and static workstation addresses.

In the case of Figure 6.6, 192.168.15.100 is a client computer with the hostname cadubvm1. The hostname is an important component of DNS and enables you to pinpoint issues with specific nodes on the network. When they are assigned IP addresses via DHCP, reports generated by many utilities, including Untangle, may provide only an IP address. Using either the Static DHCP Entries table or the Current DHCP Entries table in the Networking dialog box will enable you to associate an IP address with a human-readable hostname (for example, library_kiosk_1), assuming you have named the devices appropriately. (This is done at the device level, not on Untangle.)

It is also worth noting that the DHCP pool used by devices listed in Figure 6.6 does not include the entire range of addresses available on the subnet. This particular pool includes only 192.168.15.100–192.168.15.200. To use all available addresses in this particular subnet, you would specify a pool of 192.168.15.2–192.168.15.254, excluding only the address associated with the Untangle interface. Because the pool in this case is limited to 101 addresses, you could actually avoid assigning any static entries in Untangle and simply configure static devices individually with an IP address from the ranges 192.168.15.2–192.168.15.99 and 192.168.15.201–192.168.15.254. However, by using Untangle to assign static IP addresses to specific devices, all such assignments are centrally managed and documented.

Finally, Figure 6.6 shows a single computer (cadubvm1) assigned a static IP address from the DHCP pool automatically. Whenever the computer is turned on and requests an address from Untangle, it will always be given the address 192.168.15.100 because of the record in the Static DHCP Entries table. Thus, this computer can be set up to use DHCP (useful if it is a laptop and needs a different dynamic IP address when used elsewhere), but will always be assigned the same IP address when used on the Untangle network. Untangle identifies computers for this purpose by their MAC address rather than by computer name, adding an important layer of security for organizations that need to ensure that only specific computers can be given an address and therefore access the network. While this is not often necessary for client computers, it illustrates the flexibility and power of Untangle's DHCP server.

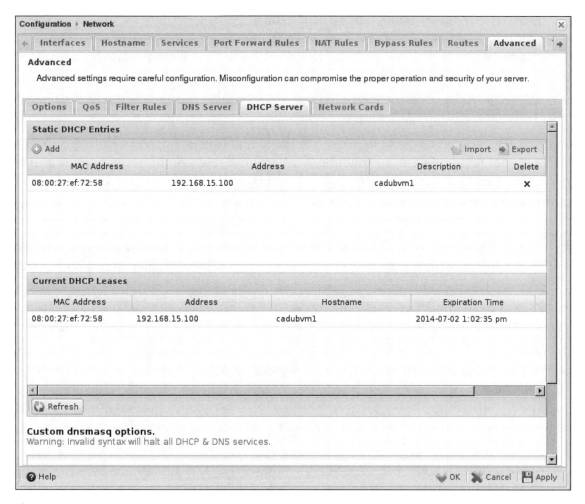

Figure 6.6
DHCP configuration.
Source: Untangle, Inc.

DNS

As you learned in Chapter 5, "Network and User Protection Best Practices," Domain Name Service (DNS) is like the phone book of the Internet, mapping IP addresses to human-readable names. Untangle has a built-in DNS server that acts as the initial lookup for addresses on the internal and/or DMZ networks, as well as for any external addresses on the Internet or other outside networks that may be stored (or cached) in Untangle's DNS.

By default, DNS is enabled in Untangle but not configured. Often, a modem or router will already be providing DNS for the network; alternatively, a previously installed server may have that role. Untangle doesn't need to be the DNS server on a network; leaving it unconfigured will essentially make it inactive. However, in the spirit of simplicity and ease of administration, in most cases it makes sense for Untangle to handle DNS. DNS by its very nature, though, is intended to be redundant and distributed, so other DNS servers can exist on the network and—again by design—Untangle can and will look to upstream servers for additional resolution.

That said, DNS configuration remains one of the least intuitive aspects of Untangle, partly because it can be modified from multiple locations and relies on both the operating system and the Untangle virtual machine (see the upcoming section "Bypass Rules") for correct operation. Fortunately, recent updates to the Untangle NG Firewall have made DNS configuration relatively straightforward and automated, if not completely transparent.

Successful configuration of the Untangle DNS server assumes that the gateway's external interface is already pointing to a valid "upstream" DNS server, whether a public DNS server on the Internet (for example, one provided by Google, OpenDNS, etc.), a DNS pre-configured on a router or modem provided by an ISP, or another DNS server between Untangle and the router/modem. This upstream DNS server is usually configured automatically if the external interface is set to DHCP.

As with DHCP, most elements of DNS are configured in a subtab on the Advanced Network configuration tab (for DNS, it's the DNS Server subtab). As shown in Figure 6.7, there are two types of DNS records that users can add or modify: Static Entries and Local Servers. Static entries are intended for efficiency and to short-circuit lookups, most often for internal servers and devices. In Figure 6.7, the address of an internal web server on the DMZ interface has been specified so that users can simply access web_server .6geeks.net instead of using the external address for the web server (presumably www.6geeks.net) and forcing traffic out of the external interface, bringing it back through external interface, and filtering it in both directions.

Local DNS Servers assign DNS duties for a particular domain to another server on the network. In Figure 6.7, I have assigned a DNS server attached to the internal interface to handle all queries related to the domain for my consulting company. Thus, if users on my network want to access the tekedu.net web server, they can enter web.tekedu.net in their browser. Then, instead of Untangle resolving that name to an IP address, the separate DNS server at 192.168.15.3 will handle the resolution. For smaller networks, this will often not be necessary, and it is likely that there won't be any static DNS servers specified.

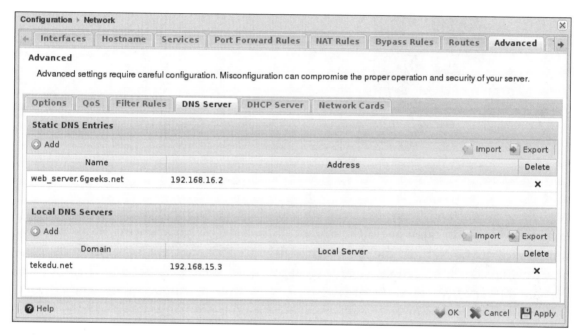

Figure 6.7
DNS configuration.
Source: Untangle, Inc.

BYPASS RULES

Bypass rules ensure that certain types of traffic pass immediately through Untangle to their appropriate destination without filtering. Untangle uses a Java virtual machine to perform content filtering and most of its gateway tasks. However, traffic like VoIP requires such low latency that even the fastest Untangle server will introduce unacceptable delays. The normal and bypass flows of data in Untangle are shown in Figure 6.8.

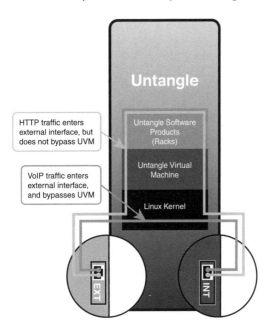

Figure 6.8
Untangle virtual machine schematic and flow of data resulting from bypass rules.

Untangle includes built-in bypass rules for the most common types of VoIP (SIP and Asterisk), so you can often avoid the advanced tools unless your organization has more sophisticated needs. Not that the tools aren't fairly user-friendly, but a goal for most readers of this book will be simplicity and set-it-and-forget-it configuration. The advanced tools add a layer of complexity that requires a more in-depth understanding of networking than many users in home, school, or small office settings will want to pursue.

Skype, though technically a VoIP application, is not compliant with either SIP or Asterisk. If an organization has just a few Skype users, then this isn't an issue because Skype can make use of ports that are open by default. However, if a business has many frequent users of Skype (and a growing number of businesses rely on Skype, especially for international communications), then bypass rules will need to be set up allowing this sort of traffic.

Similarly, Microsoft's Remote Desktop Protocol (RDP) is used to stream desktop sessions for remote access to virtual machines, terminal servers, and administrative interfaces, among other things. Creating a bypass rule so that data passing via RDP is unfiltered helps ensure a smooth experience even if bandwidth is limited.

Bypass rules are managed in the Bypass Rules tab in the Network Configuration screen. Figure 6.9 shows the setup for bypassing RDP, which uses TCP port 3389. Untangle can also identify traffic to bypass based on its source interface, destination address, etc.

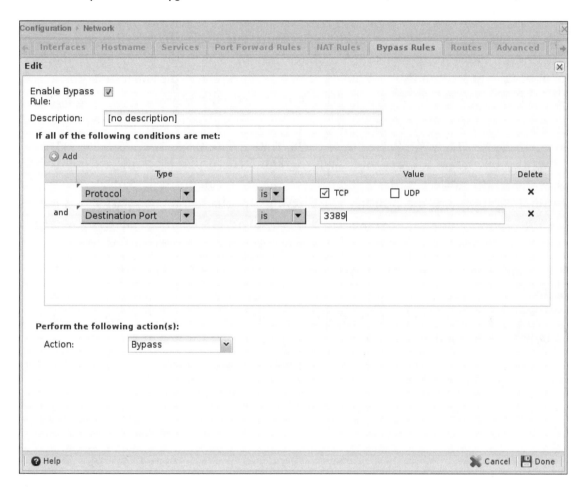

Figure 6.9
Setting up a bypass rule for RDP.
Source: Untangle, Inc.

ADVANCED CONFIGURATION

We have already explored two of the Advanced subtabs—DHCP and DNS. The Advanced tab is located in the Network Configuration screen and also provides access to packet filtering and quality of service (QoS).

Packet Filtering

Untangle offers packet filtering through its basic firewall. Packet filtering is a key element of any firewall. However, more granular packet filtering is available through the advanced tools under the Filter Rules subtab. Like the bypass rules, filter rules operate at the kernel level and don't require calls to the slower Untangle Virtual Machine.

As shown in Figure 6.10, filter rules are divided into two types: forward filter rules and input filter rules. Forward filter rules still apply to traffic even if it has been bypassed because they operate at a lower level than the Untangle virtual machine. As their name implies, these rules deal with traffic that is forwarded through the Untangle server. The Firewall application (see the section "The Firewall" in Chapter 7) also passes and blocks traffic based on a variety of conditions. Even so, there are key differences between the forward filter rules and the firewall that provide appropriate use cases for each:

- Forward filter rules apply to all network protocols instead of being limited to TCP and UDP.

- Forward filter rules apply to bypassed traffic. Bypassed traffic never reaches the firewall application.

- The firewall application has much more granular control over traffic and can support more sophisticated policies.

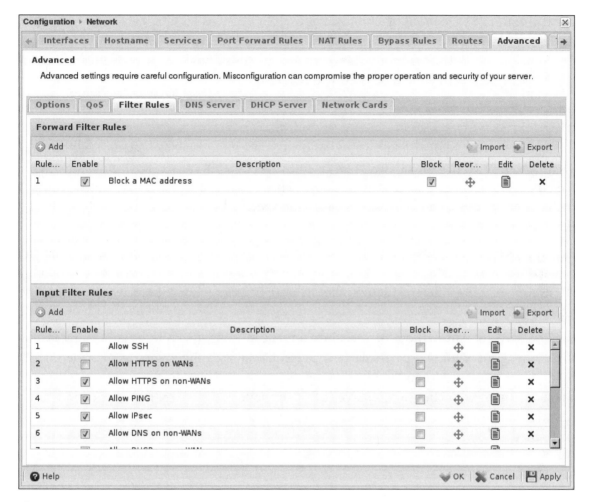

Figure 6.10
The Filter Rules interface.
Source: Untangle, Inc.

In Figure 6.10, note that a forward filter rule has been set up to block a specific MAC address. This rule will prevent all traffic to or from a specific computer regardless of its IP address or hostname. Figure 6.10 also shows several input filter rules. These rules relate to traffic that isn't forwarded by Untangle but rather accesses Untangle itself. For example, the rule to "Allow HTTPS access on WANs" allows administrators to log in to Untangle from outside the network. Input rules can create substantial security vulnerabilities if applied incorrectly and should be used with caution.

QoS

Quality of service (QoS), also known as bandwidth shaping, enables Untangle administrators to assign priorities to certain types of traffic. By default, only a small number of QoS rules are created when Untangle is installed. These apply to broad categories of content such as gaming, DNS, and TCP, as well as to the specific bypass rules discussed in "Bypass Rules" section for VoIP.

Untangle recommends that every bypass rule have a corresponding QoS rule giving the bypassed traffic the highest priority. The logic here is that if data needs to move so quickly that it shouldn't be filtered, then it should also be given top billing by the operating system.

The QoS screens mimic those of the other advanced tools, but a few features are worth calling out in Figure 6.11—particularly because, along with the ability to manage DHCP on multiple interfaces, bandwidth shaping is arguably the most important advanced feature for those who choose to enable it. It can make or break critical applications on a network, particularly as the number of users increases and/or when bandwidth is constrained.

Figure 6.11
QoS configuration.
Source: Untangle, Inc.

As you move down the configuration page, notice that QoS is not enabled by default. To enable it, click the Enabled checkbox to select it; users can then choose a default priority. This is a matter of preference, but in most cases, leaving the default as Medium allows for the most logical differentiation from normal traffic in the rules that follow.

The built-in QoS rules are straightforward and should generally be left alone with the exception of the last two (OpenVPN Priority and Gaming Priority). In organizations where remote access to internal computing resources is critical (for example, in an organization with a large number of telecommuters or a virtual office setting), the priority of OpenVPN traffic should be raised. Conversely, for most educational and professional environments, gaming should be severely limited. The last thing a business needs is to have a critical online presentation to clients lagging because some developer is taking a break playing *World of Warcraft*.

The custom rules, as noted on the dialog box, should be established only when there is a corresponding bypass rule. Otherwise, custom rules may conflict with the broad categories defined previously. New custom rules are added just as other items are defined across the Untangle network configuration pages.

The QoS priority levels are predefined. It isn't possible to add new levels. However, you can modify the existing levels by simply clicking the cell containing the reservation percentage to be changed. For example, the Limited Severely setting could be changed to 1% across the board (0% is not an allowed value). However, totals in each column must add up to 100%, as these represent total allocations of bandwidth.

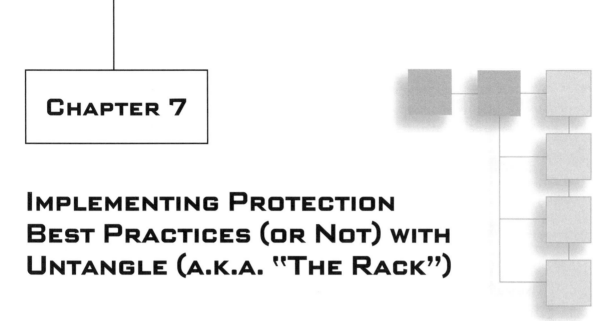

CHAPTER 7

IMPLEMENTING PROTECTION BEST PRACTICES (OR NOT) WITH UNTANGLE (A.K.A. "THE RACK")

No, "The Rack" is not a medieval instrument of torture. At least not in this context. Rather, as noted in previous chapters, the actual applications built into Untangle are presented to users through virtual server racks in the web-based GUI. The default rack contains all available applications that have been installed. In addition, each element can be turned on and off individually and is configured individually. (See Figure 7.1.)

Figure 7.1
Annotated default virtual rack.
Source: Untangle, Inc.

One topic discussed later in this chapter is the Policy Manager. This application is a paid feature of Untangle and allows for the creation of multiple racks with varying configurations and different applications (virtual application servers in Untangle nomenclature) turned on or off for different users and interfaces. In terms of free features, however, only the default rack is available, and all configurations apply across the board.

The rack is divided into two sections of virtual servers:

- **Filter applications.** Filter applications, as their name implies, facilitate the appropriate flow of traffic through the appliance and generally work in concert with the configurations in the Config tab.

- **Service applications.** Service applications, which have little relevance to end users, are centered around administrative functions. Basic Untangle implementations will rarely require you to access service applications, but administrators seeking more robust implementations will generally find that the major limitations of the free version of Untangle occur within the service applications.

THE FIREWALL

The purpose of a firewall is to control, with a fair degree of granularity, access to a network from other networks (often, but not always, the Internet itself) and outbound access to the Internet (or other networks), based on a series of rules specified by administrators. Because Untangle is also a router/gateway, much of the inbound access is already handled by the Network Address Translation (NAT) and port forwards set up via the various tabs in the Networking Configuration dialog box described in the previous chapter.

The firewall is most often used within Untangle for egress filtering, or managing outbound requests. Egress filtering can also be handled at specific levels by the Protocol Control application, but administering these levels requires different baseline skill sets and knowledge, and one skill set may be more comfortable or familiar for particular administrators than the other. Some admins, in fact, may never touch the firewall if all their needs are met by Protocol Control.

However, an important component of the firewall that isn't replicated elsewhere is the ability to decide on a blacklist versus whitelist approach to outbound network traffic. The NAT rules already established as part of the setup of Untangle's networking/routing capabilities generally limit incoming traffic to specific types and destinations. For example, all HTTP and FTP traffic might get routed through all interfaces to all users, and port 80 requests to a specific external IP address might be routed to a server on the DMZ interfaces.

By default, the Untangle firewall is set to the more permissive blacklist approach. In this scenario, all outbound traffic is allowed by default and administrators must specifically disable certain types of traffic. For example, if administrators wanted to disable SSH and FTP sessions to external servers, they could block ports 22 and 21, respectively. Similarly, they might want to prevent access from a public wireless access point on the DMZ interface to servers on any internal interfaces.

Clicking the Firewall Settings link on the virtual rack will open a list of firewall rules. Administrators can then either add a rule or edit an existing rule, as shown in Figure 7.2. In this figure, two parameters have been defined to prevent the sort of internal access described in the preceding example. These parameters are evaluated in order and all conditions must be met for the action to be completed. In this case, the first condition identifies traffic coming from the DMZ, the second condition identifies traffic bound for anywhere other than the external interface, and the action specifies that such traffic will be blocked. (Note that the names of the interfaces in this dialog box are dynamic and will reflect both the number of available interfaces and their labels assigned during network configuration, as outlined in Chapter 6, "Implementing Networking Best Practices (or Not) with Untangle."

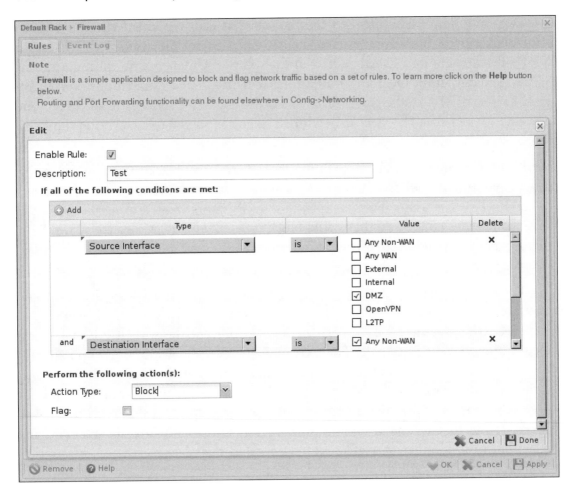

Figure 7.2
Rule set definitions in the firewall.
Source: Untangle, Inc.

Any number of these rules can be created in the firewall interface and, like the conditions that comprise them, are evaluated in order. Often, you want to block users from accessing resources on other interfaces but need to allow specific types of traffic to pass. For example, if DNS and DHCP servers reside on the internal interface (if you aren't using Untangle to handle network infrastructure in that way), then those same users you isolated on the DMZ between interfaces still need to be able to get addressing information from the server on the internal interface.

Thus, you can set up a rule allowing only User Data Protocol (UDP) traffic between any non-WAN interface and a specific IP address on the internal network. (UDP essentially offers a subset of TCP functionality and is used for services like DHCP and DNS that need to work rapidly and do not have the reliability needs of web traffic that can only be served by the full implementation of Transmission Control Protocol.) As you can see in Figure 7.3, the graphical interface makes it easy to create sophisticated logical rules in the firewall with very granular controls over types, destinations, and sources of traffic.

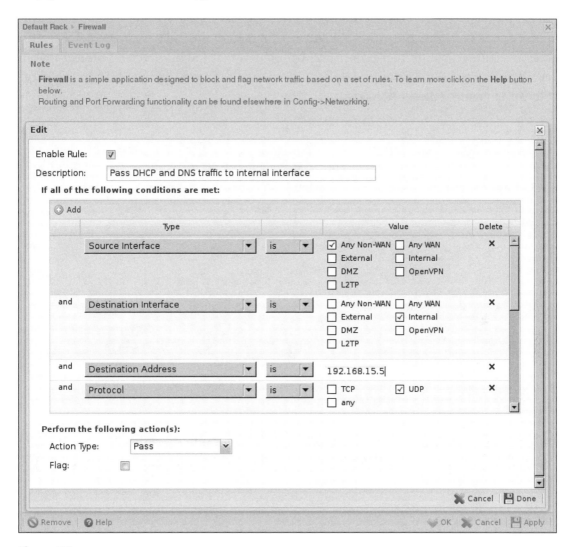

Figure 7.3
A more complicated rule.

Source: Untangle, Inc.

Note

Other standalone firewall products offer more robust tools for managing traffic that passes through the firewall. However, few can match the simplicity of Untangle.

As mentioned, the sub-rules or conditions within each firewall rule are evaluated in order and take precedence based on their order. The rule definition in Figure 7.4, therefore, must be evaluated before the rule in Figure 7.3 because the rule allowing UDP traffic would be overridden by the rule preventing traffic between the interfaces. You can manually reorder these rules by clicking and dragging on the four-way arrow icons in the Reorder column to ensure correct precedence.

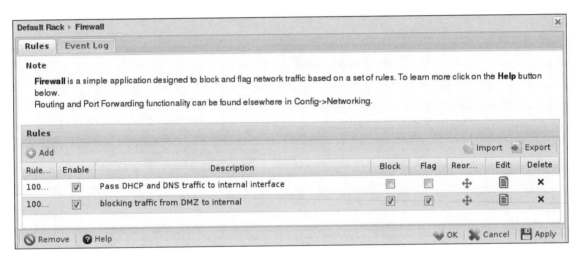

Figure 7.4
Setting precedence for firewall rules.
Source: Untangle, Inc.

Several types of firewall rules can be established, all based on criteria such as destination address, interface accessed, etc. Table 7.1 outlines the various configurations for each type of rule.

Table 7.1   Firewall Rule Types

Rule Type	Available Operators	Allowed Values	Notes
Destination Address	is is not	Any valid IP address	May be internal or external IP addresses; must use IP matcher format (see Table 7.2).
Destination Port	is is not	Any valid port number or range	Must use port matcher format (see Table 7.3).
Destination Interface	is is not	Any WAN, any non-WAN, external, internal, DMZ, Open VPN	This is the interface through which users connect to the requested server. In Figure 7.4, it was the internal interface. When blocking Internet traffic, it will normally be the external interface. The external interface is usually also the WAN interface. With the paid WAN Balancer or WAN Failover applications, DMZ interfaces can also be specified as redundant WAN connections.
Source Address	is is not	Any valid IP address	May be internal or external IP addresses but will most often be internal.
Source Interface	is is not	Any WAN, any non-WAN, external, internal, DMZ, Open VPN	This is the interface through which the requesting client computer is connected. Usually, this will be either the internal or DMZ interface.
Protocol	is is not	TCP, UDP, any	For more granular control of the specific type of traffic, requires the Application Control (paid) or Application Control Lite (free) apps.
Directory Connector: Username	is is not	A username from any connected Active Directory or RADIUS server	Requires the paid Directory Connector app.
Directory Connector: User in Group	is is not	A group name from any connected Active Directory or RADIUS server	Requires the paid Directory Connector app.

As noted in Table 7.1, the firewall requires that ports be specified in port matcher format. Policy Manager, discussed later in this chapter, also requires the use of this format. Similarly, IP addresses and ranges must be specified throughout Untangle applications using the IP matcher format. Examples of each are provided in Tables 7.2 and 7.3.

Table 7.2 IP Matcher Formats

Name	Example	Description
Any Matcher	Any	Matches all addresses
Single IP	1.2.3.4	Matches the single IP address
Range of IPs	1.2.3.4–1.2.3.100	Matches all the IPs in the range
CIDR Range	192.168.1.0/24	Matches all the IPs in that subnet
List of IP Matchers	1.2.3.4,1.2.3.5, 1.2.3.10–1.2.3.15	Matches all the IPs in the list and in that range

Table 7.3 Port Matcher Formats

Name	Example	Description
Any Matcher	Any	Matches all ports
Single Port	80	Matches that single port
Range of Ports	80–85 or 1024–65535	Matches all the ports in the range
List of Port Matchers	80,443,8080–8088	Matches all 80, 443, and 8080–8088

THE APPLICATION CONTROL

While the firewall can be used to control traffic at a high level with the rules discussed in the preceding section (and, to some extent, with the NAT policies and port forwarding discussed in Chapter 6), Application Control (both the paid Application Control and free Application Control Lite apps) provides a much greater degree of granularity and sophistication through a graphical interface. Note that these applications were previously referred to as Protocol Control, giving some indication of the manner in which they identify applications to block or allow.

An FAQ entry on the Untangle Wiki helps differentiate the capabilities of Application Control from that of the firewall:

> Q: I've already installed the firewall. Isn't Application Control redundant?
>
> A: The firewall application works to block traffic for IP addresses and/or ports. For well-behaved applications (such as legitimate web and email servers) the port can be used to identify the protocol. However, less legitimate applications may use different ports, or malicious users may deliberately use unwanted services on obscure ports.
>
> Application Control scans all traffic, looking for a match even if traffic was not transported across the expected port for that protocol.

While the paid Application Control app is quite powerful in its ability to filter applications, especially those that hop ports and intelligently try to circumvent such controls, this book is focused primarily on the free components of Untangle. The Application Control Lite app is still quite useful, allowing users to block large classes of applications with just a few clicks. It also shares most of its user interface with the paid app, so users wishing to upgrade will not be unfamiliar with its use if they have mastered the Lite app.

Untangle identifies applications by their signatures, or components of transmitted data that allow them to be handled appropriately by server and client machines. Like most Untangle apps, Application Control Lite is divided into tabs:

- Status
- Signatures
- Event Log

The Status tab provides an at-a-glance summary of the available signatures that can be controlled, the number of those currently being logged, and the number currently being blocked. It also provides an interesting note for users related to the limitations of the Lite version:

> Caution and discretion is advised using block at the risk of false positives and intelligent applications shifting protocol usage to avoid blocking.

Thus, in many settings, it is useful to simply log traffic on various protocols that might be used for non-work/non-school/inappropriate purposes and then deal with users violating any relevant policies rather than blocking the applications and running the risk of not being able to identify them or users accessing them when the applications intelligently change their signatures. The paid version of Application Control can manage these changing signatures proactively.

The Signatures tab, shown in Figure 7.5, is where most of the setup for your particular network gets done. Here, administrators choose which protocols are blocked and/or logged. About 100 protocols are available for inspection, ranging from AOL Instant Messenger to FTP to several peer-to-peer applications (often used for illegal file sharing). Blocking and logging particular protocols can be set up directly from this screen. Clicking the Edit icon on any of the signature rules allows users to change the displayed name of the protocol, provide a more useful description, and change the signature itself (represented by a string of ASCII characters). The latter is absolutely not recommended without significant expertise. New signatures can also be added from this screen, but users will need to know the ASCII code for the protocol to be monitored or blocked.

Protocol	Category ▲	Block	Log	Description	Edit	Delete
POP3	Email	☐	☐	Post Office Protocol vers	▤	✕
IMAP	Email	☐	☐	Internet Message Access	▤	✕
SMTP	Email	☐	☐	Simple Mail Transfer Prot	▤	✕
FTP	File Transfer	☐	☐	File Transfer Protocol - R	▤	✕
TFTP	File Transfer	☐	☐	Trivial File Transfer Proto	▤	✕
IRC	Instant Messenger	☐	☑	Internet Relay Chat - RFC	▤	✕
AIM	Instant Messenger	☐	☑	AOL instant messenger ('	▤	✕
MySpace IM	Instant Messenger	☐	☑	MySpace chat client	▤	✕
Jabber (XMPP)	Instant Messenger	☐	☑	open instant messenger	▤	✕
AIM web content	Instant Messenger	☐	☑	ads/news content downlo	▤	✕
MSN (Microsoft Network) Messenger file	Instant Messenger	☐	☑	MSN (Microsoft Network)	▤	✕
MSN Messenger	Instant Messenger	☐	☑	Microsoft Network chat c	▤	✕
Yahoo messenger	Instant Messenger	☐	☑	an instant messenger pro	▤	✕
NNTP	Internet News	☐	☐	Network News Transfer F	▤	✕
Shoutcast and Icecast	Music	☐	☐	streaming audio	▤	✕
pressplay	Music	☐	☐	A legal music distribution	▤	✕
live365	Music	☐	☐	An Internet radio site - htt	▤	✕
Tor	Networking	☐	☐	The Onion Router - used	▤	✕
SSDP	Networking	☐	☐	Simple Service Discovery	▤	✕
DHCP	Networking	☐	☐	Dynamic Host Configurat	▤	✕
Ident	Networking	☐	☐	Identification Protocol - RI	▤	✕
DNS	Networking	☐	☐	Domain Name System - F	▤	✕
NBNS	Networking	☐	☐	NetBIOS name service	▤	✕

Figure 7.5
The Signatures tab.
Source: Untangle, Inc.

Finally, the Event Log tab displays the following information about requests made to blocked or logged services:

- Time
- Requesting IP address or hostname
- Username of requester (if available)
- Protocol the user attempted to access
- Whether the request was blocked
- Destination server

All these data points can be used in conjunction with the content filter to prevent access to sites deemed inappropriate by a given organization.

THE WEB FILTER

Like the Application Control apps, the Web Filter app also has both a Lite (free) version and a full (paid) version. For many, content filtering is what first brings them to Untangle—especially the ability to meet filtering requirements for schools and libraries or to impose restrictions on a home network for free. While it's only a small part of the overall functionality of Untangle, Web Filter (whether free or paid), is an essential component of most Untangle use cases.

Again, this book is focused on the free components of Untangle. However, the paid version of the Web Filter is most likely a worthwhile investment for secondary schools, large libraries, and other organizations for whom content filtering is really critical. Figure 7.6 and Figure 7.7 show the Block Categories tabs of the Lite and paid versions, respectively, for comparison.

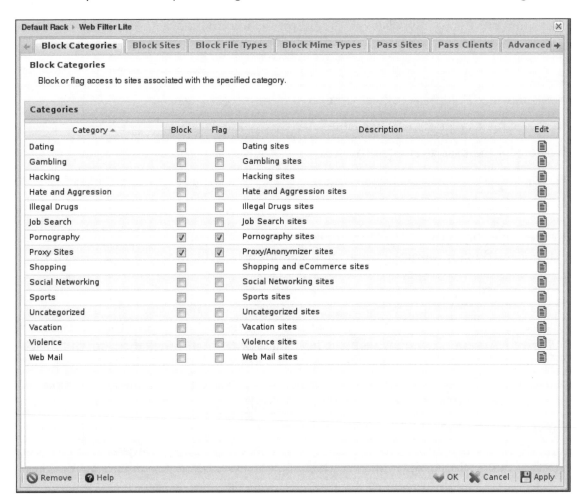

Figure 7.6
The Web Filter Lite Block Categories tab.
Source: Untangle, Inc.

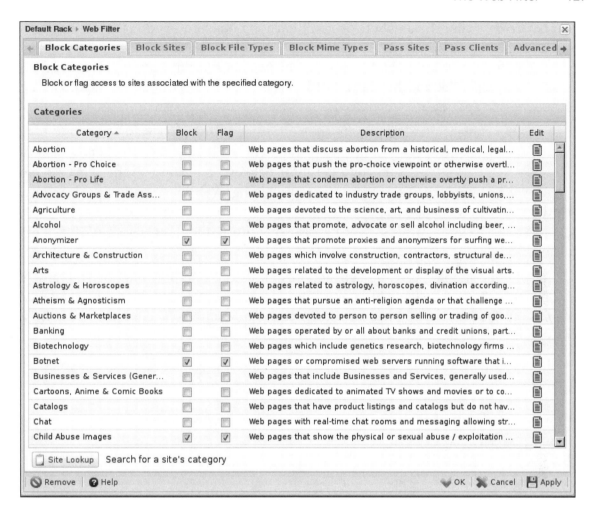

Figure 7.7
The Web Filter (paid) Block Categories tab.
Source: Untangle, Inc.

Note that, in addition to including many more categories, the paid version of Web Filter includes more intelligent filtering for sites that bypass DNS-based filtering, the ability to enforce safe search on most search engines (which block or filter search results containing mature content), and the ability to support YouTube for Schools, which prevents access to much of the non-educational video on YouTube and highlights educational channels and content.

Again, the Lite version of the Web Filter application is quite usable and works very well for settings in which users simply need to prevent access to specific categories of websites and aren't overly concerned about (or don't have the budget to address) more sophisticated attempts to circumvent the content filter. Similarly, as shown in Figure 7.6 and Figure 7.7, the interface is quite similar between the two apps, making an upgrade easy from the user perspective (although rules created in the Lite version cannot be imported into the paid version and must be re-created).

Implementing content filtering is quite straightforward if it is acceptable for all users to have the same policies applied to them. For differential filtering with the Lite version of Web Filter, some additional configuration of the network, machines on the network, and firewall will be necessary. Not surprisingly, combining Web Filter (either paid or Lite) with the paid Policy Manager application allows for the most robust configuration. (See the upcoming section "Critical Features Missing from the Free Package" for more information.")

Starting with the simplest case, though, administrators can fine-tune filtering with any of the top tabs in the Web Filter applications. The tabs are the same in both the Lite and paid versions, but the paid version has far more options in each tab. The tabs, in order from left to right, are as follows:

- Block Categories
- Block Sites
- Block File Types
- Block MIME Types
- Pass Sites
- Pass Clients
- Advanced

Categories in the Block Categories tab include such items as Dating, Illegal Drugs, and Pornography. The most common proxies, used for circumventing content filters such as Untangle, are included under the Proxy Sites category. Obviously, it's a matter of internal policy as to which categories an organization will block. However, it will be the rare situation in which the Pornography, Illegal Drugs, Proxy Sites, Hate and Aggression, Gambling, and Violence categories will contain useful information for end users. Other categories like Job Search and Sports are generally benign, but may be enough of a distraction that organizations will choose to block them as well.

In the same way, the Social Networking category can be sticky for some organizations. Fortunately, administrators can use the Pass Sites tab to add, for example, www.twitter.com as an acceptable site while still blocking social networking more generally in the Block Categories tab. The Block Sites tab also enables you to indicate specific websites that should be blocked without blocking an entire category of sites—for example, if a school wanted to block Google Images but generally allow the use of search engines.

In addition to blocking or passing specific websites, administrators can also block or pass certain file types and MIME types. File types are easily identified to most users by extension (for example, .exe for Windows executable files and .jpg for JPEG images). MIME types are similar in functionality, but more descriptive—especially for the web servers and applications that use them. A GIF image file, for example, has the file type .gif and the MIME type images/gif. Either interface could be used to block such images, but a larger cross-section of users will be able to easily manage file types.

While it would be unusual for organizations to block the majority of file or MIME types, many may choose to block those that are most likely to contain malicious payloads or be downloaded by users in an attempt to install unauthorized software. For example, EXE files or ZIP archives would be on the likely lists of files to block.

I already mentioned the Pass Sites tab. Just as particular sites can be passed, so too can particular client IP addresses and ranges of IP addresses (specified in IP matcher format) be passed. This means that, in small settings, administrators can specify static IP addresses for computers used only by people who can be exempted from filtering. Alternatively, most operating systems allow the creation of local user accounts, each of which can have different network settings.

For example, a shared Windows PC in a home with Untangle operating as a router could have logins set up for Mom, Dad, Big_Brother, and Little_Sister. The Mom and Dad accounts could be set with static IP addresses that match entries in the pass list. The kids' accounts could be set for DHCP, with the DHCP pool specifically excluding the static IP addresses in use on the parent accounts.

In larger settings, either the DMZ or additional internal networks can be used for machines that don't need to be filtered—for example, teacher PCs in a school. These can obtain their IP addresses from the DHCP pool associated with the interface or can have static IP addresses assigned in the same subnet as the chosen interface. Then the range of addresses for this interface can be added to the pass lists. It isn't a particularly elegant solution, but it's free and robust, which is all most organizations actually need.

Finally, the Advanced tab also contains a Block Pages from IP Only Hosts checkbox. This should be used with care as many organizations use IP addresses internally to point to intranet servers, test machines, file servers, etc. At the same time, end users may try to access IP-only hosts to circumvent content filtering.

The Unblock drop-down list on Advanced tab allows administrators to specify whether users can temporarily or permanently unblock a site. This feature is, in most cases, fairly worthless, because a content-filtering system that allows all users to bypass the filters, even temporarily, isn't much of a content filter. However, there are ways to filter some users while allowing others unrestricted access to the Internet. Later, this chapter discusses Policy Manager, which provides the simplest means of differentiation between groups of users (teachers and students, for example). However, there is an easier way, making use of the multiple internal interfaces supported by Untangle.

ATTACK BLOCKER (SHIELD) AND INTRUSION PREVENTION

The Attack Blocker and Intrusion Prevention apps are both free, with no paid upgrades. They are included with the basic Untangle Free package and provide the services outside of rule-based traffic control traditionally associated with firewall appliances. In version 10 of Untangle, Attack Blocker was incorporated into the Untangle platform itself and is now referred to as "Shield." It is not actually a rack application, but is referenced here because it was for a long time a critical part of the rack, it functions much like a rack app, and it seems to be conspicuously absent for users familiar with previous versions. It is now accessed via Config > System > Shield and should always be enabled. However, like Intrusion Prevention, it requires no particular configuration (although some basic exceptions are manageable by administrators). The default configuration for Shield and Intrusion Prevention will usually be adequate for most deployments.

Shield is designed to quickly identify and drop traffic involved in a denial-of-service (DoS) attack. It also intelligently monitors traffic on the network and slowly reduces available bandwidth to devices with relatively high consumption, ensuring that all users have adequate network resources available when needed. According to the Untangle Wiki:

> As the load on an Untangle Server increases, it may not have enough resources to service all requests. Rather than slow everyone down, the Attack Blocker takes action against hosts with the [greatest utilization]. In this way, hosts that hog all the bandwidth are allocated fewer resources while other less demanding hosts experience no change in service and performance levels.

Extremely high utilization is often associated with either a DoS attack or nefarious uses of network resources (for example, P2P file sharing). When utilization from particular hosts reaches a critical level, all traffic from the host is dropped, protecting the network from outage. High utilization, however, may also come from legitimate sources such as web or mail servers. It is rare that Untangle would drop a mail server, for example, but if an administrator determines that it shouldn't be subject to throttling, then it can be added to the rules list, found in the Shield interface.

The rules list was originally designed for NAT'ed IP addresses, where multiple internal IP addresses were sharing a network connection with a single IP address, making that single IP look like a heavy user of network resources. Thus, the User Count drop-down list, shown in Figure 7.8, was intended to allow administrators to specify the number of internal IPs contributing to traffic on the NAT'ed IP. However, by assigning an IP address an unlimited number of users, it is protected from any sort of throttling, regardless of how it is being used (as a server, for example).

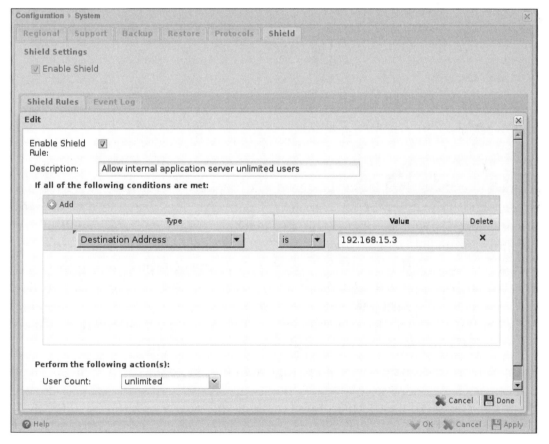

Figure 7.8
Adding a Shield rule.
Source: Untangle, Inc.

Intrusion Prevention also intelligently monitors traffic and drops connections that appear to be subject to attack or takeover. However, it uses heuristics to identify traffic signatures from known attack patterns. The various signatures and rules are based on Snort (www .snort.org). Users unfamiliar with Snort should not attempt to modify the rules or so-called rule variables. Fortunately, the rules enabled by default are unlikely to cause problems (false positives, for example) and can generally be left alone.

Security students using this book, however, will likely find this a valuable point for experimentation. In some situations, on networks on which unusually or highly industry-specific applications are being run, administrators may need to disable particular rules that are causing false positives and preventing applications from functioning correctly on the network.

Anti-Malware and Email Protection

Untangle includes several free packages for preventing malware from entering the network, either via web surfing or email. These include the following:

- Virus Blocker Lite
- Spam Blocker Lite
- Phish Blocker
- Ad Blocker

Virus Blocker Lite and Spam Blocker Lite have paid versions with richer feature sets and stronger protection. However, the Lite versions of both are more than adequate for most applications, particularly if computers on the network are already running Windows Defender (free anti-malware from Microsoft), ClamAV (free, open-source antivirus protection for all operating systems; for Windows, this is called Clamwin), or other commercial anti-malware applications. The non-Lite version of Virus Blocker was formerly known as Kaspersky Antivirus; it remains an extremely robust gateway antivirus tool and should certainly be considered in mission-critical deployments or where it is more cost-effective to rely on gateway antivirus rather than client-side tools.

Both Spam Blocker and Spam Blocker Lite operate only on email received using client software such as Outlook or Apple Mail. Encouraging users to access their email via webmail clients like Gmail or Yahoo Mail provides automatic spam protection, making these applications less relevant and certainly negating the need to purchase the non-Lite version.

The Virus Blocker interface is quite simple and should feel familiar due to other applications we've covered. Most of the default settings can simply be accepted without further consideration. Where administrators may want to modify the application is in the File Extensions control on the Web tab (which you access by clicking the Advanced Settings link). As with the Web Filter app, both MIME types and file extensions can be specified to prevent users from downloading potentially harmful files. Windows executables, certain archives, Visual Basic scripts, and others are likely to carry malware payloads. Other types, as with the Web Filter, can be blocked for policy reasons.

Administrators can also choose to block tracking and ad cookies with the Ad Blocker app. While this can have a negative impact on the performance of some legitimate websites, generally cookies provide too many hooks for potential malware as well as invasions of privacy. In many of the settings where this book will be useful (schools, legal practices, doctors' offices, etc.) privacy is not just best practice but is also the law, so in most situations, cookies should be blocked at this level.

The Pass List tab, as expected, exempts certain domains from monitoring and blocking. One example might be Google's various domains in a school that uses Google Apps, where the use of cookies adds considerable functionality for users. The same may be true of certain content management systems that require cookies. The Logs tabs are self-explanatory.

Spam Blocker Lite and Phish Blocker both operate on emails being delivered via the POP, SMTP, and IMAP protocols to email clients. It is best practice for users to access their email via a webmail client, the vast majority of which address anti-virus and anti-phishing needs before email would ever reach Untangle. The Virus Blocker application also has settings for scanning traffic using the three primary email protocols, but simply accepting the default settings for these three applications will provide sufficient protection for the shrinking number of users still relying on email clients.

CRITICAL FEATURES MISSING FROM THE FREE PACKAGE

Overall, the Untangle Free package is a robust, cost-effective set of firewall and content-filtering tools that will meet the needs of most small organizations and families and certainly provide sufficient flexibility for students studying information technology and security. However, one of the paid features available in Untangle will really be critical for many organizations that must impose different restrictions on heterogeneous groups of users: Policy Manager. Policy Manager makes differentiated handling of content filtering, malware protection, spam thresholds, etc., very simple and far more user-friendly than the workarounds described earlier.

Essentially, Policy Manager allows for the creation of multiple virtual racks, each with its own settings, apps, and associated users. Those users can be entered in the local directory or can be pulled from a RADIUS server or Active Directory if the Directory Connector app is in use. Directory Connector is also a paid application and, although not as critical for the easy, transparent operation of Untangle across users as Policy Manager, will be quite useful for organizations that have made investments in Microsoft's server architecture. Organization units defined in Active Directory, for example, can be the basis for differentiated settings; these OUs can be automatically obtained if the Directory Connector application is in place. For organizations of even modest size, these two apps—especially Policy Manager—should be the two things that take Untangle from free to very inexpensive.

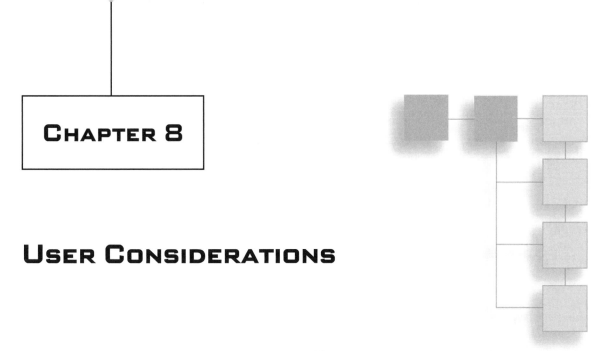

CHAPTER 8

USER CONSIDERATIONS

At its core, Untangle (indeed, any content-filtering application or appliance) is really about end users. It is designed to protect students from inappropriate content, protect business users from legal issues, protect the network and computers on which they rely from malicious software, and ensure that access to critical resources is prioritized.

Obviously, this is also a tool for the administrators responsible for the safety and security of the network, the productivity of users, and, in the case of most schools and libraries, compliance with federal regulations around the exposure of minors to offensive materials. However, the interests of users and administrators are often in direct conflict with each other, with users demanding freer and more liberal access to web-based materials and administrators seeking to maintain network control in the face of increasingly aggressive malware and concerns about the use of network resources for work/school-related activities only instead of for the myriad distractions the Internet provides.

As discussed in Chapter 7, "Implementing Protection Best Practices (or Not) with Untangle (a.k.a. 'The Rack')," Untangle provides powerful free capabilities for managing access to the Internet and, for a very moderate cost, far more capacity to differentiate filtering and monitoring between different groups of users. This chapter is devoted to management of users and finding a balanced approach to usability, compliance, access to resources, and network security.

CREATING USERS

In the free version of Untangle, only so-called local users may be created. Organizations with existing LDAP directories should strongly consider using the paid Directory Connector application. In either case, the term directory refers to a database of user accounts and their associated policies, roles, and permissions.

Local Directory

Local Directory is a very simple directory service that runs from within Untangle itself. It is accessed via Configuration > Local Directory. It cannot be used to provide authentication or login services to any other network resources outside of Untangle and is intended only to facilitate authentication and user capture for the purpose of content filtering and basic user monitoring. As you will see in the upcoming section "The Captive Portal: User Consent," the Local Directory can be used to enforce basic consent to content filtering and map specific users to their assigned IP addresses and host machines.

The Local Directory is perfectly adequate for small organizations, home/parent use, etc. Many users, in fact, simply create a finite number of user accounts in Local Directory, regardless of how many actual users access the system. In a school, for example, there might only be a Teacher and a Student account, while home users might have a Parent account and a Child account. Again, as discussed in Chapter 7, this level of differentiation is actually of limited significance because different content-filtering policies can't be imposed without physically segmenting the network across multiple Untangle interfaces or purchasing the Policy Manager add-on application. However, there will at least be some high-level associations between types of user, IP address, hostname, and the various reports that Untangle can generate. There is no technical limit to the number of users that can be added to Local Directory via the interface shown in Figure 8.1. (The inset shows the editing of individual user information.)

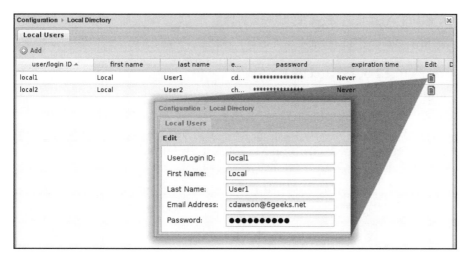

Figure 8.1
Adding and editing users in Local Directory.
Source: Untangle, Inc.

Directory Connector

Although there is no technical limit to the number of users that can be added to Local Directory, there is a practical limit. As the number of users increases, particularly when Policy Manager is used to allow differential access and filtering by user, most organizations will use an external directory such as Active Directory or OpenLDAP to manage users. Such tools allow centralized authentication services across the enterprise and connecting these to Untangle prevents the maintenance of user information in multiple directories.

For example, if a business uses Windows Server for authentication to network services via Active Directory, it is possible to manage both PCs and user roles and privileges on the server. Administrators can also fine-tune user information and create groups and organizational units, applying policies broadly across these groups. It would be trivial to create a filtered group and combine Directory Connector with Policy Manager such that all users in this group would have predefined filtering rules.

Similarly, these two modules allow any number of differentiated roles and filtering capabilities. For example, librarians could have only anti-spam filtering, adult library patrons could have only potentially malicious sites and those related to hate speech filtered, and minor patrons could additionally have pornographic and drug content filtered.

Smaller organizations can enjoy the same granularity of control using only Local Directory and Policy Manager. The differential filtering is not a function of which directory services are used for authentication. However, as enterprises grow, it becomes unwieldy to manage users in multiple directories, providing a simple business case for the use of the paid module.

THE CAPTIVE PORTAL: USER CONSENT

Captive Portal has two purposes in Untangle:

- Authenticate users against Local Directory.

- Inform users that they are subject to content filtering and obtain their consent.

When using Directory Connector, it isn't necessary to actively authenticate users. Rather, user data are passed to Untangle based on their LDAP/Active Directory login. However, when using Local Directory, there needs to be a way to stop users before they access the Internet, determine their level of filtering, receive their consent, and then provide access accordingly.

Even in settings where only a single username has been set up (for example, internetuser), Captive Portal still provides a variety of important functions:

- It is a last line of logical defense. If a user doesn't enter a username and password, then that user doesn't get access to the network.

- Users can be informed that their Internet access will be filtered and/or monitored. By logging in at the captive portal, they either implicitly or explicitly consent to such monitoring (depending upon the language used with the login page).

- Acceptable use policies for the organization can be presented to the user prior to accessing the network.

When Captive Portal is enabled, users can't access the Internet until they enter a username and password or respond to a basic message, depending upon the configuration. Captive Portal is set up in the same manner as Web Filter, Attack Blocker, and other apps: via the Apps tab of the Untangle web interface. While authentication is one primary purpose of Captive Portal, for most readers of this book (many of whom will not be authenticating against directory services or paying for the Policy Manager app), its most practical and useful feature is the ability to display a message to all users before they connect to the Internet.

Although it sounds simplistic, it actually takes care of a fair amount of coding for organizations—whether schools, coffee shops, hotels, or otherwise—that need to alert users to terms of service, use policies, and other conditions to which they should explicitly (rather than implicitly) consent. Most privacy experts agree that, while everyone should expect that their use of the Internet in public places may be monitored, it is a best practice (and legally advisable) to directly inform users of monitoring and filtering activities, even if filtering is only for the purposes of anti-malware rather than for potentially objectionable content.

Administrators define rules for Captive Portal in the Captive Hosts tab based on the following (see Figure 8.2):

- The time of day (for example, users after hours are not required to authenticate)
- The day of the week
- The interface being accessed
- The IP address of the client and/or server involved in the attempted connection

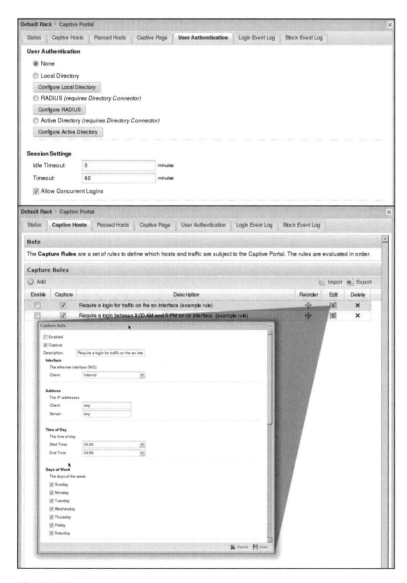

Figure 8.2
Captive Portal setup: status and rules.
Source: Untangle, Inc.

Rules must be enabled to trigger a capture. As with most other apps and services in Untangle, hosts and servers to be excluded from capture can be specified in the Passed Hosts tab. Exclusions must be specified by IP address. Hosts that are commonly excluded from capture include servers, machines that must maintain Internet connections for very long periods of time, and internal DNS or DHCP servers.

As shown in Figure 8.3, administrators can choose from a basic message, a basic login, or a custom portal page. The basic message is the simplest scenario, requiring users only to click Continue (or select an Agree checkbox if the administrator chooses) to access the Internet. However, the message itself can be customized to include links and other HTML, as well as any content the administrator wishes to display. At least linking to a terms of use or acceptable use policy at this point is highly advisable, although creating a general statement as shown in Figure 8.3 also covers an organization that is providing public Internet access.

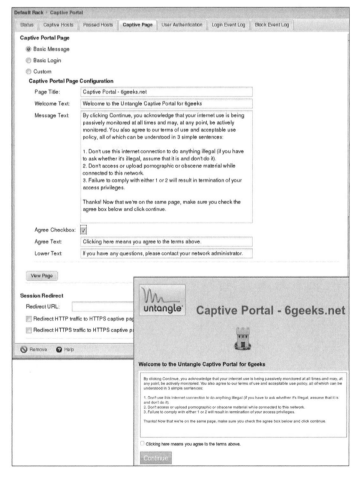

Figure 8.3
Captive Portal setup: Captive Page.
Source: Untangle, Inc.

The basic login option requires a username and password before users can access the Internet. This login can come from Local Directory or via Directory Connector, but can also contain a customized message regarding terms of service or acceptable use.

The custom page option redirects users to a web form created by the administrator that captures either a login or a simple Continue page like the basic login in Figure 8.3. This allows integration of Untangle with an intranet or other web service. This may be necessary in some regulated environments, but is unnecessary for most users.

The User Authentication tab allows the administrator to specify whether users need to log in (they can't log in if the Basic Message captive page is in use), authenticate against the Local Directory, or authenticate against a RADIUS or Active Directory server (both of which require Directory Connector). The other tabs speak for themselves.

BYPASSING CONTENT FILTERS AND PROTECTIONS

Like most content filters, Untangle can be configured to allow certain rules to be bypassed. Unfortunately, the free version of Untangle is quite rudimentary in its implementation of so-called bypass rules for various content filters and protections. When setting up Web Filter and Web Filter Lite, for example, administrators have the option of allowing users to unblock sites:

- Never
- Temporarily
- Permanently and globally

In most cases, the only reasonable choice is to never unblock sites from the user side. Otherwise, the users for whom you are trying to prevent access can simply click an unblock button every time he or she hits a website marked as blocked by Untangle. When using the paid Policy Manager app, multiple racks can be defined for different groups of users or different IP address pools. For example, teachers could have the ability to temporarily unblock a site but students could not.

However, using only free apps in Untangle, administrators can access a single rack, making such bypass rules (block lists and pass lists) inappropriate. The only robust solution in this case is to allocate IP addresses to those clients who should be able to bypass filtering and add these IP addresses to the pass lists. A network schematic for such a scenario is depicted in Figure 8.4.

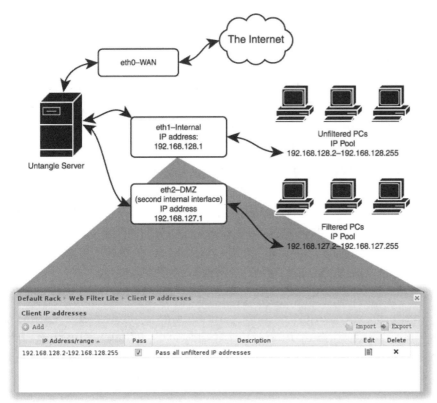

Pass list for Web Filter to ensure that unfiltered PCs are not blocked using only free software and the necessary three interfaces

Figure 8.4
Schematic for filtering network segments using only free software.
Source: Untangle, Inc.

ENFORCING CONTENT FILTERING ANYTIME, ANYWHERE (VPNs AND PROXIES)

There are many occasions when organization-owned or controlled devices are taken off premise but still need to have appropriate filtering and protection applied. Similarly, off-site computers must often access on-premises resources such as file servers, application servers, and even client PCs.

A number of content filters provide the ability—whether through locally installed applications or via a so-called remote proxy filter—to leverage the filtering and protection of an on-site filter. In most cases, computing devices outside the organization are set up to use the content filter as a proxy server via the Internet settings of the device. This can be challenging to enforce and is relatively simple to circumvent on most devices. It is also not a supported configuration for Untangle. However, a third-party, open-source proxy filter called Squid can be run simultaneously on an Untangle server and can provide this service. The configuration of Squid is beyond the scope of this book, but administrators are encouraged to examine the use of this proxy server if remote filtering is an organizational requirement. A good place to start research on the use and setup of Squid is http://www.squid-cache.org.

Untangle does support secure access to on-site resources, including content filtering, anti-malware, etc., through the OpenVPN application. Secure, filtered access to on-premises resources by remote clients is far easier to implement and enforce and is a more common use case for firewalls. While many organizations are increasingly looking to cloud-based solutions for a variety of computing needs, obviating the need for virtual private network (VPN) connections to a home office, a majority still require at least occasional, secure, remote access to on-premises hardware.

Similarly, for organizations that use thin clients, desktop virtualization, or Remote Desktop to deliver standardized and centralized computing experiences to users on premises, VPNs ensure that remote users enjoy the same computing experience regardless of where they are located. This type of computing is far less commonly deployed in the cloud and is well-supported by Untangle.

Untangle's OpenVPN application creates a secure tunnel through the firewall for authorized clients such that users can access resources as if they were on site. It can be configured in two ways:

- As a server
- As a client

The most common implementation is as a server, brokering connections between the client and the network that Untangle protects. Administrators must specify each client that will be allowed to access the network via the VPN. Although this process can be somewhat arduous if a large number of remote clients will be allowed to connect to the network, Untangle actually generates a file specific to every allowed client that can be distributed automatically via email and installed on the remote computer to facilitate access transparently. These files can be either Windows executables or configuration files that need to be converted to operating system–specific executables at openvpn.net; the latter ensures compatibility with all major operating systems. Figure 8.5 shows the function of the VPN server and client software at a high level.

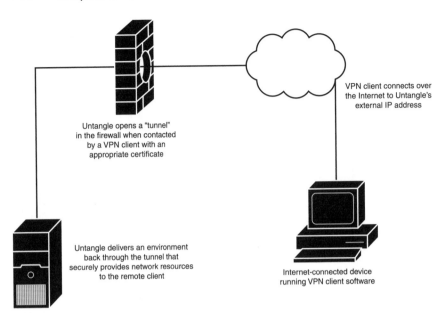

VPN client connects over
the Internet to Untangle's
external IP address

Untangle opens a "tunnel"
in the firewall when contacted
by a VPN client with an
appropriate certificate

Untangle delivers an environment
back through the tunnel that
securely provides network resources
to the remote client

Internet-connected device
running VPN client software

Figure 8.5
Untangle creating a secure connection to internal resources.
Source: Untangle, Inc.

As noted, Untangle can also run in client mode. Whether Untangle functions as a VPN server or a VPN client is determined during the initial installation of the OpenVPN application. When running as a VPN client, Untangle allows an entire network (for example, a branch office) to securely connect to a main network via VPN. Thus, all computers behind the Untangle client are automatically connected via a secure tunnel to the resources sitting behind a designated Untangle VPN server without needing to create records and install software for every individual remote machine.

Because the principle is the same in both cases, the remainder of this section focuses on individual remote client machines connecting to a network through an Untangle server with the OpenVPN application running. Once the VPN client software generated by Untangle is installed on the client device, users of this device need only launch the software; they can then map network drives, print, launch Remote Desktop sessions, and browse the web as if they were physically located within the network. Figure 8.6 diagrams and explains the various tabs and their functions in the OpenVPN configuration as well as the flow for allowing access to the network via VPN.

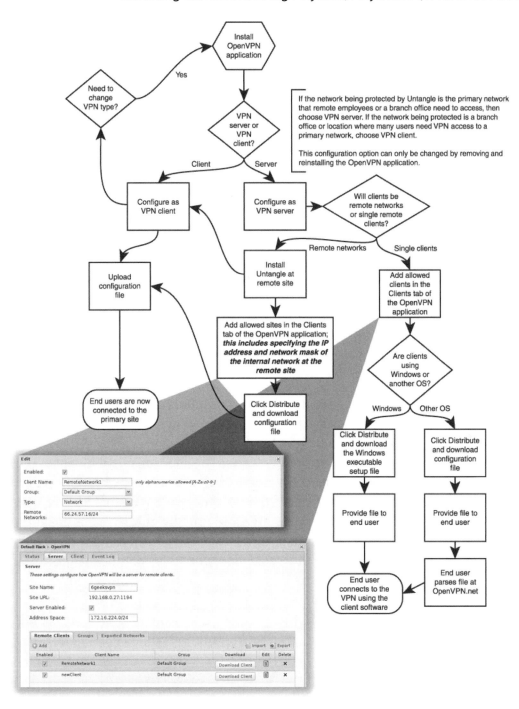

Figure 8.6
Configuration of the OpenVPN.
Source: Untangle, Inc.

A few caveats apply here. OpenVPN creates its own IP address pools for clients accessing the virtual network. It is generally advisable to leave the default IP addresses alone. Additionally, these addresses, although not generally part of the normal pools used in local area networks, functioning instead like addresses on a virtual subnet, cannot overlap with existing IP addresses used on the networks behind the Untangle gateway.

WHAT SHOULD YOU BE FILTERING?

Untangle can lock people out of basically any site on the web with a high degree of reliability and reasonable resistance to the use of external proxy filters employed to circumvent such filtering. But, to steal a phrase from *Spiderman*, with great power comes great responsibility. It's incredibly important for an organization to ask itself what it actually should be filtering.

Chapter 5, "Network and User Protection Best Practices" outlined what are considered best practices around content filtering based on the environments in which Untangle is implemented. However, as this chapter is entitled "User Considerations," it is worth noting that all the best practices in the industry are basically worthless if they are not used with careful consideration of their consequences, the business rules to which they conform, and the users that they so fundamentally affect.

In educational institutions, for example, there are two primary schools of thought that grow more distant from each other every day. The first is a very broad interpretation of government regulations (known in the U.S. as the Children's Internet Protection Act, or CIPA), which require schools to prevent student access to objectionable materials. They also require those acceptable use policies discussed earlier in this chapter in the section "The Captive Portal: User Consent." However, the term objectionable materials is open for interpretation and regulatory bodies have failed repeatedly to clarify its meaning. In this context, many schools take a very aggressive approach to filtering and prevent access to a variety of useful tools on the Internet under the guise of student protection to adhere to federal requirements that can have a significant affect on school funding through the E-Rate program (a program that reimburses for large percentages of infrastructure and Internet access expenses). Other schools take a much more *laissez-faire* approach, relying on acceptable use policies and teacher training combined with moderate filtering designed to meet basic requirements under the law. This tactic is becoming known as balanced filtering.

It isn't the purpose of this book to make judgments about the degree of filtering used in schools or other organizations where Untangle is being used, but rather to encourage what are often difficult conversations about content-filtering policies. These policies can be a major source of workplace discontent and loss of productivity by users seeking to circumvent filters or by users unable to do their jobs effectively when valuable resources are not readily accessible due to strong content filtering.

Clearly, standards and requirements will be different in a liberal arts college than in an evangelical church. Untangle provides the facilities to meet the entire spectrum of content-filtering needs, from the most restrictive to the least invasive. Yet organizations need to consider what is really being gained by blocking Facebook, for example. There are legal precedents, after all, for allowing reasonable use of business phone services for personal calls. Facebook is the 21st century version of the phone call, dominating the personal interactions of nearly a billion people.

Countless businesses and organizations block access to Facebook and other social networking sites in the name of improved productivity and reduced bandwidth utilization for non–mission critical tasks. A case can certainly be made that social media sites are a productivity and bandwidth drain, but organizations need to be able to clearly make this case to their users. For example, in some organizations, blocking Facebook could severely hamper the work of the marketing department.

One possible compromise that groups should consider as they develop clear policies around the use of the Internet (policies that should be documented, agreed upon, disseminated, and explained to all users, and then implemented in Untangle) is the use of quality of service (QoS) restrictions. Untangle, as noted in Chapter 5, supports the throttling of certain types of Internet traffic without blocking it outright to ensure that mission-critical use is not adversely affected by less critical uses (such as personal communications). Thus, users can be deterred from the use of such services by slower access without being blatantly blocked, reducing the potential for resentment and discontent, as well as attempts at circumvention, which opens the network to far more serious risks from malware.

Note

When acceptable use policies have been rigorously defined, are fully understood by users—whether students, patrons, employees, or others—and are based upon a clear set of rationale, then those who violate those policies will have absolutely no recourse.

EVENT LOGGING, OR CATCHING THEM BEING NAUGHTY AND WHAT TO DO ABOUT IT

Untangle provides extensive logging and reporting capabilities associated with the content filter as well as a separate reports facility. For example, Web Filter contains its own built-in, near real-time logs that show which clients have attempted to access blocked URLs. (See Figure 8.7.) As discussed in Chapter 5, particular URLs and categories can also be set up for flagging without blocking; these appear in the logs as well. The latter is useful when monitoring potentially inappropriate behavior or attempting to determine the impacts of blocking certain sites.

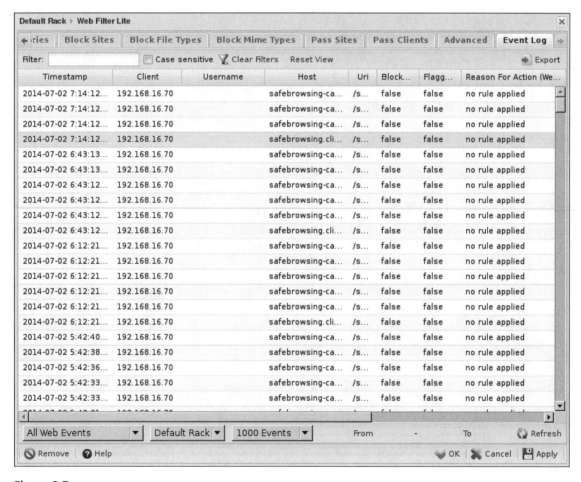

Figure 8.7
Web Filter Lite built-in log.
Source: Untangle, Inc.

The Reports service is quite a bit more extensive, with per-user logs and other means of both aggregating and disaggregating data for analysis. The summary view of the Reports service is shown in Figure 8.8.

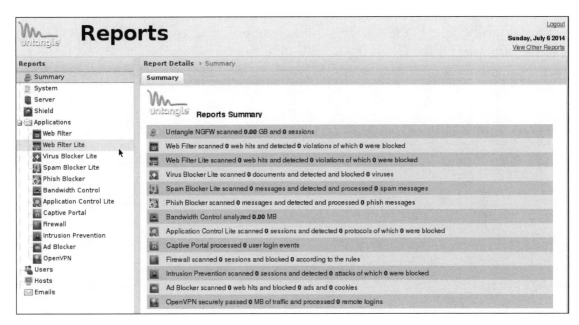

Figure 8.8
Reports Summary view.
Source: Untangle, Inc.

These reports can be set to automatically generate at specific times daily, weekly, and monthly, and can be automatically emailed to any number of recipients. Reports range from blocked pages by user to overall traffic and utilization statistics. Data can be exported to Excel for analysis as well as documentation for disciplinary action or decision-making around bandwidth allocation, filtering, and quality of service.

Note that this is one justification for the use of either complete logins established in Local Directory (that is, all users have an entry in Local Directory with a username and password) or the use of the paid Directory Connector, even if Policy Manager is not used to differentiate filtering by user group. Reports that flag excessive use, inappropriate actions, etc., by IP address only can be of limited utility. Reports by username are far more useful in identifying abusive users.

The disciplinary action is of particular note. Again, the presence of clear, well-documented, well-understood terms of use and acceptable use policies needs to be accompanied by clear consequences for their violation. When users repeatedly attempt to access blocked sites or are found to be attempting circumvention of the filters (for example, if they are accessing known proxy sites), then those consequences can be called into play, backed up by documentation from Untangle.

The most critical element here is documentation: of policy, of consequences, and of violations. The first two are the job of the organization running Untangle. The third is the job of Untangle and the administrators who monitor its logs and receive its reports.

CHAPTER 9

ADVANCED TOPICS

Untangle is a remarkably powerful tool in and of itself, particularly considering that the core system is free. For the cost of some time and extremely basic hardware, you have a full-featured router, firewall, content filter, and bandwidth-management device. However, there are a number of other features available to adventurous admins, most of which are natively supported (perhaps with paid applications), but others (sometimes referred to as "hacks") that are best left for non-production environments. Fully utilizing the Untangle software and the available hardware on which it runs also requires an understanding of the underlying architecture of Untangle and ways to optimize its performance.

WHY UNTANGLE DOESN'T BEHAVE LIKE AN AVERAGE LINUX SERVER

Untangle is generally meant to stand alone, with the underlying operating system dedicated to running two things:

- A web server that presents the Untangle interface to users (both administrators and those encountering the Captive Portal as end users)
- The Untangle software

Untangle is usually fairly efficient in its various operations, leaving what seems to be excess capacity on many custom-built and repurposed computers running the gateway software. Because Untangle is really just a highly customized version of Debian Linux, most administrators new to Untangle but familiar with Linux immediately begin to wonder what else the system can do besides process Internet traffic.

In particular, many schools, non-profits, small businesses, and home users may not have the means to maintain multiple computers to act as web servers, file servers, print servers, etc., and will want to make full use of the hardware hosting Untangle. While this is completely reasonable, and while the ability to customize and extend the functionality of most Linux systems is nearly endless, it is a mistake in most cases to use an Untangle installation for anything other than an Internet gateway. As many experienced Untangle administrators will attest, although Untangle is based on Debian Linux, it isn't Debian—it's Untangle.

As shown in Figure 9.1, with Untangle—as with many Linux-based operating systems designed to power computing appliances—customizations are deep and extensive, in this case touching many areas of the Debian software stack.

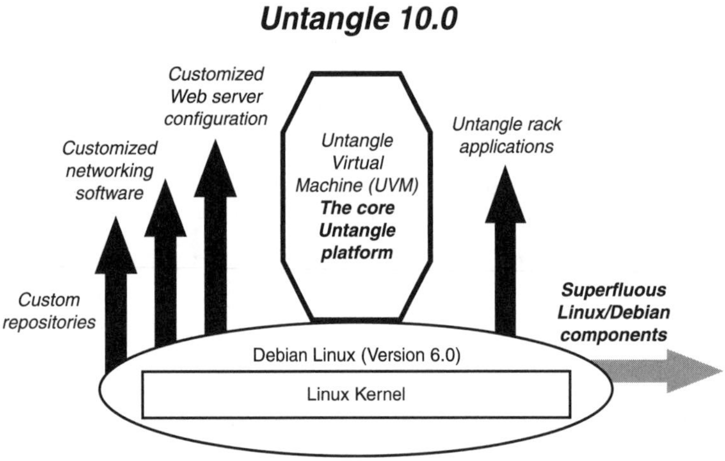

Figure 9.1
The Untangle software stack and customizations from stock Debian Linux.

The end result of these customizations, especially in the latest version of Untangle, is that while it is quite possible to add extra Linux applications directly to an Untangle install, these extra applications often behave unpredictably. It also requires substantial knowledge of Linux file systems and the ability to manually edit configuration files—both those used by Untangle and those associated with new applications. Many of the configuration files used by Untangle are in non-standard locations and either conflict with or aren't properly referenced by the new applications.

Additionally, notice that Untangle itself runs in a Java virtual machine called the Untangle Virtual Machine (UVM). The UVM handles all the network traffic coming into the box (except traffic that is specifically bypassed, like VoIP data) and then interacts with both the underlying OS and the ancillary applications. The presence of the virtual machine allows Untangle's core functionality to be updated regularly without needing to rebuild or update the underlying Debian components. It can also, however, introduce unexpected interactions between Untangle and user-installed Linux software.

This may seem a lengthy way of recommending against installing additional Linux software on an Untangle machine. However, people often turn to Untangle in the first place for the following reasons:

- To save money

- Because they are familiar with Linux

- Because they want a DIY solution to managing network and Internet traffic

All these qualities often have users looking for (and unexpectedly finding) the limits of Untangle as a flavor of Linux. Quick searches related to adding applications to Untangle litter Linux, security, system administration, and Untangle forums on the Internet, most of which reveal users hitting dead ends. The bottom line is that Untangle needs to stand alone.

That being said, there are occasional circumstances in which very specific pieces of software need to be added to Untangle's underlying Debian back end. For example, administrators may need to do the following:

- Add hardware drivers for components in DIY Untangle machines.

- Create a custom rack application for Untangle.

- Add software such as caching tools that can be leveraged by Untangle but aren't directly supported by the gateway.

- Add network data-handling capabilities for traffic that is defined as bypassed by Untangle.

REMOTE ADMINISTRATION AND SSH

Before enabling the Debian software repositories or making extensive use of the terminal interface to administer Untangle, it is necessary to understand the use of SSH for remote access to the Linux back end of the gateway. Aside from software installation, Untangle administrators more commonly need to use the command line or terminal to remotely do the following:

- Restart specific services on a gateway.

- Examine log files.

- Restart the gateway itself or restart the Untangle UVM.

- Otherwise maintain the gateway with minimum impact on end users, especially if the web client is unavailable.

This may be the first time it is necessary to launch the command line (or terminal) in your interaction with Untangle. This must be done either on the Untangle box itself or via a Secure Shell (SSH) session. SSH is a protocol that allows for remote access to the command line on Unix-like systems (including Untangle). You must enable SSH through the Filter Rules on the Configuration > Network > Advanced page by selecting Allow SSH, as shown in Figure 9.2. Consult the documentation for your particular SSH client to find out how to launch a remote terminal session if using this option. Once connected, the procedure is the same via SSH or in a direct terminal session.

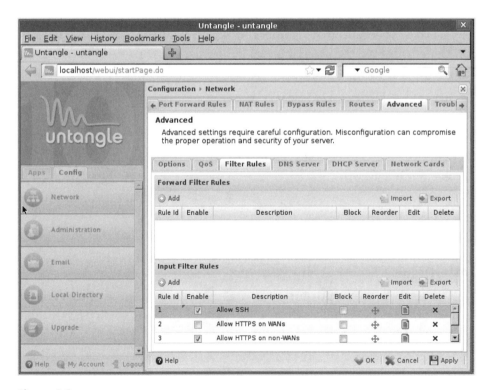

Figure 9.2
Enabling SSH.
Source: Untangle, Inc.

To access the terminal directly on the Untangle server, close the web browser window if it is open and click the Terminal icon on the menu bar. You will be prompted to create a root user password if this is the first time launching the terminal. (As noted previously, the first use of the terminal shell must occur on the Untangle server itself rather than via SSH.)

Note

Once the terminal shell is running, you will have what is called "root access" to the server. As noted in previous chapters, the root user has unfettered access to the workings of the operating system. While this is convenient, it also makes it relatively easy to do serious damage to a production server. Proceed with caution.

Enabling the Debian Repositories

Because Untangle runs on top of Debian Linux (a popular distribution in its own right and the basis for such mainstream Linux distributions as Ubuntu and Mint), there is a very large body of free software that can be installed directly on Untangle, albeit with all of the aforementioned caveats. Instructions for unlocking this additional Debian software is provided for reference and exploratory purposes only and should not generally be done in production environments. Users are encouraged to experiment on non-production gateways and are left to determine whether adding particular Debian software applications to Untangle is necessary and/or appropriate. Adding software from Linux repositories is not supported by Untangle.

All Linux systems use the concept of repositories to distribute software. Most of the software, like Linux and Untangle itself, is free and open source. Thus, adding new software (and thereby new capabilities) is largely a matter of the following:

- Enabling these repositories
- Using the command line to install new software from the repositories
- Configuring the new software, again from the command line

The latest version of Untangle runs on version 6 of Debian Linux, code named "Squeeze." (Notice that many of the commands that follow refer to Squeeze repositories to differentiate them from other versions of Debian, each of which has its own repositories.) To begin enabling these repositories, enter the following command:

```
nano/etc/apt/sources.list
```

This will launch a terminal-based text editor called Nano and will display the current list of repositories to which Untangle has access.

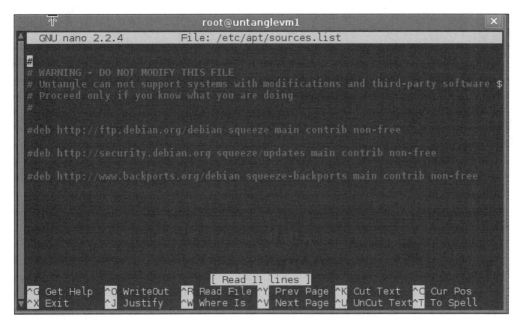

Figure 9.3
The default sources.list file.
Source: Untangle, Inc.

Note that all three of the primary Debian 6.0 repositories are listed but commented out (the hash mark at the beginning of each line designates that line as a comment that is not read by the operating system). Using the arrow keys (the mouse is not operational in the terminal window), navigate to each line of the file that begins with #deb and delete the hash mark. Now press the Ctrl and O keys together to save the file. (Available commands are listed at the bottom of the Nano window; the caret character represents the Ctrl key.) Press Enter to confirm that the old file is to be overwritten with the same name. Then press Ctrl+X to exit Nano.

Untangle must now be told to update its available software with the new repositories with the following command:

`apt-get update`

The Untangle gateway is now ready to have additional Debian software installed. It is also possible to add more lines to sources.list that provide access to even larger libraries of software. Again, though, while all of this is possible, it is rarely easy, predictable, or advisable.

VIRTUALIZING UNTANGLE (THE RIGHT WAY TO RUN MULTIPLE SERVICES ON AN UNTANGLE GATEWAY)

There is a method of adding functionality to an Untangle gateway that is both supported by Untangle and will behave in far more predictable ways than merely installing software from Debian repositories. This involves running Untangle as a virtual machine with a proper hypervisor alongside other virtual servers dedicated to the particular functions you want the Untangle box to serve.

A Virtualization Primer

Virtualization is an increasingly popular means of managing processing, storage, and networking in a way that abstracts computing from the physical hardware on which it is performed. Through virtualization, it is possible to run multiple logical servers, for example, on a single piece of physical hardware. Other possible uses for virtualization include the following:

- Running multiple instances of a desktop operating system like Linux or Windows on a single server or cluster of servers and then giving users access to these desktops through thin clients or mobile devices

- Unifying storage across multiple physical and virtual devices such that users see only a single large, highly scalable storage medium

- Running multiple instances of server operating systems on a single server or high-performance cluster to discretely manage their functions and/or rapidly scale server infrastructure

Any of these scenarios (and many others) are made possible through the use of a so-called "hypervisor." Hypervisors are either dedicated operating systems (type 1 hypervisors) or standalone applications (type 2 hypervisors) that act as hosts for instances of other operating systems. Type 1 hypervisors are often referred to as "bare-metal hypervisors" because they are installed on clean servers with no pre-existing operating systems. While bare-metal hypervisors tend to be more efficient in terms of system resources, they generally require greater experience and expertise to set up and manage than their application counterparts.

In either case, the system on which the hypervisor is installed is referred to as the host and the operating system(s) running under the hypervisor is (are) called the guest(s). Several of each type of hypervisor are available on the market today, with VMWare VSphere, Microsoft HyperV, Citrix XenServer, and multiple offerings from IBM and Novell being the most important commercially. In keeping with the use of free and open source tools like Untangle in this book, further examples and discussions will focus on the most widely used free hypervisors:

- Linux KVM (type 1)
- VMware vSphere Hypervisor ESXi (type 1)
- Oracle VirtualBox (type 2)

In particular, because VirtualBox can run on Windows, Mac OS X, and Linux, it provides a powerful testing solution for Untangle in a virtualized environment.

Virtualization is not without its limits. The number of guest operating systems (including Untangle) and the performance of each are limited by the overall memory and processor specifications of the host machine. Similarly, because Untangle is designed for high-throughput, bandwidth-intensive networking applications, sharing a single network connection on a host between Untangle and other virtual machines can create bottlenecks for both Untangle and other guests. However, whether for testing purposes or to support increasingly common virtualized computing environments, virtualizing Untangle is worth understanding and considering as a solution for a growing number of network administrators.

Note

Every screenshot in this book was captured from virtualized instances of Untangle running in Oracle VirtualBox hosted on Mac OS X.

Typical Virtualization Scenarios with Untangle

As noted, virtualizing Untangle using a type 2 hypervisor is especially useful for testing Untangle configurations and settings. Most hypervisors have the additional benefit of "snapshots" in which various states and configurations of virtual machines can be saved, further increasing their utility in test environments.

Untangle does not actually recommend virtualizing its gateway but will provide support for specific configurations, even in production environments. Many users, including the author, have successfully virtualized Untangle, however, and there are many situations in which it can be quite valuable:

- **Testing.** Whether testing new settings, rack apps, or upgrades before rolling them into production or building entire virtual networks to simulate production environments, virtualizing Untangle makes testing and demonstration safe and relatively straightforward. This also works well for instructional purposes.

- **Differential policies and virtual subnetworks.** Because the easiest way to differentiate filtering policies and traffic processing with Untangle is to create multiple physical subnets, the same is true in virtual environments. However, creating multiple virtual networks is generally far easier via a hypervisor interface than in physical buildings.

- **VDI.** Virtual Desktop Infrastructure (VDI) refers to creating multiple virtual instances of desktop operating systems on a single server or cluster of servers operating together. Entire computer labs, office desktop deployments, etc., can be served to very inexpensive end user hardware. Virtualizing Untangle in this setting centralizes gateway functions with desktop delivery.

- **Improving resource utilization.** One of the original purposes of virtualization (and the primary reason that this book began exploring the topic of adding functionality to an Untangle box) was ensuring that excess capabilities on a server weren't wasted. Thus, a server that consistently ran at only 25% capacity processing network traffic could easily act as a low-volume print, file, or web server simultaneously if the functions were virtualized.

- **Leveraging existing virtual infrastructure.** In environments that have already invested in virtualization, whether for servers, storage, or VDI, the best way to maximize the return on that investment is to use it to capacity. Adding services such as content filtering instead of adding new physical hardware may make sense in such a situation.

This list is by no means comprehensive; ways to use Untangle in virtualized environments are largely limited by the imagination and equipment available to users, subject to the caveats described in the previous section.

Virtual Network Setup

As noted, all of the screen shots in this book were captured using an Untangle virtual machine in the Oracle VirtualBox type 2 hypervisor. In addition to a dedicated physical server purpose-built for this book and an Untangle appliance supplied by the company, the virtual machine was used for extensive testing of multiple versions of Untangle.

Figure 9.4 is a schematic of the virtual network connections and virtual machines used for testing purposes and screen capture in this book.

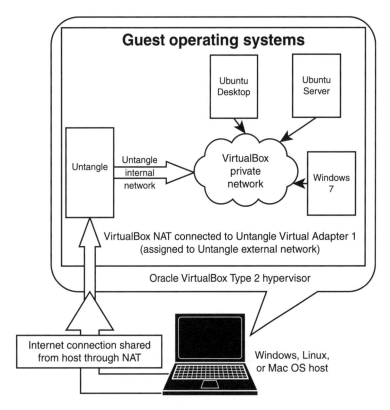

Figure 9.4
Virtualized test environment using Oracle VirtualBox.

In particular, testing included running a web server and two desktop operating systems in parallel with the Untangle virtual machine on a virtual network created through VirtualBox. This setup is a very useful test bed and instructional platform for users interested in both Untangle and virtualization. Complete setup instructions for this test environment are provided in Figure 9.5.

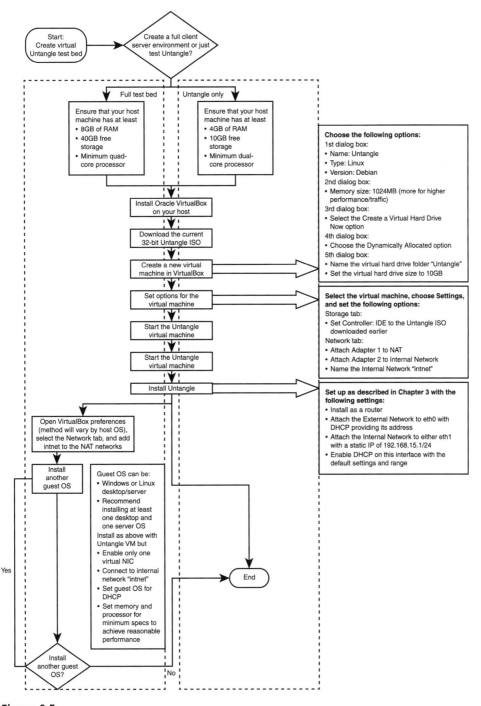

Figure 9.5
Flowchart for setting up a virtual test environment.

OPTIMIZING UNTANGLE

Much of this chapter has dealt with ways to use excess capacity on Untangle machines. However, it's worth taking time to examine ways to optimize Untangle's performance, especially in scenarios where the problem isn't too much capacity but too little. This is especially common in DIY settings where older computers have been repurposed as gateways and lack either the necessary throughput on their network cards or the processing horsepower to handle specific intensive workloads.

While even fairly modest hardware performs work well in most situations, as networks grow or more bandwidth-intensive applications are added to a network, optimizing Untangle becomes increasingly important. Even with a well-equipped gateway, administrators need to be aware of bottlenecks that can occur and understand how to address them efficiently.

Several applications that have a greater impact on system performance and resource requirements are listed in Table 9.1 (data adapted from the Untangle Wiki).

Table 9.1   Hardware Load by Untangle Component

Application	Memory Footprint	CPU Utilization	Disk I/O
Web Filter Lite	High	Low	Low
Virus Blocker	Medium	Medium	Medium
Virus Blocker Lite	Medium	Medium	Medium
Spam Blocker	Medium	Medium	Medium
Spam Blocker Lite	Medium	Medium	Medium
Phish Blocker	Medium	Medium	Medium
Web Cache	Medium	Low	High
Bandwidth Control	Low	Medium	Low
Application Control	Low	Medium	Low
Application Control Lite	Low	Medium	Low
Intrusion Prevention	Low	Medium	Low
Reports	Medium	Medium	Very High

Thus, Untangle optimization has two primary components:

- Hardware optimization
- Software optimization

Organizations that rely on Untangle's extensive reporting capabilities or the paid Web Cache application, for example, need to ensure that their gateways have high-speed disks installed. Administrators who find that the Web Filter Lite application is consuming too much memory should either upgrade the physical memory available on the gateway or switch to the premium Web Filter application, which has a much smaller memory footprint. The daily and weekly reports natively available in Untangle can provide significant insight into resource utilization, and administrators can consider hardware adjustments based on the preceding guidelines.

In terms of software optimization, most administrators agree that the most important (and often the only) adjustments should occur in the Bypass Rules. As discussed previously, Bypass Rules are accessed via the Configuration > Network panel. There is a fair amount of traffic that Untangle doesn't need to process and some that it absolutely shouldn't. Voice and video over IP, for example, should be bypassed, as it causes significant performance issues for Untangle, is negatively affected by scanning, and is of no risk to the network, making scanning unnecessary anyway.

The System reports available in the Untangle reporting module can also point to specific ports that are generating large numbers of sessions. Perhaps a peer-to-peer networking service is being used for research purposes or to distribute legitimate software. Bypassing the port used for this service will dramatically reduce the load on the gateway and improve network performance for the P2P application and for other traffic as well. On the other hand, these same system reports can reveal ports with substantial illegitimate traffic, such as illegal file sharing or malware connecting to external servers. Administrators could then block these ports entirely using the Forward Filter Rules or the Firewall Application.

Note

Note that Bypass Rules let the kernel (the low-level core of Untangle and all Linux systems) process traffic very quickly and prevent the Untangle VM or any rack applications from seeing the traffic. If this traffic still requires a degree of processing (e.g., blocking specific ports only for a subset of IP addresses), then administrators should use Forward Filter Rules, which operate at the kernel level.

Advanced Network Architectures with Untangle

Untangle can support very sophisticated network topologies. Three technologies in particular support improved usability and increased functionality even with completely free Untangle implementations.

VLANs

Virtual local area networks (VLANs) are a relatively new means of creating logical subnets on a single physical network. VLAN traffic is differentiated and completely segregated on a single wire using so-called VLAN IDs. These IDs are attached to packets associated with each VLAN and ensure that traffic remains independent even though the virtual networks are sharing physical infrastructure.

Because Untangle supports only seven physical interfaces, and many Untangle servers are limited to just two or three, VLANs are very useful for segmenting traffic beyond what can be achieved with physical network interfaces. For VLANs to function correctly, the NICs installed on the Untangle server and any hardware switches connected to the Untangle box must support VLANs. VLAN configuration on switches and other hardware is beyond the scope of this book, but readers are encouraged to check with their vendors or consult their documentation before proceeding.

In Untangle, VLANs are managed in the same way as physical interfaces. Under the Configuration > Network > Interfaces panel, simply select Add Tagged VLAN Interface. In the dialog box that follows, give the new virtual interface a name and assign it a parent interface. The parent interface must be a physical interface on the Untangle server. VLAN IDs should be assigned sequentially as multiple VLANs are created on a given interface.

The VLAN may be set to Addressed mode or Bridged mode, or may be disabled. Bridged mode simply connects the VLAN straight through to the physical interface. The setup becomes more useful in Addressed mode, where it can be treated in the same way as an addressed internal network with full support for its own DHCP range and options.

Multiple Physical Subnets or VLANs and Easy Differentiated Filtering

Whether defined via direct connection to a physical Untangle interface or as a VLAN, subnets allow substantial differentiation in terms of filtering and traffic handling without the purchase of premium Untangle rack applications like Policy Manager. Because subnets are associated with a range of IP addresses, these ranges can be added to pass lists in the Web Filter Lite application and be added to Passed Hosts in the Captive Portal.

The interfaces themselves can have specific rules applied to them in the Firewall, Bypass Rules, and Forward Filter Rules. Although the Policy Manager application provides a robust means for applying different rules and policies to user groups, for those users looking at completely free implementations of Untangle, thoughtful subnetting provides a workaround by applying different rules to ranges of IP addresses and physical and virtual interfaces on an Untangle server.

For example, a school may wish to provide different levels of filtering for students, teachers, and guests. The Policy Manager application presents entirely different racks for groups of users, which is the most granular means of differentiating filtering rules. Many schools have budget constraints that may preclude adding paid applications that carry an annual cost. In this case, if the school has VLAN-aware switches, an administrator can define a teacher and a student VLAN on an internal interface. Teacher computers would be configured to connect to the teacher VLAN, which could be set to bypass Untangle. Student computers could be configured to connect to the student VLAN and would pass through all configured rack applications. Finally, a series of wireless access points could be connected to Untangle's DMZ interface. The DMZ could be set within the firewall application to allow access only to port 80 (standard HTTP) and would also receive all of the web and application filtering to which the student subnet was subjected.

This is only one possible scenario, but it should be clear that interfaces and IP address ranges are powerful means of selecting traffic to process, bypass, or otherwise control without using paid applications.

Dealing with Wireless

Users of previous versions of Untangle found workarounds by which they could add a wireless network interface card to turn their Untangle servers into wireless access points. This is no longer supported and absolutely not recommended. It is also largely unnecessary due to the low cost of high-quality wireless access points and routers. Similarly, although the external interface can theoretically be a wireless NIC, making Untangle a wireless bridge, the use of a dedicated wireless bridge (if necessary) to connect Untangle to a WAN link is far more reliable.

In general, wireless access points should be added to a network managed by Untangle in one of two ways:

- By plugging the access point into a switch connected to an Untangle physical interface
- By plugging the access point directly into an Untangle physical interface

In both cases, any DHCP functionality in the access point should be disabled. In addition, if it can act as a gateway, gateway functions should also be disabled. It should be given a static IP address associated with the subnet or interface to which it is connected and should be connected via one of its LAN ports instead of a WAN/uplink port if it has an integrated Ethernet switch. This configuration will ensure that Untangle handles the underlying networking and that the access point merely connects clients directly to the network.

Note

Untangle must always be upstream of wireless access points. If a cable modem or other WAN connection has its own wireless router, this should be disabled because any users connecting to the modem via WiFi will not have their traffic captured and filtered by Untangle.

Using DynDNS

Most Internet service providers (ISPs) charge a premium for a static, dedicated IP address. A static external IP address is necessary if organizations host high-volume websites, require absolute reliability for external access to network resources, or need to establish rock-solid connections between branch offices. Often, though, Untangle users simply need to remotely administer their servers or set up simple VPN access for a small number of users. In these less-demanding scenarios, dynamic DNS services alleviate the need to purchase static IP addresses from an ISP.

DynDNS is perhaps the best-known dynamic DNS provider, although many others are available and supported by Untangle. Regardless of the particular provider, though, dynamic DNS works by continually updating the IP address associated with a domain name such that the domain always points to the correct network, even if that network has an address dynamically assigned by an ISP. The dynamic DNS services require that an agent be installed on a computer on the network that transmits the current IP address back to the provider. Thus, a user could simply enter chrisdawson.dyndns.org (the assigned domain is usually a canonical domain made available by the provider), for example, and be directed to whatever service was port forwarded on the network, regardless of the actual address assigned by the ISP. This practice is especially useful for home users who would otherwise need to upgrade their Internet service to much more expensive business-class service to get a static IP address.

Untangle has several agents preinstalled that connect to six of the most popular dynamic DNS services (EasyDNS, ZoneEdit, DynDNS, Namecheap, DSL-Reports, and DNSPark). Simply choose one of these hosts, create an account, and enter the account information in Untangle under Configuration > Network > Hostname.

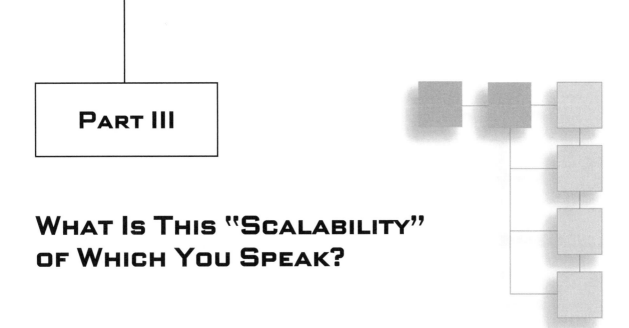

PART III

WHAT IS THIS "SCALABILITY" OF WHICH YOU SPEAK?

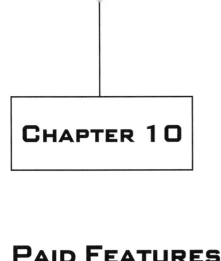

CHAPTER 10

PAID FEATURES

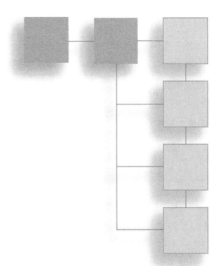

Until now, we have largely been concerned with all of the capabilities that are freely available in Untangle. Many of these features are built directly into the core of Untangle and process traffic right in the Linux kernel itself, bypassing the Untangle Virtual Machine and achieving very high performance even on moderately capable hardware. In fact, Untangle can act as a very passable router without ever touching the rack applications. To review, these core features include the following:

- DNS
- DHCP
- Quality of service (QoS)
- Traffic bypassing and basic filtering
- Port forwarding
- Network address translation (NAT)
- Static routing

Not surprisingly, though, most users also leverage rack applications to turn the router/gateway into a firewall and content filter. For traffic that isn't bypassed, the firewall rack application provides more granular blocking and flagging of traffic; the Captive Portal allows user-based reporting and basic differentiation of traffic management; and so on. However, most of the free rack applications have distinct limitations in the following:

- Options
- Granularity
- Integration with third-party platforms
- Speed and performance, including their memory footprint
- Differentiation among user groups
- The depth of traffic inspection and management

The Untangle core and the free applications included with Untangle NG Firewall (particularly in the aptly named Free package) are adequate for home users, students, hobbyists, and smaller organizations. A coffee shop, for example, could use Untangle to provide basic control of public WiFi access. A library could ensure basic levels of compliance with regulations required to access specific state and federal subsidies. Even larger organizations could achieve adequate performance and throughput simply using Untangle as a router. As organizations grow or as content-filtering needs become more complex, adding one or more paid applications to the Untangle rack can turn a basic router and content filter into a full-featured, all-in-one firewall, gateway, and network appliance.

PAID VERSUS FREE FEATURES

Paid rack applications can be added *à la carte* or in packages. While using packages is more cost-effective than adding all their included features individually, often users will need only one or two particular paid functions. This represents a major advantage for Untangle because organizations can add (and pay for) precisely the features they need. For schools, non-profits, and government entities, Untangle offers substantial discounts on packages, but not on individual application purchases. Qualifying institutions should evaluate overall costs, even if they need only a few additional applications.

Paid applications are added to the rack in the same way as free features. Simply clicking the Install link on the application list on the left side of the Untangle UI will begin a 14-day free trial. After the trial, applications are sold in a subscription model with tiered fees based on the number of users or clients, depending on the application.

Untangle recently simplified its package offerings, condensing all of the rack applications into Free and Complete packages. The special pricing noted for certain institutions is available for the Complete package. It is simplest to compare the features and applications of both packages, as in Table 10.1, to get a sense of where paid applications offer advantages worth the cost over the freely available suite of applications included with Untangle NG Firewall. As a general rule, the applications in the Complete package are focused on network performance and reliability, while those in the Free package offer more basic firewall/content filter functionality.

Table 10.1 Comparison of Free and Complete Packages

Application	Complete Package	Free Package
Virus Blocker	×	
Virus Blocker Lite	×	×
Firewall	×	×
Intrusion Prevention	×	×
Phish Blocker	×	×
Web Filter	×	
Web Filter Lite	×	×
HTTPS Inspector	×	
Spam Blocker	×	
Spam Blocker Lite	×	×
Application Control	×	
Application Control Lite	×	×
Ad Blocker	×	×
Web Cache	×	
Bandwidth Control	×	
WAN Balancer	×	
WAN Failover	×	
IPsec VPN	×	
OpenVPN	×	×
Captive Portal	×	×
Policy Manager	×	
Directory Connector	×	
Reports	×	×
Branding Manager	×	

Table created from information found here: https://www.untangle.com/software-packages

In addition to extra applications, live support is also included with the Complete package. Any other scenarios (purchasing individual applications or using only free components of Untangle) do not include any support outside of access to the Untangle forums.

The Directory Connector, Policy Manager, WAN Balancer, and WAN Failover applications are covered in detail later in this chapter. They are the *à la carte* applications that Untangle users most often install to meet relatively common networking needs. However, a few other paid applications are worth a closer look.

Virus Blocker Versus Virus Blocker Lite

Virus Blocker and Virus Blocker Lite look identical in the Untangle rack. Options for scanning web, email, and FTP traffic are minimal, and in both cases, the application works transparently and automatically without configuration. However, the underlying virus-scanning engines are substantially different. Virus Blocker Lite runs on the open-source ClamAV antivirus engine, which is quite effective at scanning most web and email traffic. In contrast, the paid Virus Blocker application runs on the proprietary Commtouch AV engine and achieves higher performance, especially when scanning large compressed files. It can also decompress and scan a larger variety of archives than Virus Blocker Lite. In general, as the number of users increases, Virus Blocker becomes a more attractive option. For most readers of this book, Virus Blocker Lite is more than adequate gateway antivirus protection.

One advantage of using Virus Blocker is that it is not mutually exclusive with Virus Blocker Lite. When Virus Blocker passes traffic, Virus Blocker Lite automatically scans it as well. Because they rely on different engines and separately maintained virus definitions, this provides an additional layer of protection against viruses, Trojan horses, and the like. As network traffic increases, though, this may cause performance issues. In that case, users may want to consider disabling Virus Blocker Lite if they subscribe to the paid Virus Blocker application.

Web Filter Versus Web Filter Lite

Web Filter Lite meets federal regulations for schools and libraries, including the Children's Internet Protection Act (CIPA), and is sufficient for home users and others looking to limit access to broad categories of potentially objectionable websites. Using the coffee shop example again, the Lite version would prevent most users from accessing pornographic sites that other patrons might find objectionable.

The paid Web Filter application, though, provides some significant enhancements that many organizations may find useful. Figure 10.1 shows the main configuration screens for each application. Web Filter includes options for scanning HTTPS traffic, limiting YouTube to the generally PG-rated YouTube for Schools subset of content, and ensuring that users can search only for content that meets "safe search" criteria on various search engines.

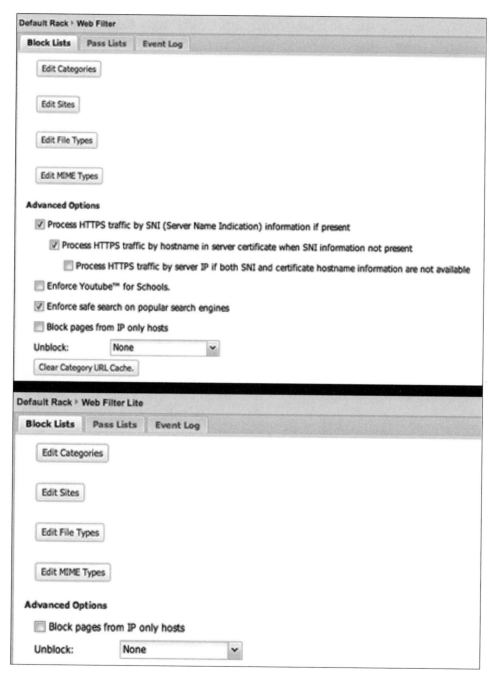

Figure 10.1
Web Filter options (top) versus Web Filter Lite options (bottom).
Source: Untangle, Inc.

Web Filter also includes a subscription to the HTTPS Inspector application described in the next section. Because many search engines, social media sites, and even pornographic websites (among others that may be objectionable) can be accessed via HTTPS instead of the standard HTTP (Internet port 80), users can often bypass web filters without this capability. This capability alone may be sufficient reason for schools, churches, and other organizations to subscribe to the paid Web Filter application. Recent enhancements to Web Filter Lite do natively allow a degree of HTTPS inspection, but the limitations without the use of HTTPS Inspector (including the certificate errors described in the next section) are significant.

HTTPS Inspector

As noted, HTTPS Inspector integrates with Web Filter and several other applications to enable Untangle to scan encrypted traffic. This capability is not unique to Untangle but is unusual in relatively inexpensive network appliances. HTTPS Inspector acts as a so-called man-in-the-middle agent, decrypting traffic on Internet port 443 (typically identified by HTTPS instead of HTTP in the URL of a site) and passing unencrypted traffic to applications in the Untangle rack.

Aside from Web Filter, in which specific options call out this functionality, HTTPS Inspector works transparently with other applications. Both Virus Blocker applications, for example, can only scan content from secure websites when HTTPS Inspector is installed but don't need to have any particular options selected to scan encrypted as well as unencrypted pages. Individual administrators will need to assess whether this capability is necessary for them to adequately protect their networks and users.

An important consideration relates to the use of webmail. In the past, many users accessed email via client software like Outlook. Messages sent and received with an email client used the SMTP, POP, and IMAP protocols, all of which are easily scanned for phishing, viruses, and other malware. More recently, users have eschewed client software in favor of webmail that primarily uses HTTPS instead of SMTP, POP, or IMAP. As a result, the protection offered by many gateways and firewalls (including the Phish Blocker and Virus Blocker applications available in Untangle) were rendered useless. Adding HTTPS Inspector to Untangle enables these applications to scan secure webmail traffic and protect users from a common source of compromise.

HTTPS Inspector does add a bit of administrative overhead. When HTTPS Inspector is enabled, users will begin seeing certificate errors if they browse secure websites. These can range from e-commerce sites to Facebook to Google, so the errors will become quite frequent. Untangle can generate a certificate that must be installed on each client computer to avoid these errors. Once installed, the certificate will rarely need to be updated.

Spam Blocker Versus Spam Blocker Lite

Because of the declining popularity of email client software and the rise of webmail, anti-spam software has declined considerably in its utility and necessity. For many readers, the Spam Blocker Lite application can actually be uninstalled with no need to consider subscribing to the paid Spam Blocker. There are a couple of notable exceptions to this guideline:

- Organizations running their own mail servers
- Businesses with a large percentage of users who rely on email client software

In these cases, even if the mail servers or email clients have built-in spam detection and quarantine capabilities, both Spam Blocker applications actually prevent spam from reaching the network. This is desirable because the volume of spam can degrade network performance and can potentially be transmission vectors for malware. The choice between Spam Blocker Lite and Spam Blocker largely comes down to volume. If Untangle is used on large networks with heavy email traffic, the higher-performance engine behind the paid Spam Blocker application may be useful.

Application Control Versus Application Control Lite

Like the Web Filter and Web Filter Lite duo, the paid Application Control application offers significant performance and manageability enhancements over its Lite counterpart. Application Control Lite is sufficient for blocking a basic set of protocols like BitTorrent that use disproportionate amounts of bandwidth. Libraries, schools, and small businesses looking to limit access to instant messaging, gaming, and other services that use protocols other than HTTP will rarely need more that the Lite version of the application.

Application Control Lite also supports custom definition of new protocols, but administrators must be able to specify the regular expression (called a *signature*) for a particular protocol. The expression for DHCP, for example, is as follows:

```
^[\x01\x02][\x01- ]\x06.*c\x82sc.
```

Application Control Lite uses the open-source L7-filter. This project maintains a list of detectable application signatures. However, an examination of the list (see http://l7-filter .sourceforge.net/protocols) and the associated detection times for each signature makes it clear that manually entering signatures is onerous and unreliable. Moreover, the performance levels in detecting many of these signatures may be too low as network utilization increases.

The paid version of Application Control uses a proprietary filter, achieving much better performance on a much wider range of built-in protocols. Administrators who deal with large volumes of traffic—especially traffic that might violate the organization's policies—will want to seriously consider subscribing.

Bandwidth Control

Bandwidth Control has no specific free alternative among the Untangle rack applications. At a very basic level, the quality of service (QoS) features in the Untangle core can provide some of the functionality of Bandwidth Control by assigning priorities to various services, users, and network addresses. However, Bandwidth Control provides much finer, point-and-click control for true bandwidth shaping. The application also enables user quotas, throttling of users and applications consuming excessive bandwidth, and enforcing differential usage policies among users and groups.

As is the case with many of the paid applications, most readers of this book will be able to achieve reasonable results using free components of Untangle (in this case, the QoS controls). Yet as organizations rely increasingly on web-based services or seek to deliver services to outside users, the ability to detect and manage network utilization that interferes with these critical services becomes more important. In such cases, neither version of Application Control is sufficient to ensure that these services are properly prioritized on the network because most use HTTP. Bandwidth Control, then, is the most efficient means of conserving bandwidth at the individual device/user level.

Web Cache

Web Cache is another performance-enhancing rack application that is really only useful at scale. Web Cache stores frequently requested content, including Microsoft software updates, such that the data can be downloaded from the local network rather than repeatedly from the Internet. As shown in Figure 10.2, Web Cache updates statistics regarding its performance in near real time.

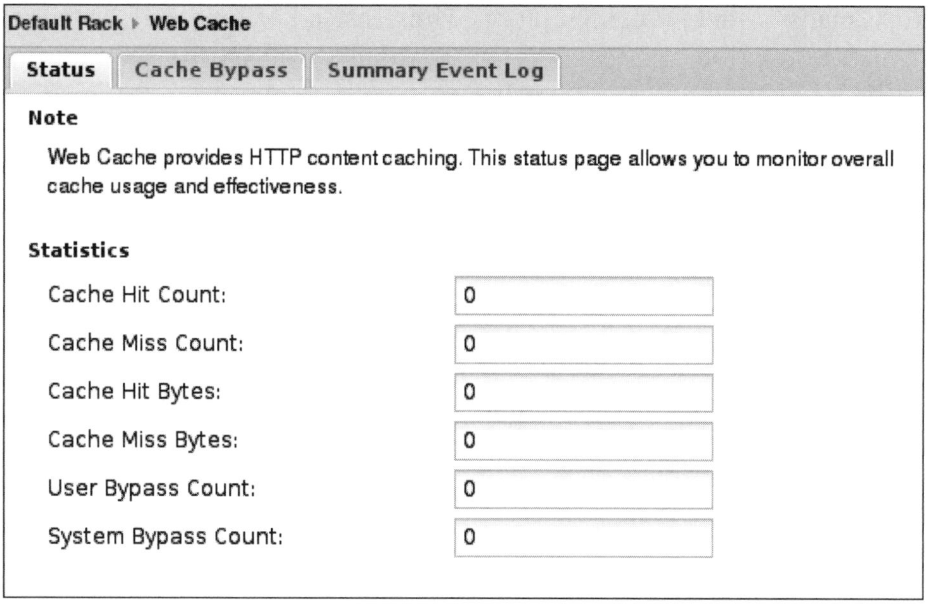

Figure 10.2
Web Cache monitoring statistics.
Source: Untangle, Inc.

This feature is very useful for organizations evaluating whether they need to subscribe to the application. During the 14-day free trial that accompanies every paid rack application, users can monitor whether enough duplicate content is downloaded to justify using Web Cache.

IPsec VPN Versus OpenVPN

Untangle engineers and system administrators from a variety of fields frequently recommend OpenVPN (which is included free with every Untangle distribution) for use in virtually all situations requiring a virtual private network (VPN) connection. As noted, VPNs enable remote users to connect securely to a network or for remote networks to connect to each other. In the first scenario, OpenVPN creates a point-to-point tunnel, enabling remote users to access file servers, printers, etc., behind an Untangle box protecting a network. In the second scenario, OpenVPN gives a branch office or remote network access to the same protected resources.

Internet Protocol Security (IPsec) VPN is useful when multiple networks need to be connected to each other. Whereas OpenVPN uses a hub configuration in which all external networks connect to a single "master" Untangle gateway, IPsec VPN connects the networks in a star or "many-to-many" configuration. Thus, instead of connecting network B to network C via network A (the "master" network), as occurs with OpenVPN, network B can connect directly to network C with IPsec VPN.

Where multiple networks require secure interconnectivity, IPsec VPN is a clear choice for performance. Otherwise, it isn't worth the added expense of licensing, especially because it must be licensed on all Untangle gateways to be connected.

Branding Manager

Readers of this text will rarely have a need for the paid Branding Manager application. Branding Manager enables administrators to replace the Untangle logo and other references to Untangle from user-facing pages, including the following:

- Captive Portal login
- Untangle login
- User reports and quarantine digests
- Block pages
- The Untangle rack visible to end-users

While this may be useful in some instances, most end-users are familiar with content filter blocks and would not be surprised to see application-specific pages for logins or blocked content. Individual pages can also be "re-skinned" or customized with graphics and text without paying for Branding Manager. Although it is outside the scope of this text to describe skin customizations, Untangle provides downloadable templates and instructions on re-skinning on their website.

UNIQUE AND CRITICAL (FOR SOME) PAID APPLICATIONS

While all of the applications described previously may be useful in specific cases, four additional paid applications will likely be useful and/or necessary for many users of Untangle beyond hobbyists, students, parents, and so on. They are as follows:

- Directory Connector
- Policy Manager
- WAN Balancer
- WAN Failover

Directory Connector and Policy Manager

User accounts in Untangle work via the Captive Portal to associate particular functions and behaviors with specific users or groups of users. In a hotel, for example, staff may be able to access the Internet without restrictions, while guests may be prevented from using peer-to-peer or other bandwidth-intensive web applications. Installing Untangle using settings with differentiated groups of users usually works best with one of two approaches:

- Using the paid Policy Manager application to create unique virtual racks with individualized settings for each group

- Physically segmenting a network and building rules in rack applications and the configuration tab to differentiate between these networks (in the hotel example, hotel staff computers could run from switches attached to one Untangle interface, while a wireless network for guests could be connected to another Untangle interface)

The second approach is free in terms of Untangle but is inflexible and relies on the ability to physically segment a network, which may not always be possible. The first method, in contrast:

- Is extremely flexible

- Is easy to implement

- Provides a means for controlling how each group uses the network at a very granular level

Policy Manager relies on the presence of defined users and groups that can be created in the Untangle Local Directory. However, as the number of groups and users increases, using a second paid application, Directory Connector, is often more convenient. Directory Connector enables Untangle to use a Windows Active Directory domain or a separate RADIUS server for user and group identification and authentication.

Frequently, when Untangle is used in a production environment, an Active Directory or RADIUS server will already be in place. Adding Directory Connector means that administrators don't need to re-create users and groups in the local directory. User maintenance and provisioning is handled centrally as appropriate in an organizational setting. When combined with Directory Connector, Policy Manager provides a complete solution for differentiated content filtering, application control, and other elements of Untangle's network control in common networking scenarios.

Users can then log in to the Captive Portal or Untangle interface using their Active Directory or RADIUS usernames and passwords. Alternatively, Active Directory domain administrators can download the Active Directory Login Script (ADLS) from the

Directory Connector application and install it on the domain controller. When users authenticate in Windows, they are automatically authenticated in Untangle, providing the level of access assigned to their Active Directory user group in the Policy Manager application.

Load Balancing and Bandwidth Aggregation

One of Untangle's most powerful features is its ability to provide load balancing and failover between multiple connections to the Internet. However, these are both paid features contained in the WAN Balancer and WAN Failover rack applications, respectively.

Although not true bandwidth aggregation—in which, for example, two 10 Mbps connections are actively bonded to provide a single 20 Mbps pipe to the Internet—WAN Balancer can intelligently distribute traffic among as many as six ISP connections. (Untangle supports up to seven network interfaces, so at least one must be used for the internal network.) WAN Balancer maintains a cache of active routes to various sites and services and will attempt to maintain connections to specific applications on a single ISP to avoid potential conflicts generated by multiple IP addresses using the same service for the same user.

WAN Balancer also allows administrators to specify whether certain types of traffic should use an individual interface. For example, Voice over IP (VoIP) is far more sensitive to latency than to bandwidth, so administrators may designate low-latency connections as targets for VoIP traffic. Even if rules like these aren't specified, administrators can manually designate percentages of overall traffic that Untangle should send to each interface. In the simplest scenario, a 5 Mbps DSL connection can be assigned 25% of the traffic, while a 15 Mbps cable connection can be assigned 75% to balance the remaining bandwidth.

WAN Failover is designed to work in conjunction with WAN Balancer to automatically use active connections in case any available interfaces go down. In the preceding example, if the DSL connection fails, 100% of the network traffic would be directed to the cable connection and Untangle would ignore the rule that pushes 25% of the traffic to the failed DSL line.

WAN Failover can work independently without WAN Balancer. It simply leaves a secondary connection to the Internet inactive until it is needed in the event of a failure. This is reasonable if the secondary connection is very slow and intended for use only in emergencies, but it is generally not the best use of redundant connections that WAN Balancer allows Untangle to utilize simultaneously.

HIGH AVAILABILITY

Version 10.1 of Untangle included enhancements for high availability. In network terms, *high availability* refers to a set of redundant systems that ensure little or no downtime for applications or access to network resources (including the Internet). For Untangle specifically, high availability is implemented with the Virtual Redundancy Router Protocol (VRRP). Using VRRP, users can set up multiple Untangle servers that fail over to maintain network connectivity. In this scenario, one server acts as the master and any others in the VRRP group act as slaves that take over routing activities if the master fails.

Like many of the paid rack applications, high availability is not something that users in smaller or less demanding environments will need to set up. High availability is, however, a critical part of scaling Untangle to larger networks that rely on Internet connectivity and the networking functions that the server provides. Because Untangle servers are relatively inexpensive to set up, setting up high availability is cost-effective even for schools or non-profits to implement, and the technology is a welcome enhancement to the Untangle operating system. VRRP is set up in the Edit Interface dialog box, accessible via Configuration > Network, as shown in Figure 10.3.

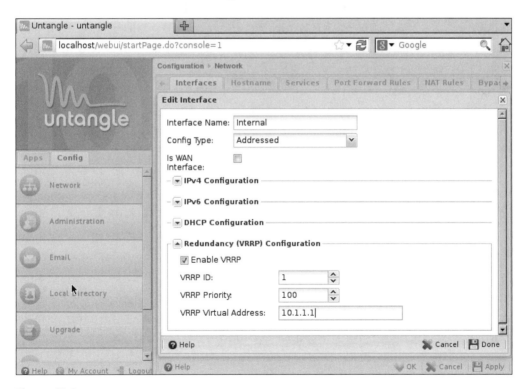

Figure 10.3
Turning on and configuring VRRP.
Source: Untangle, Inc.

VRRP can be configured on both internal and external interfaces, either separately or at the same time. Before configuring VRRP, administrators should set up two or more identical Untangle servers. These boxes should be identical in terms of interface configuration, networking setup, and application setup, but the underlying hardware can be different. A master-slave relationship is created when interfaces on multiple Untangle servers are assigned the same VRRP ID and the same virtual IP address. They must also have static individual IP addresses on the same subnet.

The virtual IP address is the address used by all nodes on the network when referring to the gateway. It allows a single IP address to refer to any number of physical Untangle servers in a master-slave group. The master is always responsible for routing functions at any given time, handling all traffic to and from the virtual IP address. However, in the event of a failure on the master (power loss, hardware failure, etc.), the virtual IP address is immediately associated with one of the slaves, which becomes the new master and begins handling routing tasks. This happens transparently to the other devices on the network because the gateway address they are assigned to use (the virtual IP address) hasn't changed.

VRRP differentiates the master from the slave(s) and chooses the new master in case of a failure based on the VRRP priority. VRRP priority is defined on a scale of 0 to 100, with 100 being most likely the master. Administrators can actively demote a master and force a failover to a slave by changing the master's VRRP priority. For example, if an organization's primary Untangle server had been assigned a priority of 100 and the backup assigned a priority of 90, operators could reduce the priority of the master to 80 to cause the backup to immediately begin handling routing, DHCP, content filtering, and any other configured services.

If VRRP is set up for external interfaces, each must have separate, static IP addresses provided by the ISP or external network to which the Untangle boxes are connected. Any NAT rules, port forwards, etc. (see Chapter 6, "Implementing Networking Best Practices [or Not] with Untangle") should be set up using the virtual IP address associated with the external interfaces.

While VRRP can be set up on either internal or external interfaces, it usually makes the most sense to set it up for both as diagrammed in Figure 10.4. Untangle's VRRP implementation automatically releases the master status on both internal and external interfaces if one or the other goes down. A complete failover on both internal and external interfaces is the only way to ensure high availability in case of any type of failure instead of the subset of failures that may affect only one interface.

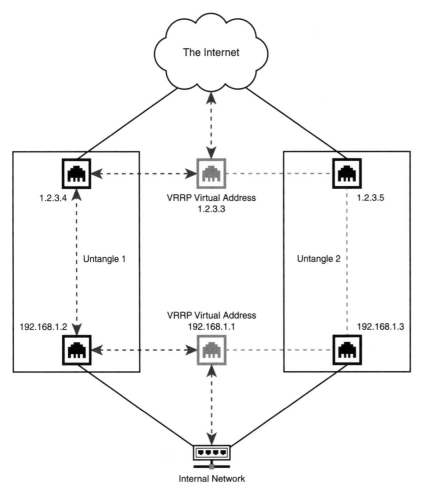

Figure 10.4
Schematic for sample VRRP configuration on both internal and external interfaces. (Based on an image provided by Untangle, Inc.)

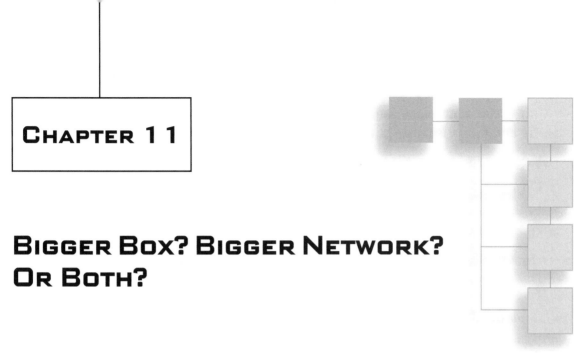

Chapter 11

Bigger Box? Bigger Network? Or Both?

You can significantly extend Untangle's features and functionality by adding paid features. Some of these features, such as WAN Failover and Directory Connector, are critical in larger networks or enterprise settings. However, some elements of Untangle performance and scalability simply can't be addressed by adding new functions. Rather, they require new hardware and/or network optimization to deal with bottlenecks and poor performance in more demanding network environments.

As noted in Chapter 10, "Paid Features," some of the paid Untangle modules perform better than their free counterparts. Virus Blocker is considerably faster at scanning content than Virus Blocker Lite, for example. More often than not, though, poor performance on any network with an Untangle gateway results from three significant factors unrelated to Untangle's underlying code:

- Increasing numbers of users and associated increases in network traffic
- Increasing utilization of network resources
- Network infrastructure issues

All three of these factors can exacerbate or expose the others. A network that functioned acceptably despite suboptimal configuration or legacy switching hardware with 20 users may become unacceptably slow with 40 users even if the Untangle gateway can handle the extra traffic. Rolling out new web-based applications to users may cause a spike in traffic and reveal that a network has inadequate bandwidth and that the existing gateway can't support the new levels of utilization.

In either scenario, the administrator is left to determine the root cause(s) of the bottleneck and make appropriate corrections. First, though, it is worthwhile to outline signs of poor network performance that would prompt an administrator to investigate both network capacity and the capabilities of the Untangle firewall:

- Slow-loading web pages for users
- Unacceptable performance of video and VoIP applications like Skype and Google Hangouts
- Slow-loading web pages for servers hosted behind the Untangle firewall
- Slow VPN connections for workers connecting remotely to the network
- Slow loading of Captive Portal or blocked content pages

Assuming that Untangle itself is configured optimally, any of the above are sufficient reason to take a closer look at network infrastructure, including Untangle.

CAN I JUST MAKE A BIGGER, FASTER UNTANGLE GATEWAY?

Untangle's performance is primarily dependent on four parameters:

- Processor speed
- Interface speed
- Available memory
- Disk speed

As described in Chapter 9, "Advanced Topics," in the section "Optimizing Untangle," different components of Untangle place varying demands on the CPU, memory, and I/O subsystems. The reporting module and disk-caching feature benefit from fast disks, while Web Filter Lite uses a substantial amount of memory. Network interfaces, on the other hand, will be most affected by traffic volume. As a result, administrators must first determine whether Untangle is the source of network performance issues and, if so, whether traffic or particular modules are taxing the system. This information will inform upgrade choices or future system design if the system needs to be replaced entirely.

It is worth noting that processor clock speed is the least important of the four parameters noted. The nature of routing, packet inspection, etc., is such that bottlenecks will tend to occur in disk and network I/O or as a result of insufficient memory far sooner than on the

CPU. These also tend to be the easiest components to upgrade, making complete replacement of the Untangle box unnecessary in many situations.

While it isn't possible to determine precisely which Untangle applications are causing system issues, Untangle includes reporting features that operators can use to determine whether I/O, memory, or CPU load is exceeding reasonable thresholds. Open the Reports application, click Settings, click the View Reports button, and choose Server from the menu on the left. Graphs showing CPU load, free memory, swap usage, and disk usage can give important information about hardware bottlenecks.

CPU load is a measure of processor free capacity. A value of 0 means that the CPU is not being used, while a value of 1 indicates that the processor is operating at full capacity. Values greater than 1 are a measure of how many processes are waiting for CPU resources. In general, CPU load shouldn't exceed 0.5, with occasional spikes toward 1. If CPU load appears to frequently approach or exceed 1, then a CPU upgrade is in order.

Free memory and swap usage are closely related. As the amount of free memory approaches 0, Untangle will begin using a dedicated partition on the disk as temporary memory. This slows down the machine considerably because disk storage is much slower than RAM. In general, there should be little or no swap usage, and this metric is a red flag for a potential memory upgrade.

The disk usage metric shows remaining free space on Untangle's hard drive(s). As with most computer systems, a good rule of thumb is to have at least 10% of the drive's capacity free to ensure reasonable performance.

Turning to the system report (again, selected from the left pane in the Reports application), operators can determine average throughput on the interfaces over time. While this report isn't particularly specific, if throughput is regularly hitting 50 to 75% of the speed of the interfaces, then upgrading interface speeds or the number of interfaces may also improve performance. Fortunately, this is a fairly inexpensive upgrade on most DIY systems, so if there is any suspicion that throughput may not be adequate for network requirements, dividing throughput among more interfaces is a reasonable approach.

This still doesn't answer the ultimate question, though, of whether to upgrade or replace an Untangle firewall in the event of poor performance. If network infrastructure has been ruled out as the root cause (see the next section), then it's important to fully assess network and performance requirements as well as budget constraints before choosing between replacement and upgrade. Schools, for example, frequently use repurposed servers or computers as Untangle firewalls because it is an affordable solution. An upgrade, if the original computer or server will support it, will most likely be the most cost-effective way to address emerging performance problems.

Because CPU clock speed is considered the least important contributor to Untangle performance, operators can often forego CPU upgrades, which also tend to be the most costly and frequently aren't well supported, especially on repurposed OEM PCs (i.e., a computer originally purchased from a major manufacturer). However, most desktop PCs and servers less than three years old will support memory upgrades, installation of additional network interfaces, and replacement of standard hard drives with solid state drives, all of which will substantially boost Untangle performance.

Where cost is less of an issue (and performance can affect mission-critical systems in business settings), replacement may be a better option. Whether the replacement is purpose-built as an Untangle firewall or organizations purchase a server-class machine, full replacement will often be easier, faster, and more trouble-free, and will ensure higher performance than upgrading an aging firewall.

What If I Just Improve My Network Infrastructure?

Untangle Firewall generally performs acceptably with fairly basic hardware. Untangle sells a series of appliances (see the upcoming section "When It's Time to Move to Untangle Hardware, Pay for Support, and Give Your First Box to Your Grandmother") that, on the low end, support up to 64,000 network nodes with a single dual-core Intel processor. Granted, these are dedicated devices purpose-built and optimized by Untangle, running their latest proprietary suite of content-filtering software, but the point remains that hardware requirements tend to be quite reasonable for average-sized networks. Thus, before looking at hardware upgrades and expensive servers, operators should first look at their network infrastructure as the source of performance issues.

Particularly because many readers of this book will be interested in Untangle as an inexpensive, DIY solution for content filtering and network protection, budget constraints may well have led to suboptimal network architecture. Again, schools are an excellent example of networks that may not be designed to support growing traffic needs. As with many small and medium businesses, schools may still be using legacy network hardware like hubs or low-speed switches, which may have been cobbled together over the years with excessive distances between nodes, aging cabling, and consumer-grade parts obtained because of their low cost.

Too often, modern best practices in network design and management aren't implemented or maintained because of budget, staff turnover, or lack of expertise. The following is a list of common networking problems that, if solved, will usually have a far more dramatic impact on network performance than any upgrades to the Untangle firewall:

- **The use of Cat5 Ethernet cabling instead of Cat5e or Cat6 cabling:** Cat5 Ethernet cables can only support a maximum of 100 Mbps data transfer instead of the gigabit speeds that more modern cables can support. Even if desktops, servers, switches, and the Untangle box itself support higher throughput, Cat5 cables will limit data transmission to 20th-century speeds. Moreover, Cat5 cables are often fairly old and may have been kinked, nicked, or otherwise degraded over many years of inattention, further reducing throughput.

- **Ethernet hubs:** While most network operators have eliminated hubs from their infrastructure, it is surprising how many can be found lurking in wiring closets, computer labs, and other areas where they are easily overlooked for upgrade. Hubs do a very poor job of managing traffic on a network and, where they still exist, tend to be sources of significant collisions. They should be replaced immediately, even with inexpensive switches if budgets don't allow for more costly managed switches.

- **Legacy switches:** Even the slowest switch is preferable to an Ethernet hub. However, like Cat5 cables, older switches often run at 10 or 100 Mbps, limiting transmission speeds on a network regardless of the throughput that other nodes and endpoints can support. Newer switches often have improved switching algorithms, more intelligent traffic-management capabilities, and configurable features that can further improve network performance.

- **Consumer-grade wireless access points:** As WiFi has become an expected feature in most network environments, many small and medium businesses (SMBs), schools, and other smaller organizations have simply plugged consumer-grade wireless access points into the network. These are not designed to have more than a few devices connected at once, often can't achieve adequate range in settings with metal or concrete structures, and may not have appropriate firmware for management in critical settings. Upgrading to wireless devices designed for business and institutional settings can help businesses accommodate the rapidly growing number of wireless devices, maintaining speed and performance across the network.

- **Architectural issues:** Efficient networks rely on a strong, high-speed backbone of switches, with less expensive switches connected to the backbone by "home runs." These inexpensive switches (and often wireless devices) are used to connect individual PCs, printers, and other nodes on these networks to the backbone.

This architecture ensures low-latency connections to servers and the Internet, the latter via the Untangle firewall. However, it isn't uncommon to see the following:

- Very long home runs. Ethernet standards specify that a single run of either Cat5e or Cat6 cable can't exceed 100 meters.

- Repeated hops between switches instead of home runs that introduce much more complicated paths for data on a network.

- The use of bridges and repeaters to get around the 100 meter length limit. These still introduce unacceptable latency, however.

Improving and simplifying architecture can pay big dividends in terms of overall performance.

Untangle users should embark on upgrades only after major networking issues like those just described are addressed. Untangle should be part of a holistic approach to ensuring the health and performance of any network.

VIRTUALIZATION REVISITED

In Chapter 9, the section "Virtualizing Untangle (The Right Way to Run Multiple Services on an Untangle Gateway)" introduced the idea of operating Untangle in a virtual environment. There, the focus was maximizing utilization of a server and making use of a single, relatively expensive machine for potentially several purposes (e.g., a web server, a file server, etc.). However, virtualization also has two important implications for scalability and performance.

The first is that virtualization essentially eliminates the notion of hardware upgrades in this context. While the server on which the Untangle virtual machine is running may be upgraded, the actual hardware is abstracted from the Untangle OS. This gives operators the ability to upgrade the virtual hardware on which Untangle runs whenever necessary and reconfigure interfaces to optimize traffic flow through the virtual network. Assuming that the host for the Untangle virtual machine has sufficient resources, the hypervisor can allocate additional memory, more processor cores, and greater storage if performance problems related to the content filter and gateway emerge in the virtual environment.

In virtualized settings, it is also much simpler to add network interfaces, segmenting traffic and managing network infrastructure. Figure 11.1 shows one possible deployment of Untangle virtual desktops and virtual servers deployed across two physical servers.

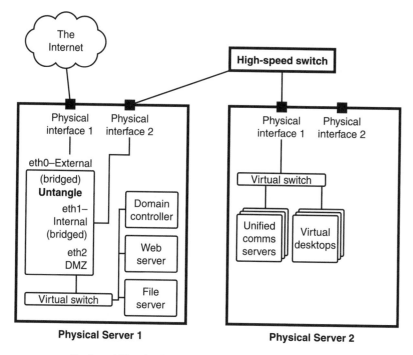

Figure 11.1
Sample virtual environment with Untangle and a variety of OS images on two physical servers.

This is only one of many possible implementations. In this case, the virtual switching appears as it would in the Microsoft Hyper-V hypervisor, but the same concepts could be applied with any hypervisor. Similarly, in more sophisticated environments, engineers might connect an Internet router directly to a managed switch and create direct routes to the server's physical interfaces instead of connecting the router itself to one of the servers. Virtual switch configurations could also be set up flexibly, while the Oracle VirtualBox hypervisor could be used to define internal networks instead of virtual switches. Regardless of the exact configuration of the virtual environment, virtualizing Untangle is a useful means of increasing the capacity of the firewall and content filter, especially in conjunction with other virtualized desktops and servers.

The second implication of using Untangle in virtualized settings relates more generally to heavily virtualized environments. Organizations can potentially deliver virtual end-user desktops, a variety of servers, and even storage from a cluster of physical servers with an Untangle firewall deployed as just one more virtual server. In this scenario, even the

Internet gateway is virtual, as are the network connections between the gateway and the other virtual nodes. The key takeaway here is that reliability and scalability within this type of deployment require a robust, well-planned underlying hardware infrastructure.

WHEN IT'S TIME TO MOVE TO UNTANGLE HARDWARE, PAY FOR SUPPORT, AND GIVE YOUR FIRST BOX TO YOUR GRANDMOTHER

Many people are initially skeptical about Untangle. How can something this powerful be free? How does Untangle make money if it just gives its software away? As discussed in Chapter 10, Untangle sells subscriptions to premium rack applications that are add-ons to the core Untangle Next Generation Firewall. This so-called "freemium" model, in which basic software is free and users can then pay for upgrades, is common among modern software vendors.

However, Untangle also sells hardware appliances that have their Next Generation Firewall software pre-installed and configured. As shown in Figure 11.2, these appliances range from the U10, designed for small workgroups, to the M3000, a rack-mountable model that can easily support 3,000 users with high usage.

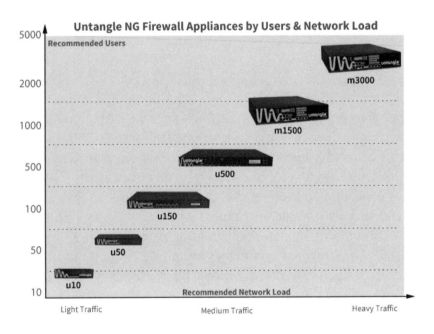

Figure 11.2
Untangle Next Generation Firewall Appliances.
© 2014 Untangle, Inc.

For some organizations, even the Next Generation Firewall appliances may not meet all their needs. Most likely, this won't be the result of inadequate hardware; the M3000 appliance is sufficient for very large businesses. Instead, these organizations will be looking for a degree of control, management, reporting, and granularity that the Untangle NG Firewall can't deliver. The firewall scales extremely well with the right underlying hardware, but managing the rack applications in very large network environments, particularly across distributed campuses and multiple sites, becomes unwieldy.

To address the needs of more complex networks and requirements for better management, insight, and analytical capabilities, Untangle also offers high-end Internet Content (IC) Control appliances. The largest of these devices supports as many as 200,000 network nodes, gigabit throughput, up to 10,000 simultaneous filtering requests, and 250 custom rules for managing bandwidth and traffic types. Beyond raw horsepower, though, IC Control appliances give administrators a "single pane of glass" interface to view everything from security threats to user activity (see Figure 11.3). Application management is centralized and far more granular than what is available in the Untangle NG Firewall.

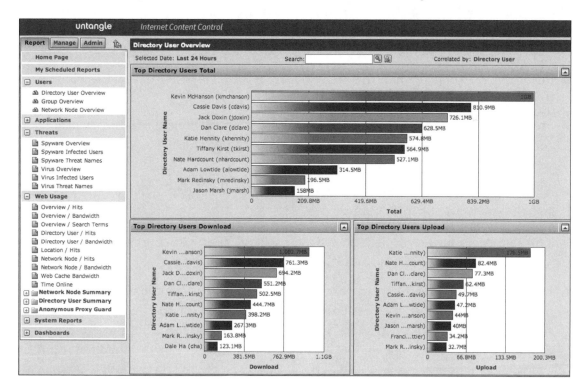

Figure 11.3
Untangle Internet Content Control user interface.

Source: Untangle, Inc.

Where the focus for the NG Firewall is network protection and regulatory compliance, the focus for the IC Control appliances is complete visibility, robust network management, and high availability. NG Firewall recently added support for high availability, but Untangle sells a dedicated IC Control Manager appliance that can manage multiple IC Control nodes at different sites, on redundant WAN connections, and in other distributed environments where centralized administration is critical. The IC Control Manager allows operators to push configurations to multiple IC Control appliances or respect local settings—for example, in a school district where building IT staff may set different policies appropriate for elementary, middle, or high school students rather than using a blanket policy set at the district level.

This book has been largely concerned with building DIY firewalls and gateways using Untangle software to achieve very cost-effective content filtering and network gateway services. With repurposed computers, families, schools, small businesses, and so on can often achieve their content-filtering, user-safety, and network-security goals for free with the Untangle NG Firewall. Untangle's appliances, on the other hand, are not cheap (although they are highly competitive with similar appliances on the market). For most readers of this book, they will probably be overkill at best and unattainable at worst. However, they are discussed here for a few important reasons:

- Readers may eventually find themselves in environments where cost is less of an issue than performance or reliability.

- Free implementations of Untangle may work for instructional purposes or proofs of concept but production needs may exceed what can practically be done with free software and DIY hardware.

- All the appliances—even low-end models suited to small deployments—have certain advantages over their free counterparts.

This last item bears further explanation. Readers shouldn't be discouraged from building their own firewalls, but should be aware of the following caveats:

- **Licensing costs:** Operators can purchase either "free" or "complete" packages with the NG Firewall appliances. Free packages include the standard Lite/free apps and the core of Untangle, and are included with the base hardware price of the devices. Complete packages include all free and paid applications at a substantial discount over the subscription costs for the applications available to DIY Untangle users. The annual subscription price for the complete package is also fixed instead of charged per user (or group of users), so costs never go up, regardless of how many users are serviced by the appliance.

- **Energy:** Although the appliances are essentially just servers, they are strategically sized for their expected workload. Repurposed computers and DIY servers—especially those based on older hardware—are frequently going to consume more energy than equivalent appliances, the cost and footprint of which can be significant in an always-on device.

- **Hardware optimization and integration:** The latest version of Untangle has broad compatibility with a variety of hardware. However, there is no guarantee that DIY hardware—particularly inexpensive or off-brand components like network cards or graphics chips—will work easily (or at all) with Untangle. This can be particularly challenging when repurposing computers or attempting to build an Untangle box from the least expensive available parts. Appliances are built with standardized components whose compatibility is obviously a foregone conclusion. When time and ease of deployment are of paramount importance, simply using an appliance built by Untangle can save headaches, even if it won't necessarily save money.

- **Network interfaces:** Untangle NG Firewall appliances come with at least four network interfaces. Higher-end models have six or eight Ethernet ports ready to use out of the box, all in a chassis no larger than two rack units in height. Enabling eight interfaces may simply not be possible on repurposed hardware or on small form-factor PCs, or may require the use of expensive multi-port expansion cards. Of course, Untangle works with as few as two network interfaces, but having more ports offers greater possibilities for network failover, WAN balancing, network segmentation, and DMZs. Moving up to IC Control appliances provides options for high-speed fiber connections, better integrating with robust network backbones as described in the section "What If I Just Improve My Network Infrastructure?" earlier in this chapter.

It is also worth noting that both the appliances and paid subscriptions to packages of premium rack applications come with live technical support. Access to the technical support team can also be purchased on a subscription basis. This alone may be reason enough to upgrade. The Untangle user community provides useful support and documentation for those wishing to build and maintain their own Untangle gateways, but as environments become increasingly sophisticated and critical to the functioning of larger organizations, technical support directly from Untangle can be invaluable.

WHEN IT'S TIME TO LOOK BEYOND UNTANGLE

With the introduction of Internet Content Control appliances, Untangle offers a relatively complete line of content-filtering, firewall, and Internet gateway products. At the lowest end, the Next Generation Firewall can be had as a free download that can be installed on almost any computer with two Ethernet ports. The NG Firewall on a repurposed or DIY computer will meet basic regulatory requirements for schools and libraries, offer parents considerable control over Internet usage for their children, and give reasonable gateway network protection to small businesses.

Stepping up to key paid rack applications for the NG Firewall can improve performance in many areas, simplify management with connections to directory services on the network, and increase network reliability and availability. Whether run on a DIY box or an Untangle appliance, NG Firewall and selected subscription services like those described in Chapter 10 in the section "Unique and Critical (for Some) Paid Applications" should serve the majority of mid-sized organizations well with little need for additional specific gateway appliances.

Larger organizations or those with much more specific or stringent network management needs can further upgrade to one or more Internet Content Control appliances. These devices can implement filtering and bandwidth-management policies on mobile devices as well as standard Mac and Windows PCs. As described in the previous section, IC Control appliances provide very high levels of visibility and control over network traffic, and can be centrally managed by an additional dedicated appliance.

So what else could an organization need in terms of network management and control? As with many of the advanced topics covered in the final part of this book, few readers will encounter situations where an Untangle solution won't fulfill requirements for the following:

- An Internet firewall
- Content filtering
- DHCP, DNS, and other networking fundamentals
- Consent to monitoring and filtering
- User tracking and monitoring
- Bandwidth shaping and quality of service implementation

In many networks, these functions may be handled individually by multiple dedicated appliances. In general, the simplicity of managing each of these elements of computer networking and security through a single interface is quite valuable, especially when IT resources are limited.

That being said, Untangle is not without its limits, even with the IC Control appliances. Untangle actually publishes a page on their support wiki entitled "Why Untangle Sucks." The title is a bit tongue-in-cheek, but as the page explains:

> *No software is perfect, and no solution is right for everyone.*
>
> *The goal of this page is to be up-front and realistic about some common complaints about Untangle. This may help you save some time and determine if Untangle is ultimately right for you.*
>
> *We strive to keep things simple and not introduce more settings than necessary. We want things to "just work." However, this is not right for everyone—for example, power-users who like to customize and tweak settings. Often, power-users coming from other solutions are sometimes frustrated by not being able to tweak the spam engine's settings inner workings or how the web filter categorizes sites. Whether Untangle's approach is right for you or not depends on your goals.*

Even if Untangle's approach isn't an issue, it is important to evaluate competitive solutions. At the lower end, there are no competitors who provide such a robust set of network management tools for free or allow users to build their own firewall and content filter as easily as Untangle does. As users begin looking at high-end appliances, though, the market becomes somewhat more crowded. Network administrators should evaluate offerings from a variety of vendors to ensure that IT budgets are spent wisely on solutions that will satisfy current and future requirements.

Solution providers often bundle routers, firewalls, and content filters with complete data center systems, communications infrastructure, etc. Similarly, operators looking to new technologies like software-defined networking, big data analytics, and high-performance computing will likely need to look elsewhere. Significant automation and orchestration of network services (again, most often seen in data center applications) should be left to hardware and software ecosystems designed for these approaches.

Despite these limitations at the high end of networking technology, Untangle NG Firewall brings an incredible array of network tools within reach of users who could not otherwise afford hardware with similar capabilities. This is why Untangle has been so widely adopted in schools and continues to intrigue students, home users, and small business owners who want to protect their users and their computer resources and better understand the inner workings of IP networks.

Part IV

Appendixes

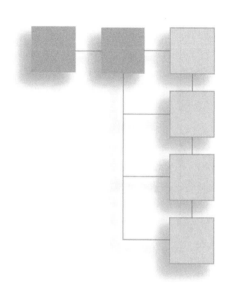

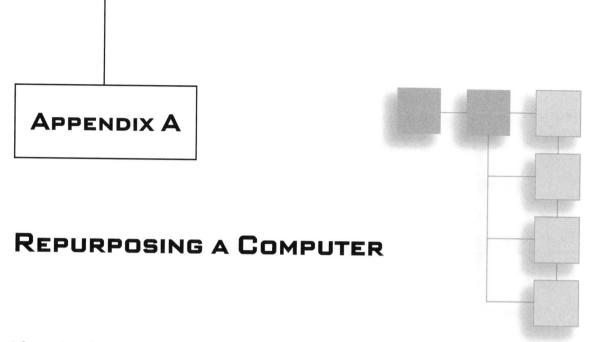

APPENDIX A

REPURPOSING A COMPUTER

The easiest, least expensive way to begin using Untangle Next Generation Firewall (aside from using a virtual machine) is to simply repurpose an existing computer. While virtually any used PC or server can be used with Untangle, some work better than others.

A repurposed machine should meet the following minimum requirements, assuming a relatively small workload (10 to 15 users with average utilization):

- Intel Pentium 4, Intel Atom, or equivalent processor
- 1 GB RAM
- 80 GB hard drive
- The ability to support at least two NICs or a single NIC with at least two ports

Exact hardware requirements can be found at http://wiki.untangle.com/index.php/Hardware_Requirements, although in practice, the minimum requirements are only sufficient for basic utilization.

More robust specifications will improve performance, but overall reliability is more important than exact hardware if the gateway is to be used in a production setting. If possible, repurposing server- or workstation-class hardware will often yield the best results. Most form factors will also be acceptable, but a tower will generally be easier to modify or repair, especially if more than two NICs are to be installed.

Repurposing a computer is a simple matter of evaluation, modification, and installation.

EVALUATION

Repurposing a computer for use with Untangle begins with careful evaluation of the hardware.

1. Ensure the following:

   - The PC meets the minimum hardware requirements for the intended level of utilization.

   - The computer boots and recognizes a hard drive.

   - BIOS settings indicate that all installed RAM is recognized.

   - The hard drives don't contain any data that can't be erased when installing Untangle.

2. Determine the physical condition of the computer.

3. Determine whether, when the computer is turned on, it runs relatively quietly and stays on without producing excessive heat.

4. Open the computer and check for dust, broken or disconnected components, and any fans that aren't running smoothly.

5. Determine whether the processor is 32-bit or 64-bit. Most AMD processors are 64-bit, as are the majority of Intel Core series and Xeon series processors. Others may require a bit of research after you identify the actual processor model.

Note that the interior of the PC shown in Figure A.1 is clean and dust-free and all cables are connected and tied. All fans are free of obstructions. One PCIe XI slot and two PCI slots are free for potential expansion with additional NICs.

Figure A.1

This picture shows both standard PCI slots and a newer PCIe X1 slot.

Image courtesy of Wikimedia Commons (http://upload.wikimedia.org/wikipedia/commons/thumb/7/7b/Computer_case.JPG/596px-Computer_case.JPG).

Modification

After you have determined that the computer meets the basic requirements for repurposing as an Untangle server, it's time for some basic maintenance and the addition of appropriate networking hardware.

1. If necessary, clean the interior of the computer thoroughly with compressed air and/or an electronics vacuum.

2. Check and tighten all cable connections.

3. Replace any fans that are worn or not functioning properly.

4. If the computer has only a single network interface, install one or more cards from the Untangle Hardware Compatibility List (http://wiki.untangle.com/index.php/

Hardware_Compatibility_List#Network_Interface_Cards). Network cards are fairly inexpensive components (aside from specific high-end NICs such as Intel's server-class cards listed on the HCL), so it is reasonable to install more than the requisite two NICs if expansion slots are available. Gigabit NICs (instead of 10/100 cards from the list) will help maximize the performance and scalability of the repurposed machine. While these are both suggestions rather than requirements, Untangle users will quickly discover new uses for additional fast interfaces.

5. Upgrade RAM or the hard drive if necessary. (This will most likely be necessary only if a component has failed and needs to be replaced.)

INSTALLATION

Finally, you are ready to install Untangle. Boot the computer and install Untangle as described in Chapter 3, "Downloading and Installing Untangle." Based on your evaluation of the processor, install either the 32-bit or 64-bit version of Untangle. If you chose NICs from the Untangle HCL, installation should proceed smoothly. Potential problems during install include the following:

■ Incompatibility with video hardware either installed as a standalone card or integrated with the motherboard

■ Incompatibility with an existing network interface (for example, the Ethernet port typically on the motherboard)

■ Problems with hardware (such as aging hard drives) that were not obvious during the inspection

Because older computers are so cheap (and often freely available in large quantities in schools and similar institutions), it is usually better to simply move on to another computer instead of investing significant time, energy, and money attempting to make an aging computer suitable for use with Untangle.

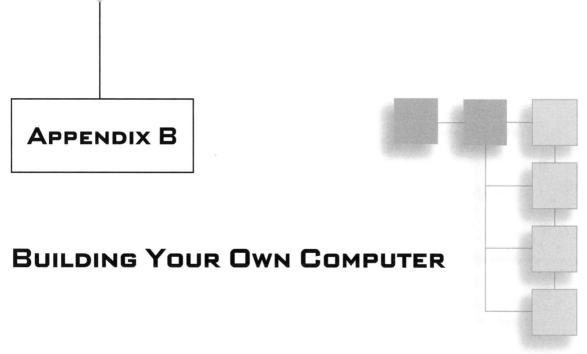

APPENDIX B

BUILDING YOUR OWN COMPUTER

Instructions for assembling a computer from parts can be found online. They are also typically included with most kits purchased from online retailers such as Newegg and TigerDirect or brick-and-mortar stores like Fry's. For this reason, such instructions are not provided here. Instead, this appendix includes examples of kit components for three different use cases:

- A budget test machine
- A compact home system
- A mid-range server

Because prices on individual components can vary considerably from week to week, prices provided are estimates for the completed kits. TigerDirect and Newegg frequently have sales on complete computer kits to which you can simply add inexpensive network cards. By purchasing one of these discounted kits, you can potentially save a considerable amount. Most kits will include the following components:

- Case
- Power supply
- Cabling
- Motherboard

- Processor with fan and heat sink. It is easiest to purchase a processor with a compatible fan and heat sink; they are frequently sold together.

- Necessary screws and fasteners.

- Thermal paste. This is used between the processor and heat sink, per manufacturer directions.

Some kits may include some of the following components. If they do not, you must ensure that you also purchase them.

- A hard drive.

- RAM.

- Network cards. Even inexpensive motherboards include a basic Ethernet port, so only one more card should be required. More can be added as necessary.

Be aware that specific processors are compatible only with particular motherboard "sockets" (the pin configuration into which the processor fits). Check the specifications for any processors against those for the motherboard using the chart at http://www.cpu-world.com/Sockets/.

Note

Specific brands noted here do not constitute a recommendation or endorsement. Rather, they are examples of a particular class of hardware.

Budget Test Machine

This computer will be appropriate for between five and 10 heavy users or up to 20 light users. It is inexpensive to purchase and easy to modify, allowing you to begin testing Untangle quickly. All the components should be available for under $200. They include the following:

- **An ATX full-tower or mid-tower case:** Either will have sufficient room for expansion and will be easy to work on.

- **ATX motherboard with on-board video and networking:** ATX refers to the size. ATX is the largest and will have the most room for expansion. If a smaller motherboard is included with a given kit and has adequate room for expansion, it won't cause problems and may be less expensive.

- **AMD A-series or Athlon processor:** These are generally the least expensive PC processors. A-series processors are more energy efficient and use a newer architecture.

- **2 GB RAM:** Also check the RAM specifications and ensure that they are compatible with the motherboard.

- **DVD drive:** This can be a very inexpensive component. It will be used a handful of times to install software, and there are no specific requirements other than low cost and a SATA interface.

- **Power supply:** Power supplies are rated by the number of watts of power they can deliver. For this system, any size is appropriate.

- **SATA hard drive:** SATA refers to the interface with the motherboard and is the current standard. An inexpensive hard drive with at least 80 GB is acceptable.

- **Network card:** Choose one that appears on the Untangle HCL (http://wiki.untangle .com/index.php/Hardware_Compatibility_List#Network_Interface_Cards).

COMPACT HOME SYSTEM

This computer will be appropriate for demanding home use but will be very compact, quiet, and energy efficient. It could fit unobtrusively in a media room, entertainment center, or home office. The budget for this machine is approximately $400. It should include the following:

- **Mini-ITX case:** These can be challenging to work with because they are very compact but they do provide the smallest possible form factor.

- **Mini-ITX motherboard:** Some minis are specifically designed to work without fans and to fit in a very compact case.

- **Intel Celeron or Atom processor:** At the very least, you need a dual core processor. These are low-power options meant for systems of this type.

- **DVD drive:** This can also be an inexpensive component, but ensure that it is compatible with the Mini-ITX case. Again, it should have a SATA interface.

- **4 GB RAM:** 4GB RAM should suffice.

- **Power supply:** This must be compatible with a Mini-ITX case. A low power rating is expected and acceptable.

- **Solid state SATA hard drive:** This should be at least 80GB. The solid state drive uses very little power and produces far less heat than a standard magnetic hard drive.

- **Network card:** Choose one from the Untangle HCL. This will need to be a low-profile NIC to fit in the case.

Mid-Range Server

This computer will be appropriate for demanding use by hundreds of users in a school or business setting. It will not be silent and is intended to be housed in a server room or area where some fan noise is not a problem. There are more compact, energy-efficient ways of configuring a machine with this much power, but this will provide an easy, cost-effective solution that can be expanded and upgraded to meet future needs. The budget for this machine is approximately $750. It should include the following:

- ATX full tower or mid-tower case.

- ATX motherboard. For this server, it is unacceptable to substitute a smaller motherboard because of the lack of expandability. The motherboard should support RAID 1 because you will be using two hard drives for fault tolerance.

- AMD FX series or Intel Core i7 processor.

- 16 GB RAM.

- DVD drive. Again, this can be an inexpensive component.

- Power supply. This should be at least 650 watts.

- Two SATA hard drives, at least 250 GB each. As noted, these will be configured with RAID level 1 so they are mirror images of each other. See the motherboard manual for setup instructions.

- At least two network cards from the Untangle HCL, up to the number of PCI slots supported by the motherboard.

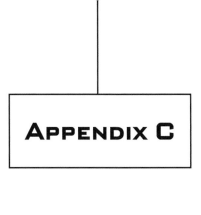

APPENDIX C

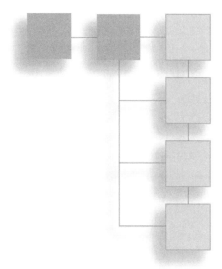

GLOSSARY

American Standard Code for Information Interchange (ASCII) A system of characters used by most computers, composed of letters, numbers, punctuation, and special symbols.

central processing unit (CPU) The hardware in a computer that actually executes computing instructions.

channel service unit/data service unit (CSU/DSU) A digital interface that connects a data line such as a T1 or T3 line to a router.

DIY Short for "do it yourself."

driver Software used to provide an interface between an operating system and a particular hardware component in a computer.

dynamic DNS A method by which dynamic IP addresses can be assigned to a static domain name with DNS records updated automatically by software. Frequently used to provide remote access to a computer or network that has an IP address assigned via DHCP by an ISP.

Dynamic Host Control Protocol (DHCP) A system by which computing devices are automatically assigned IP addresses from a given pool.

edge device A networking device (for example, a router, gateway, firewall, etc.) that provides and/or controls traffic between two networks (typically the public Internet and a private network).

Ethernet   A set of network communications standards relying on the principle of Carrier Sense Multiple Access with Collision Detection (CSMA/CD) to negotiate redundant, reliable connections between computing devices. Includes standards for both wireless and wired communications.

heuristics   In the context of information security, intelligent algorithms used to detect previously unknown malware based on the presence of certain markers, conditions, and characteristics associated with categories of security threats.

Hypertext Transfer Protocol (HTTP)   The protocol by which web pages are requested and sent from a web server to a web browser.

Hypertext Transfer Protocol Secure (HTTPS)   A secure, encrypted version of HTTP.

hypervisor   Software that abstracts an operating system (or systems) from the underlying hardware, allowing a variety of operating systems to run on a single host server. Hypervisors may be either type 1 or type 2. Type 1 hypervisors, also known as bare-metal hypervisors, are installed directly on a server without an underlying operating system. Type 2 hypervisors are applications that run on top of an existing operating system on the host server.

Internet service provider (ISP)   A telecommunications company that provides businesses and individuals with access to the Internet, usually by means of phone, cable, or fiber optics and an associated modem.

intranet   A website or sites accessible only within an organization. Used to facilitate internal communications, documentation, and collaboration.

kernel   A computer program that manages input and output requests from software and connects software to the underlying hardware (for example, the CPU, RAM, etc.).

latency   In this context, refers to network latency, or the time between sending a packet of information from one network destination to another and receiving a response back at the origin. Latency is frequently measured with the ping utility.

network address translation (NAT)   A technique used on IP networks to modify addressing information in individual data packets to appropriately route external traffic to internal nodes.

network interface card (NIC)   An expansion card attached to a PC motherboard that enables Ethernet communications on the computer. May also refer to an embedded chip attached to the motherboard for Ethernet connections.

off-premises   Refers to software and/or hardware infrastructure that is hosted at an external site rather than in an onsite, internal data center or server.

on-premises Refers to software and/or hardware infrastructure that is hosted in an onsite data center or server under internal control.

original equipment manufacturer (OEM) In the context of information technology, hardware manufacturers that generally sell wholesale computers and components to resellers. Some, like Dell and Lenovo, may sell directly to businesses and consumers.

packet The smallest chunk of information sent over an IP network. A common analogy is sending a multipage document one page at a time via the postal service, with each page individually addressed and reassembled at the destination. The envelopes and their contents are equivalent to packets on a network.

Peripheral Component Interconnect (PCI) A standard for connecting computers and internal components.

port forward A technique for automatically and transparently sending packets destined for one network location to another based on rules set at the edge of a network.

random access memory (RAM) High-speed data storage hardware in a computing device used to temporarily store data, programs, and instructions.

Remote Authentication Dial In User Service (RADIUS) A protocol for user authentication used on some networks and commonly supported by firewalls, access points, and routers.

scalability The ability to expand services or capacity based on need.

Secure Shell (SSH) A network protocol for encrypted communication between computers. Frequently used for remote access to command lines on servers.

uniform resource locator (URL) A human-readable address for a network node, website, etc.

Untangle Virtual Machine (UVM) The primary software environment of Untangle, which runs on top of the Debian Linux kernel. Rack applications run in the UVM while software defined in the configuration area of the Untangle interface run in the kernel.

Virtual Desktop Infrastructure (VDI) Hardware and software that hosts desktop operating systems on a centralized server infrastructure for simplified deployment and management of computing environments.

virtual local area network (VLAN) A logical partition of a physical network used to create subnets and isolated domains on a single network.

Virtual Redundancy Router Protocol (VRRP) A system by which multiple routers can be made available to act as a gateway for a network, increasing availability and creating failover capability at a network's edge.

virtualization   A set of technologies that abstracts operating systems and other software functions from underlying hardware, allowing multiple guest operating systems to run on a single host computer. Virtualization can also be applied to networking and storage, providing greater flexibility on a variety of hardware.

wide area network (WAN)   An architecture commonly used by larger businesses to connect multiple sites and networks.

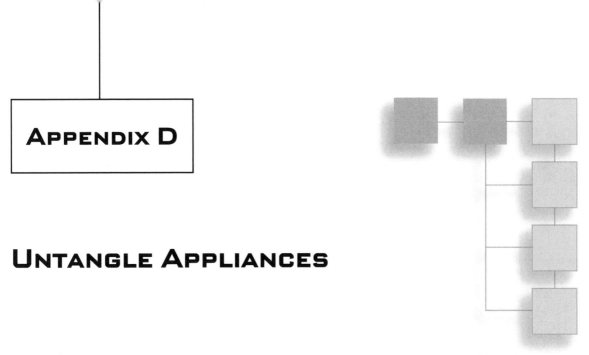

Appendix D

Untangle Appliances

Untangle offers several pre-built appliances that run either the NG Firewall or the new IC Content Control software. The section "When It's Time to Move to Untangle Hardware, Pay for Support, and Give Your First Box to Your Grandmother" in Chapter 11, "Bigger Box? Bigger Network? Or Both?," covered the appliances briefly, but this appendix lists the available devices and their intended use in greater detail.

Untangle NG Firewall Appliances

The Untangle NG Firewall appliances run the same software that has been the subject of this book and can be purchased either with the Free package or the Complete package. The appliances are purpose-built gateway/firewalls and, depending on their size, can sit on a desktop or in a server rack. Table D.1 outlines their capacities, technical specifications, and intended usage. Models and specifications are current as of July 2014.

Table D.1   Untangle NG Firewall Appliance Models and Specifications

Model	Max # Users	Hard Drive Capacity	RAM	Ethernet Interfaces	CPU Model	Rack Mount	Front Panel LCD	Base Price
u10	10	160 GB	1 GB	4	Atom single core	No	No	$795
u50	50	160 GB	2 GB	4	Atom dual core	No	No	$995
u150	150	500 GB	4 GB	6	Pentium dual core	Yes	Yes	$1,395
u500	500	500 GB	16 GB	8	Xeon quad core	Yes	Yes	$2,995
m1500	1,500	1 TB	16 GB	8	2x Xeon quad core	Yes	Yes	$6,995
m3000	3,000	1 TB	16 GB	8	2x Xeon six core	Yes	Yes	$8,495

UNTANGLE IC CONTROL

As noted in Chapter 11, Untangle's new Internet Content (IC) Control appliance bring deeper content-filtering and gateway-management services with a much more robust interface for monitoring and control. These appliances are designed for demanding environments where their increased cost can be justified. At the same time, the included software is not available freely or via subscription from Untangle. IC Control is available only when purchasing one of the appliances listed in Table D.2.

Table D.2 Untangle IC Control Appliances and Specifications

Model	Max # Users	Hard Drive Capacity	RAM	Max Through-put	CPU Model	Max Conc. Filtered Web Requests	Base Price
LX20	20	500 GB	8 GB	20 Mbps	Intel dual core	800	$2,998
LX50	50	500 GB	16 GB	50 Mbps	Intel quad core	1,500	$5,298
LX200	200	500 GB	16 GB	200 Mbps	Intel quad core	2,000	$8,498
DX500	500	500 GB RAID 1	40 GB	500 Mbps	Intel 8 core	6,000	$16,298
DX1000	1,000	1 TB RAID 1	96 GB	1 Gbps	2x Intel 8 core	10,000	$25,998

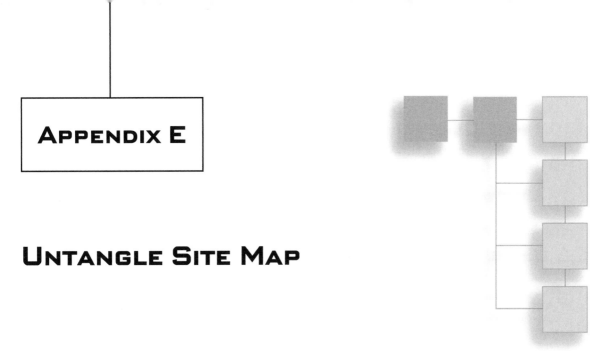

Appendix E

Untangle Site Map

Throughout this book, I have referred to the rack and configuration areas of the Untangle user interface. The application, though, is fairly intricate beyond these two main sections, and Untangle does not currently offer a full site map. The following site map is provided for reference as you look for specific parameters and functions. It is presented as an outline for simplicity.

Home (italics indicates a tab)

I. *Apps* (far left tab) (contains only links for installing new rack applications)

II. *Config* (second tab in left pane)

  A. Network

    i. *Interfaces*

      1. Edit (on each interface record)

    ii. *Hostname*

    iii. *Services*

    iv. *Port Forward Rules*

      1. Edit (on each Port Forward Rule record; same UI/screen to add records)

    v. *NAT Rules*

      1. Edit (on each NAT Rule record; same UI/screen to add records)

   vi. *Bypass Rules*

     1. Edit (on each Bypass Rule record; same UI/screen to add records)

  vii. *Routes*

     1. Edit (on each Route record; same UI/screen to add records)

 viii. *DNS Server*

     1. Edit (on each Static DNS Entry and Local DNS Server record; same UI/ screen to add records)

  ix. *DHCP Server*

     1. Edit (on each static DHCP; same UI/screen to add records)

   x. *Advanced*

     1. *Options*

     2. *QoS*

       a. Edit (on each QoS Custom Rule record; same UI/screen to add records)

     3. *Filter Rules*

       a. Edit (on each Forward Filter and Input Filter Rule record; same UI/screen to add records)

     4. *DNS & DHCP*

     5. *Network Cards*

  xi. *Troubleshooting*

     1. Connectivity Test

     2. Ping Test

     3. DNS Test

     4. Connection Test

     5. Traceroute Test

     6. Download Test

     7. Packet Test

B. Administration

  i. *Admin*

    1. Add

    2. Change Password

  ii. *Public Address*

  iii. *Certificates*

    1. Generate Certificate Authority

    2. Generate Server Certificate

    3. Create Signature Signing Request

    4. Import Signed Server Certificate

  iv. *SNMP*

  v. *Skins*

C. Email

  i. *Outgoing Server*

  ii. *Safe List*

    1. Add

  iii. *Quarantine*

    1. Edit (on each Quarantinable Address record; same UI/screen to add records)

    2. Edit (on each Quarantine Forwards record; same UI to add records)

D. Local Directory

  i. *Local Users*

    1. Edit (on each Local Users record; same UI/screen to add records)

E. Upgrade

  i. *Upgrade Settings*

F. System

  i. *Regional*

  ii. *Support*

  iii. *Backup*

  iv. *Restore*

  v. *Protocols*

  vi. *Shield*

   1. Edit (on each Shield Rule record; same UI/screen to add records)

 G. About

  i. *Server*

  ii. *Licenses*

  iii. *License Agreement*

III. Help (first link at the bottom of the left pane)

IV. My Account (second link at the bottom of the left pane)

 V. Logout (third link at the bottom of the left pane)

VI. Default Rack (right pane)

Note

The following assumes all available apps are installed. You access all apps by clicking their respective Settings button on the rack.

 A. Web Filter

  i. *Block Categories*

   1. Edit (on each Categories record)

  ii. *Block Sites*

   1. Edit (on each Sites record; same UI/screen to add records)

  iii. *Block File Types*

   1. Edit (on each File Types record; same UI/screen to add records)

  iv. *Block MIME Types*

   1. Edit (on each Sites MIME Types record; same UI/screen to add records)

  v. *Pass Sites*

   1. Edit (on each Sites record; same UI/screen to add records)

     vi. *Pass Clients*

        1. Edit (on each Client IP addresses record; same UI/screen to add records)

    vii. *Advanced*

   viii. *Event Log*

B. Web Filter Lite

     i. *Block Categories*

       1. Edit (on each Categories record)

    ii. *Block Sites*

       1. Edit (on each Sites record; same UI/screen to add records)

   iii. *Block File Types*

       1. Edit (on each File Types record; same UI/screen to add records)

   iv. *Block MIME Types*

       1. Edit (on each MIME Types record; same UI/screen to add records)

     v. *Pass Sites*

       1. Edit (on each Sites record; same UI/screen to add records)

     vi. *Pass Clients*

       1. Edit (on each Client IP addresses record; same UI/screen to add records)

    vii. *Advanced*

   viii. *Event Log*

C. Virus Blocker

     i. *Web*

       1. Edit File Extensions (expand Advanced Settings)

         a. Edit (on each File Extensions record; same UI/screen to add records)

       2. Edit MIME Types (expand Advanced Settings)

         a. Edit (on each MIME Types record; same UI/screen to add records)

    ii. *Email*

   iii. *FTP*

    iv. *Pass Sites*

        1. Edit (on each Pass Sites record; same UI/screen to add records)

    v. *Web Event Log*

    vi. *Email Event Log*

    vii. *Ftp Event Log*

  D. Virus Blocker Lite

    i. *Web*

        1. Edit File Extensions (expand Advanced Settings)

           a. Edit (on each File Extensions record; same UI/screen to add records)

        2. Edit MIME Types (expand Advanced Settings)

           a. Edit (on each MIME Types record; same UI/screen to add records)

    ii. *Email*

    iii. *FTP*

    iv. *Pass Sites*

        1. Edit (on each Pass Sites record; same UI/screen to add records)

    v. *Web Event Log*

    vi. *Email Event Log*

    vii. *Ftp Event Log*

  E. Spam Blocker

    i. *Email*

    ii. *Event Log*

    iii. *Tarpit Event Log*

  F. Spam Blocker Lite

    i. *Email*

    ii. *Event Log*

    iii. *Tarpit Event Log*

G. Phish Blocker

    i. *Email*

    ii. *Event Log*

H. Web Cache

    i. *Status*

    ii. *Cache Bypass*

        1. Edit (on each record; same UI/screen to add records)

    iii. *Summary Event Log*

I. Bandwidth Control

    i. *Status*

        1. Run Bandwidth Control Setup Wizard (wizard interface with four sequential screens)

        2. View Penalty Box and View Quotas buttons (both lead to the Hosts Viewer screen)

            a. *Current Hosts*

            b. *Penalty Box Hosts*

            c. *Penalty Box Event Log*

            d. *Current Quotas*

            e. *Quota Event Log*

    ii. *Rules*

        1. Edit (on each Rules record; same UI/screen to add records)

    iii. *Prioritize Event Log*

J. HTTPS Inspector

    i. *Configuration*

    ii. *Rules*

        1. Edit (on each Rules record; same UI/screen to add records)

    iii. *Event Log*

K. Application Control

   i. *Status*

   ii. *Applications*

   iii. *Rules*

      1. Edit (on each Rules record; same UI/screen to add records)

   iv. *Event Log*

   v. *Rule Event Log*

L. Application Control Lite

   i. *Status*

   ii. *Signatures*

      1. Edit (on each record; same UI/screen to add records)

   iii. *Event Log*

M. Captive Portal

   i. *Status*

   ii. *Capture Rules*

      1. Edit (on each Rules record; same UI/screen to add records)

   iii. *Passed Hosts*

   iv. *Captive Page*

   v. *User Authentication*

      1. Configure Local Directory (redirects to Local Directory setup)

      2. Configure RADIUS (redirects to Directory Connector)

      3. Configure Active Directory (redirects to Directory Connector)

   vi. *User Event Log*

   vii. *Rule Event Log*

N. Firewall

   i. *Rules*

      1. Edit (on each Rules record; same UI/screen to add records)

   ii. *Event Log*

O. Intrusion Prevention

    i. *Status*

    ii. *Rules*

        1. Edit (on each Rules record; same UI/screen to add records)

        2. Edit (on each Variables record; same UI/screen to add records)

    iii. *Event Log*

P. Ad Blocker

    i. *Status*

    ii. *Ad Filters*

        1. *Standard Filters*

        2. *User Defined Filters*

            a. Edit (on each record; same UI/screen to add records)

    iii. *Cookie Filters*

        1. *Standard Cookie Filters*

        2. *User Defined Cookie Filters*

            a. Edit (on each record; same UI/screen to add records)

    iv. *Pass Lists*

        1. Edit Passed Sites

            a. Edit (on each record; same UI/screen to add records)

        2. Edit Passed Client IPs

            a. Edit (on each record; same UI/screen to add records)

    v. *Event Log*

    vi. *Cookie Event Log*

Q. Reports

    i. *Status*

        1. View Reports

            a. Summary

    b. System

       i. *Summary Report*

      ii. *Administrative Login Events*

    c. Server

       i. *Summary Report*

    d. Shield

       i. *Summary Report*

      ii. *Shield Events*

    e. Web Filter

       i. *Summary Report*

      ii. *Violation Events*

     iii. *All Events*

     iv. *Site Events*

      v. *Unblock Events*

    f. Web Filter Lite

       i. *Summary Report*

      ii. *Violation Events*

     iii. *All Events*

     iv. *Site Events*

    g. Virus Blocker

       i. *Summary Report*

      ii. *Web Events*

     iii. *Mail Events*

     iv. *FTP Events*

    h. Virus Blocker Lite

       i. *Summary Report*

      ii. *Web Events*

     iii. *Mail Events*

     iv. *FTP Events*

    i. Spam Blocker
       i. *Summary Report*
       ii. *Spam Events*
       iii. *Spam Events (all)*

    j. Spam Blocker Lite
       i. *Summary Report*
       ii. *Spam Events*
       iii. *Spam Events (all)*

    k. Phish Blocker
       i. *Summary Report*
       ii. *Phish Events*
       iii. *Phish Events (all)*

    l. Web Cache
       i. *Summary Report*
       ii. *Web Cache Events*

    m. Bandwidth Control
       i. *Summary Report*
       ii. *Quota Events*

    n. Application Control
       i. *Summary Report*
       ii. *Detection Events*

    o. Application Control Lite
       i. *Summary Report*
       ii. *Detection Events*

    p. Captive Portal
       i. *Summary Report*
       ii. *Capture User Events*
       iii. Capture Rule Events

    q. Firewall
       i. *Summary Report*
       ii. *Firewall Events*

    r. Intrusion Prevention
       i. *Summary Report*
       ii. *Intrusion Events*

    s. Ad Blocker
       i. *Summary Report*
       ii. *Cookie Events*

    t. Policy Manager
       i. *Summary Report*

    u. Directory Connector
       i. *Summary Report*
       ii. *AD Authentication Events*

    v. WAN Failover
       i. *Summary Report*

    w. WAN Balancer
       i. *Summary Report*

    x. OpenVPN
       i. *Summary Report*
       ii. *Login Events*

    y. Configuration Backup
       i. *Summary Report*
       ii. *Backup Events*

    z. Users

   aa. Hosts

   bb. Emails

 ii. *Generation*

    iii. *Email*

       1. Add

       2. Change Password

    iv. *Syslog*

    v. *Name Map*

       1. Edit (on each record; same UI/screen to add records)

R. Policy Manager

    i. *Policies*

       1. Edit (on each Racks record; same UI/screen to add records)

    ii. *Rules*

       1. Edit (on each record; same UI/screen to add records)

    iii. *Event Log*

S. Directory Connector

    i. *User Notification API*

    ii. *Active Directory Connector*

    iii. *RADIUS Connector*

    iv. *Event Log*

T. WAN Failover

    i. *Status*

    ii. *Tests*

       1. Edit (on each Failure Detection Tests record; same UI/screen to add records)

    iii. *Test Event Log*

    iv. *Event Log*

U. WAN Balancer

    i. *Status*

    ii. *Traffic Allocation*

    iii. *Route Rules*

       1. Edit (on each Route Rules record; same UI/screen to add records)

V. IPsec VPN

   i. *Status*

   ii. *IPsec Options*

   iii. *IPsec Tunnels*

      1. Edit (on each record; same UI/screen to add records)

   iv. *L2TP Options*

   v. *L2TP Events*

   vi. *IPsec State*

   vii. *IPsec Policy*

   viii. *IPsec Log*

W. OpenVPN

   i. *Status*

   ii. *Server*

      1. *Remote Clients*

         a. Edit (on each record; same UI/screen to add records)

      2. *Groups*

         a. Edit (on each record; same UI/screen to add records)

      3. *Exported Networks*

         a. Edit (on each record; same UI/screen to add records)

   iii. *Client*

   iv. *Event Log*

X. Configuration Backup

   i. *Status*

   ii. *Event Log*

Y. Branding Manager

   i. *Settings*

Z. Live Support

   i. *Support*

APPENDIX F

APPLICABLE LAWS AND RULES REGARDING CONTENT FILTERING

While content filtering is merely a policy decision for many corporations, other organizations are required by various rules, laws, and regulations to implement specific levels of content filtering. Some of these regulations explicitly require content filtering (specifically CIPA and E-rate guidelines), while others create environments in which content filtering is implicitly required to maintain information security. Although other rules and regulations besides those listed here have implications for the use of content filters and firewalls, the following are most relevant for those working at schools, non-profits, and small businesses, who are most likely to be using this book.

CIPA AND E-RATE

The Children's Internet Protection Act (CIPA) was designed to prevent minors from accessing objectionable content on the Internet with government-funded hardware and Internet connections. E-rate is a public program to reduce the cost of Internet access. All schools and libraries that receive E-rate funding must comply with CIPA.

The full text of CIPA can be found at http://ifea.net/cipa.pdf. The FCC (which administers E-rate) also provides a summary of the salient points of the legislation at http://www.fcc.gov/guides/childrens-internet-protection-act. The most important elements of this guide are as follows:

> *Schools and libraries subject to CIPA may not receive the discounts offered by the E-rate program unless they certify that they have an Internet safety policy that includes technology protection measures. The protection*

measures must block or filter Internet access to pictures that are: (a) obscene; (b) child pornography; or (c) harmful to minors (for computers that are accessed by minors)...

Schools subject to CIPA have two additional certification requirements: 1) their Internet safety policies must include monitoring the online activities of minors; and 2) as required by the Protecting Children in the 21st Century Act, they must provide for educating minors about appropriate online behavior...

Schools and libraries subject to CIPA are required to adopt and implement an Internet safety policy addressing:

(a)   access by minors to inappropriate matter on the Internet;

(b)   the safety and security of minors when using electronic mail, chat rooms and other forms of direct electronic communications;

(c)   unauthorized access, including so-called "hacking," and other unlawful activities by minors online;

(d)   unauthorized disclosure, use, and dissemination of personal information regarding minors; and

(e)   measures restricting minors' access to materials harmful to them.

Schools and libraries must certify they are in compliance with CIPA before they can receive E-rate funding.

FERPA

The Family Educational Rights and Privacy Act (FERPA) regulates the disclosure of student information to agencies, organizations, or individuals other than the student and his or her guardians (if the student is a dependent). Unlike CIPA, FERPA does not include specific requirements for Internet content filtering. However, security threats on the Internet, ranging from malware designed to steal personal information to phishing schemes, can lead to potential violations of the legislation. Implementing appropriate content filtering to prevent users from accessing potentially compromised sites, helping avoid malware in e-mail and web traffic, etc., are critical parts of ensuring compliance.

The full text of FERPA can be found here: http://www2.ed.gov/policy/gen/guid/fpco/pdf/ferparegs.pdf. The U.S. Department of Education provides a summary of FERPA here: http://www2.ed.gov/policy/gen/guid/fpco/ferpa/index.html. Its FERPA guide specifically calls out requirements for student/guardian consent for release of information:

Generally, schools must have written permission from the parent or eligible student in order to release any information from a student's education record. However, FERPA allows schools to disclose those records, without consent, to the following parties or under the following conditions (34 CFR § 99.31):

■ *School officials with legitimate educational interest;*

■ *Other schools to which a student is transferring;*

- *Specified officials for audit or evaluation purposes;*
- *Appropriate parties in connection with financial aid to a student;*
- *Organizations conducting certain studies for or on behalf of the school;*
- *Accrediting organizations;*
- *To comply with a judicial order or lawfully issued subpoena;*
- *Appropriate officials in cases of health and safety emergencies; and*
- *State and local authorities, within a juvenile justice system, pursuant to specific State law.*

Not surprisingly, none of these exceptions to the consent rules include nefarious bodies or purveyors of malware.

HIPAA

Like FERPA, the Health Insurance Portability and Accountability Act (HIPAA) doesn't include language that specifically requires content filtering. However, unlike FERPA, robust network security is explicitly required, and content filtering and gateway anti-malware improves the ability of administrators to ensure the safety of personal healthcare information. Doctor's offices, hospitals, clinics, insurance agencies, etc., all need appropriate security measures to protect confidential information and avoid running afoul of recent HIPAA updates that impose substantial fines on violators.

The full text of HIPAA can be found here: http://www.hipaasurvivalguide.com/hipaa-regulations/hipaa-regulations.php. In particular, the Department of Health and Human Services provides guidance on "Protection from Malicious Software" in an administrative safeguards document here: http://www.hhs.gov/ocr/privacy/hipaa/administrative/securityrule/adminsafeguards.pdf. The document specifically describes this protection as follows:

> One important security measure that employees may need to be reminded of is security software that is used to protect against malicious software. Where this implementation specification is a reasonable and appropriate safeguard for a covered entity, the covered entity must implement:

> "Procedures for guarding against, detecting, and reporting malicious software."

> Malicious software can be thought of as any program that harms information systems, such as viruses, Trojan horses or worms. As a result of an unauthorized infiltration, EPHI [electronic patient health information] and other data can be damaged or destroyed, or at a minimum, require expensive and time-consuming repairs.

Malicious software is frequently brought into an organization through email attachments, and programs that are downloaded from the Internet.

Thus, not only should healthcare organizations and providers implement gateway anti-malware software, but they should also be limiting access to broad categories of websites that might potentially be compromised and deliver infected payloads to client computers.

OTHER REGULATIONS

There are many other regulations of critical importance to the industries to which they apply with implications for content filtering and anti-malware devices. Sarbanes-Oxley, for example, regulates many aspects of the financial services industry, while PCI-DSS regulates credit-card processing. Particularly for smaller organizations who are potentially affected by such regulation, which often carries substantial penalties for non-compliance, implementing content filtering like that offered in the Untangle NG Firewall is an important part of creating a safe and secure IT environment. Even where content filtering is not required, businesses working in regulated environments should carefully review their security infra-structure and assess the potential role for content filters and firewalls.

INDEX